D1463189

UNIVERSITY OF WINNIPEG (LIBRARY), 515 Portage Avenue, Winnipeg, MB R3B 2E9 Canada

LEAVING
BIRMINGHAM

ALSO BY PAUL HEMPHILL

King of the Road

Me and the Boy

The Sixkiller Chronicles

Too Old to Cry

Long Gone

The Good Old Boys

Mayor: Notes on the Sixties (with Ivan Allen, Jr.)

The Nashville Sound

F
334
B69
N44
1993

LEAVING BIRMINGHAM

Notes of a Native Son

Paul Hemphill

VIKING

VIKING
Published by the Penguin Group
Penguin Books USA Inc., 375 Hudson Street,
New York, New York 10014, U.S.A.
Penguin Books Ltd, 27 Wrights Lane, London W8 5TZ, England
Penguin Books Australia Ltd, Ringwood, Victoria, Australia
Penguin Books Canada Ltd, 10 Alcorn Avenue,
Toronto, Ontario, Canada M4V 3B2
Penguin Books (N.Z.) Ltd, 182–190 Wairau Road,
Auckland 10, New Zealand

Penguin Books Ltd, Registered Offices:
Harmondsworth, Middlesex, England

First published in 1993 by Viking Penguin,
a division of Penguin Books USA Inc.

10 9 8 7 6 5 4 3 2 1

Copyright © Paul Hemphill, 1993
All rights reserved

PHOTOGRAPH CREDITS
Insert two: page one, page two (top), and page three (below): The Bettmann
Archive; page two (below) and page three (top): Charles Moore/Black Star;
page six (top and below): George Tames/*The New York Times*; page eight
(top and below) courtesy of Birmingham Civil Rights Institute.
All other photographs from the author's collection.

LIBRARY OF CONGRESS CATALOGING-IN-PUBLICATION DATA
Hemphill, Paul.
Leaving Birmingham : notes of a native son / by Paul Hemphill
p. cm.
ISBN 0-670-84778-X
1. Birmingham (Ala.)—Race relations. 2. Afro-Americans—Civil
rights—Alabama—Birmingham. 3. Civil rights movements—Alabama—
Birmingham—History—20th century. 4. Hemphill, Paul.
I. Title.
F334.B68N44   1993
305.896′0730761781—dc20   93-18809

Printed in the United States of America
Set in Adobe Old Style Number Seven
Designed by Francesca Belanger

Without limiting the rights under copyright reserved above,
no part of this publication may be reproduced, stored in
or introduced into a retrieval system, or transmitted, in
any form or by any means (electronic, mechanical,
photocopying, recording or otherwise), without the
prior written permission of both the copyright
owner and the above publisher of this book.

For Joyce

Contents

Illustrations follow pages 82 and 226.

LEAVING
BIRMINGHAM

A Day
in the Park

It had been nearly three decades since Birmingham dominated the news, and that was fine with everybody, those of us who had fled and those who had stayed, for the news had always been shocking, urgent, calamitous, shrieking with visceral hate. The numbing litany of racial violence during the fifties and sixties in a city that once had proudly called itself "the Magic City" and "the Pittsburgh of the South" had seemed endless: redneck thugs leaping onstage at the city's auditorium to pummel the black singer Nat "King" Cole; Ku Klux Klansmen randomly kidnapping and emasculating and leaving to die a man guilty only of having black skin; the torching of integrated "Freedom Rider" buses; Police Commissioner Eugene "Bull" Connor's answering the protests of young black demonstrators with police dogs and water cannons; Dr. Martin Luther King, Jr.'s arrests as an ordinary "outside agitator"; the chanting of "nigger lover" and the flailing of baseball bats by sallow sawmill yahoos incensed by the television cameramen who had come to expose Birmingham's dark soul to the world; and, finally—in an act so heinous that even the Klan and Connor had to back off—the dynamiting of a church that killed four young black girls as they were slipping on their choir robes one Sunday morning in September of 1963. Those were still the images that came to mind all across America, and, indeed, around the world, when the name Birmingham came up, and not without justification. That grim old steel town, choking on its own bile and smoke in the ferrous folds of the Appalachians as they peter out in northern Alabama, sulking like a volcano likely to erupt at the slightest provocation, was the most blatantly segregated city of its size in the United States of America, and most of us regarded it with the same morbid fascination that causes us to slow down and gawk at a bloody wreck on the highway.

But the city's long absence from the evening news, ever since the dynamiting of the church on that sobering Sunday morning, had left the impression that, on the surface at least, there just might be a "new" Birmingham as we entered the last decade of the twentieth century. The majestic statue of the Roman god of metallurgy, Vulcan (origin of the word "volcano"), the city's logo during its heyday as a steel town, had become a forlorn figure, ironically overlooking a twenty-mile valley of battened steel mills and blast furnaces that once were Birmingham's heartbeat but now resembled slain dinosaurs choked by kudzu, victims of union greed and environmental concerns and cheaper Japanese steel. The most spectacular of them, the open-hearthed Sloss Furnace, only eight blocks from dead-center downtown, whose rivers of slag and showers of sparks and strobe-light glimpses of men making steel through the night had made it the best show in town, was now a museum where involuntarily retired steelworkers led tour groups, like veterans revisiting the battlefields. Replacing the thousands of steelworkers were academics and medical technicians, *outsiders,* to staff the renowned University of Alabama at Birmingham (UAB) medical and educational complex. The smoke had cleared, and a pleasant new face could be seen: hotels and office buildings; a gussied-up main drag called Birmingham Green; an expanded airport taking some of the overflow from that of bitter old rival Atlanta; interstate highway ribbons soaring above the old bricked streets and rusty, abandoned tin-roofed warehouses. And finally, more germane to the Birmingham that the world knew, there was this: a black mayor, a black-majority city council, black faces everywhere downtown except in the highest suites. The playing field, one might infer, had been made more nearly level.

But then, in the summer of 1990, came a blip. Birmingham's white flight, for those who could afford it, had occurred southward, literally behind Vulcan's back, "over the mountain," beyond the genteel all-white villages of Mountain Brook and Homewood and Vestavia Hills (founded early in this century by the Big Mules, the barons of steel and iron and coal), onward into the lush hills and bottomlands, where not just new towns but new golf communities had sprung up overnight. One of these was Shoal Creek, twenty miles from where Bull Connor had done his dirty work, and people who play golf were all aglow that, come August, the Professional Golfers Association tournament would be held at the Shoal Creek Country Club. *Right here in Birmingham!* Network television, the Goodyear Blimp, a new day for Birmingham—all of this and Jack Nicklaus, too. There was a giddiness in the air until a local reporter casually asked the head of the country club, Hall Thompson, a former good old boy now rich from dealing in earth-moving equipment, whether Shoal Creek had any black members. "Of *course* not," he said, surprised that he would be asked. "That just isn't done in Birmingham."

Oh, Birmingham. Those idiots, I thought, of the hometown I had left at the age of twenty-five, just ahead of the big trouble in the sixties. Won't they ever learn? Birmingham roared back onto the front pages and the six o'clock news, those jerky black-and-white newsreels of Bull Connor's dogs and hoses and billy clubs reminding us again of Prague and East Berlin and Soweto, and the flap took its predictable turns. "Why Birmingham?" said Hall Thompson and most of the city's whites, backpedaling and finger-pointing; and sure enough, a half-dozen other country clubs on the PGA tour, in more "enlightened" places such as Michigan and California, were similarly threatened to clean up their act or else. Shoal Creek in Birmingham, like the others, quickly corralled a token black member ("It's not because I like golf, but for the good of the community," said the black businessman who agreed to join Shoal Creek, in a sweet irony), and the boys played on. But the damage had been done. The soul of Birmingham remained the same.

If the whites wouldn't offer some sign to the world that things had changed, then the blacks, now in power, would. Thus it was that twenty-nine years after the dynamite blast that had killed the four black girls at the Sixteenth Street Baptist Church —10:22 a.m., September 15, 1963, stood frozen as the city's moment of infamy—Birmingham's new black leadership and the tight little knot of white liberals they had learned to trust were planning to pay homage to those who had fought and died by launching a day of dedications that they hoped would tell the world that there had been some degree of reconciliation. What once had been dismissed as "Niggertown," the traditional black business area four blocks west of City Hall where the most visible violence had occurred in '63, now was being designated the Birmingham Civil Rights District. In a situation not unlike the one unfolding at the same time in Dachau, Germany—arguments over whether to build a memorial or forget that the Nazi concentration camp there had ever existed—the city had been divided once again along racial lines. "Whenever somebody told me we ought to forget about that stuff," said David Vann, quite likely the city's last white mayor, who had proposed the district before passing the gavel to Richard Arrington in 1979, "I told 'em the best way to forget it is to declare it history and put it in a museum." They had done that now, building a soaring twelve-million-dollar Civil Rights Institute and landscaping Kelly Ingram Park, where the dogs and hoses had been used, and converting the old Carver Theater into a home for the Alabama Jazz Hall of Fame (Birmingham was the birthplace of Lionel

Hampton and Erskine Hawkins, whose "Tuxedo Junction" celebrated a nearby black dance hall), and even laying broad new steps in front of the stately old church where the girls had died.

For most of 1992 I had maintained an apartment in Birmingham, a base of operations, as it were, whence I would emerge every morning for my serendipitous wanderings; and the irony was not lost on me that I had been rummaging around in my hometown, trying to make something positive of my past, precisely at a time when the city itself was on a similar mission. Perhaps with that in mind, as though the city and I were in this thing together, I had made it a ritual to begin each day by cruising past Kelly Ingram Park, where the first of the series of dedications would take place in the fall, to see how things were coming along. Since the beginning of the year, from the barren, wintry nights of January through those steamy, breath-sucking days of summer that only a southerner can love, work on the modest little park had continued in a relentless rush toward this day when, it was hoped, there might be some facing up to the past. In January the city's black mayor, Richard Arrington, had spent a night in prison to protest a lingering federal investigation into the alleged mishandling of Civil Rights Institute funds; the herringbone sidewalks were laid for "Freedom Walk" anyway. In April the city was revisited by the past when a gang of Klan-type "skinheads" murdered a homeless black man; flatbed trucks delivered burlap-balled trees to the park anyway. In May there was rumbling in the black housing projects after the acquittal of the white cops who had beaten Rodney King in Los Angeles; the statues of Martin Luther King and of three kneeling black preachers were nestled into place anyway. It was payback time in Birmingham, and nothing was going to stop it.

The morning of Tuesday, September 15, 1992, had broken fine and clear. Not surprisingly, since the local newspapers have always been a part of the problem in Birmingham, there had been no notice of the day's events in Monday afternoon's *News* and only a mention in agate type under the "Short Takes" calendar in that morning's *Post-Herald* (by way of explaining why the city council's regular meeting wouldn't be held). But the planners of "A Salute to Unsung Heroes of the Civil Rights Movement" weren't deluding themselves into thinking that white foundry workers from Tarrant City and Republican moneychangers from Vestavia Hills would drop what they were doing and come tooling into town—where they seldom ventured anymore these days, anyway—put down their asbestos gloves and their putters and their copies of *Southern Living* magazine, to go downtown in order to embrace their African-American brothers and sisters. The black leaders knew who their friends were, and, sadly, not many of them were white.

The day's opening ceremony was a breakfast at the old city auditorium, the same place where Klansmen had jumped Nat Cole in 1956. It was now refurbished and named for Albert Boutwell, the moderate white who had served briefly as mayor when the electorate—black *and* white—had kicked Bull Connor and his cronies out of office. One had only to look around at that sea of smiling faces, the black elite in their dark suits and Sunday dresses, to see that this was not going to be a "reconciliation" in the textbook definition of the word. Of the 850 people seated in folding chairs at tables draped with white linen, paying five dollars a head for cold sweet rolls and coffee and juice and fruit, less than one hundred were white. Only the day before I had been told by a white matron from Mountain Brook, relatively liberal for her age and station, that she had stopped attending the annual Martin Luther King Day celebration because it had become "too black" and made her feel excluded.

If the crowd wanted some old-time alliterative preaching, a taste of some of that grand Christian rhetoric that had sustained southern blacks during the darkest hours of the civil rights movement, they got it when the Reverend Joseph E. Lowery of the Southern Christian Leadership Conference headquarters in Atlanta stepped to the podium after an endless round of remarks and prayers and gospels and introductions. "It was Birmingham where spirituality met brutality," he began, and he was off and running. "This was a strange and devilish environment, but we did not hang our harps on the willow tree. . . . Singing the Lord's song means doing the right thing. . . . There's ceremony and then there's sacrament. It's ceremony when you're putting a ring around her finger. It's sacrament when you're wrapping her with love for all of her days. . . ." Soon, Lowery had veered away from what had brought him to town and moved to a larger arena: the Rodney King verdict, drugs, economic inequities ("Thirty-five years later, after all the sit-ins, the kneel-ins, the pray-ins, and the march-ins, the median income for blacks is still sixty percent what it is for whites"). Lowery had come up with a new technique for stirring a lethargic audience, replacing the old "Do I hear an 'amen'?" with a coy "Helloooo?" straight from the Comedy Channel, but the crowd didn't need any prodding when he wound up and closed it out. "Heard some fool on the radio the other day talking 'bout how they oughta send all the niggers back to Africa. Well, in the first place, most of us never been to Africa. But I get over there every now and then—got me some bucks now, you know, I can do that sort of thing. Africa's lovely, all right, but let me tell you something. I don't go over there to Africa without checking my tickets first to make sure it says 'round trip.'" Folding chairs squeaked on the slick concrete as everyone rose to give the old warrior an ovation, and while they were up they began to sing "We Shall Overcome," and soon they were leaving the hall and walking toward Kelly Ingram Park, en masse, beneath the white man's skyscrapers and behind the City Hall that had been Bull Connor's bunker and past the bus station where Freedom Riders had been clubbed to the floor, some of them holding hands and singing that old freedom song, going over to check out a little green spot in the belly of the city that now, at last, they could claim as their very own.

Kelly Ingram Park had been named for a white man, Oswald Kelly Ingram, the first American sailor to die in the First World War, but over the years had evolved as a buffer between the black and white business areas of downtown Birmingham. It was during the first week of May in '63 that it became the focal point of the war between Bull Connor and his cops and firemen and Martin Luther King and his demonstrators, mostly preachers and students. Every morning hundreds of blacks would walk across the street from Sixteenth Street Baptist and begin milling about in the park, queuing up for a march on City Hall, four blocks away. Facing them would be Birmingham's all-white police force with their riot gear and paddy wagons and K-9 dogs and the firemen with water cannons capable of stripping bark off a tree at one hundred yards. Soon enough, the battle was joined, with network television crews there to record it all for the world to see: chanting crowds; stumpy little Bull Connor in his short-brimmed straw hat shrieking orders to his troops; frightened young blacks fleeing for safety from the snarling dogs and the water cannons; paddy wagons being loaded with so many demonstrators that ultimately people were being jailed behind fences at the state fairgrounds. Those days in May created the most chilling television images recorded during the civil rights movement in America. When they were over, on May 10, King had won. A tentative agreement was reached that the city's white leaders would release all prisoners and begin to desegregate public accommodations and hire blacks as clerks and, for the first time, actually sit down and start listening to the black people who constituted forty percent of the city population.

No wonder, then, that on this bright summery day nearly three decades later the words "hallowed ground" would be heard over and over from the two dozen dignitaries seated in a semicircle before a bandshell in the park, in the shadow of the AT&T Tower. When the group from the auditorium had made it over, following the strains of "Tuxedo Junction" being played by a group of old black men hastily assembled as the Birmingham Heritage Band, their numbers swelled the crowd to more than a thousand. Again, no more than ten percent of them were white. Many of them were black schoolchildren, romping on the newly laid sod, skipping along Freedom Walk, playing hide-and-seek among the sculptures depicting demonstrators cowering before vintage water cannons mounted on tripods and kids languishing behind prison bars (not yet in place was a wall from which would spring sculpted police dogs), or posing at the base of the statue of Dr. King while their parents took pictures. Catty-corner from the park were, in one direction, the Sixteenth Street Baptist Church and, in another, the mammoth hulk of the Civil Rights Institute, where workmen on scaffoldings were rushing to finish in time for the museum's dedication in late November. And as always, up on the forbidding ridge of Red Mountain, the natural barrier that is Birmingham's Berlin Wall, there was the sulking statue of Vulcan looking down on it all.

Two hours had been set aside for the dedication ceremony, and the organizers could be forgiven for using up every minute of them. The music and the prayers and the readings and the remarks began anew. "The tragedy of Birmingham wasn't the brutality of bad men," said Richard Arrington, "but the silence of good men." Someone else quoted Santayana: "Those who cannot remember the past are condemned to repeat it." There were rambling reminiscences from half a dozen of the old warriors, including the jaunty and combative Reverend Fred Shuttlesworth, a local preacher who was going to jail and being bombed before it became a fact of life: "Those children kept coming at Bull and his police until there was no more room at the inn." There was applause for David Vann, recognized as one of the few "good" white men in those days. There was more music, from an all-black elementary school choir. And at exactly 10:22 a.m., there was a solemn pause to remind the crowd of what had happened at that very moment twenty-nine years earlier; all eyes turned slowly to glimpse the twin cupolas of Sixteenth Street Baptist across the way.

Then, finally, as the crowd grew restless in the intensifying heat of the late morning, yet another black preacher stepped to the microphone to underscore what all this was about. He was the Reverend Abraham Woods, both a pastor and a professor at little Miles College in Birmingham, another of these black men whose hair was turning gray as they reached their sixties, veterans of the battlefield who had lost count long ago of how many times they had been beaten, bombed, jailed, and cursed. For a moment, the children who had been playing on the statues were hushed by their parents, and the Muslims who had been hawking T-shirts on the sidewalk paused, and the workmen across the street rose up to listen; for they all knew Abe Woods well, had heard him many times, knew he could set things right. "This park is the Jerusalem of the civil rights movement," he said, "the Mecca of the civil rights movement, the Iwo Jima of the civil rights movement." His voice flowed from the bandshell and tolled like a bell, over saplings still secured by guy wires and the bubbling fountain and the newly laid walkway and the fresh green sod. The crowd was silent. "From now on, when we come here and hear the birds sing, they will be singing 'freedom.' When the water runs, it will run 'freedom.' When the crickets chirp, they will chirp 'freedom.' When the wind blows, it will blow 'freedom.' When footsteps touch the walk, they will say 'freedom.' " And soon the crowd began singing "We Shall Overcome" once more; and surely some of them noticed, as they dispersed and began to stroll through the park, that the only dogs in sight this time were stray mongrels sniffing for scraps, and the only water hoses to be seen were spraying fine mists on the beds of chrysanthemums planted beside a granite marker proclaiming the park a "Place of Revolution and Reconciliation."

Part One

VULCAN'S CHILD

CHAPTER ONE

Bad Birmingham

Never for a moment in its brief and tortured life has Birmingham been a genuinely "southern" city. True, it lies in the north-central part of Alabama, "the Heart of Dixie," only a hundred miles up the road from Montgomery, "the Cradle of the Confederacy." True, people there say "y'all" and on the surface would seem to share many traits with the rest of the Old Confederacy: they are churchgoing, flag-waving, slow-moving, and conservative to the point of being paranoid about people and ideas that deviate from the status quo. True, Birmingham has been associated with many icons that are considered, for better or for worse, southern: Bear Bryant, the Ku Klux Klan, the "Dixiecrats," George Wallace, the Confederate flag. But even southerners know that on the one hand there are Memphis and Charleston and Mobile and Natchez, old cities truly tied to the agrarian South, that gossamer myth of *Gone With the Wind,* and then there is Birmingham. No, Birmingham isn't southern except by geography. It was conceived as a gawky stepchild, more northern than southern, and was nurtured by outsiders to become the only industrial giant that ever developed below the Mason-Dixon line. It was masculine, not feminine; a hard lump of coal, not a soft boll of cotton; a miner's shack, not a plantation; a banjo, not a violin; gritty red iron ore, not damp black loam; mine shafts lit by carbide lamps, not antebellum salons bathed in candlelight. Its major blessing, that it nestled like a hen on deep lodes of all the minerals necessary for the production of steel, would turn out to be its curse.

The word "southern" implies a past, a connection to slavery and cotton and the Civil War, but Birmingham never had that past. Indeed, the city didn't even exist when Union general William Tecumseh Sherman razed Atlanta on his march to the sea. Up to that point, the area that would become Birmingham had been a scraggly wilderness at the southern end of the Appalachians, sparsely populated by pioneer farmers who didn't know exactly what to make of the sorry red earth except that it wouldn't grow much besides corn and that the departed Creeks and Choctaws had used it to make dyestuff. The big money in the South, of course, was in the cotton grown in the lush Black Belt south of there. In 1850, throughout what was known as the Cotton States, about one thousand families divided more than fifty million dollars. There was no middle class to serve as a buffer between them and the slaves, who earned not a penny for themselves, and the great sprawling mass of poor whites, whose average income was less than one hundred dollars a year. Little wonder, then, that when the call to arms was sounded, when time came for Alabama to secede from the Union, the slaves and the dirt farmers were much more interested in killing planters than in killing Yankees. Thus was born the Free State of Winston (near Walker County, whose seat is Jasper, an old lumbering and mining town on the railroad lines some fifty miles northwest of Birmingham), on the grounds that, as they say in those parts, "we ain't got no dog in that fight."

But while those poor farmers were cursing the infertile land where they had hoisted their cabins, some other men had taken a closer look at it, and doubtless their hearts had quickened. They were geologists, men who knew something of the great iron mills now pulsating in the North, men who knew that there were other uses for soil than growing crops. Thus, before the war, here and there in the dark gullies of Jones Valley in Jefferson County, whose population had been only four thousand when Alabama gained statehood in 1819, they began gouging coal and iron ore out of the ground and slapping together primitive charcoal furnaces to produce ingots of crude iron that, in the beginning, were sold to blacksmiths and to farmers who did their own smithing. By 1860, on the eve of the war, there were just twelve thousand souls living in the county, whose seat was a village called Elyton, which held one hundred and five families, a school, a courthouse, and a race track. Once the war began, the Confederacy set up an ironworks at Selma, near their capital in Montgomery, and subsidized an Alabama engineer by the name of John Milner to build a railway northward to fetch the minerals and bring them back to Selma. He didn't make it. Before Milner's men could complete the line, the Selma ironworks fell; and when the Union raiders traced the proposed line to its head in Jones Valley, which would become Birmingham, it took them only eight days in March of 1865 to destroy the furnaces and excavations that had represented the South's first tinkerings at iron production.

The war ended a month later, leaving the South in shambles. Atlanta, the queen city, had been leveled. The cotton economy was in ruins. Roaming across the wasted countryside were crippled veterans, widows and orphans, vandals and pillagers, former slaves wondering what to do with their "freedom," and a band of vultures known as carpetbaggers and scalawags and—ominously, euphemistically—northern "investors." The latter, salivating at the prospects, knowing full well what treasures lurked below the surface of the scarred earth, swooped down with their money, both real and imagined, in frenzied schemes and speculations. Land that had been worth fifty dollars an acre before the war was now going for as little as three dollars; and they bought up all they could in the knowledge that when the furnaces and mines were rebuilt, and railroads were laid to haul the coal and iron out of the valley, a whole new day would dawn in this part of the South.

Reenter John Milner, who had never given up on his dream of building a city from scratch in the middle of Jones Valley's rich veins of coal and iron ore and limestone. Milner hooked up with a shadowy Boston promoter named John Stanton in a lengthy game of cat-and-mouse involving the construction of railroads that would cross near Elyton; and when Stanton's fortune was found to be bogus, the victory went to the craftier and better-financed Milner. The railroads met, the Elyton Land Company was organized, and a new city was born. The date was January 26, 1871.

They named it Birmingham, after the grim old manufacturing center in England, and it was a stark contrast to the antebellum cities of Montgomery and Mobile in the southern part of the state. This was more like the Wild West than the Deep South. The records show that in September of '71 Birmingham proper consisted of "fifty-seven wooden houses, eighteen brick stores, two planing mills, and one hotel," but that tells little. "Now in the mud roads that pass for streets," it was written in 1937 in *Harper's Monthly*,

> the speculators hurry back and forth giving sales talks to one another. "There's millions in it. Nobody knows much about what the mineral is or where, but it's there." They have got their railroad, such as it is, built to the town site and a little beyond, but they have no Northern connection. They live in a couple of boxcars beside the railroad track and make plans. "Cincinnati money has already showed up and annexed a furnace. Do you know where there's some money?" . . . Grant is in the White House, the gilded age is dawning, and as they watch it the Birmingham speculators' mouths water. . . . The age of iron and steel, of rampant industry and the greedy gutting of a continent, has begun. . . .

As new furnaces and foundries and mills and mines sprang up in the piney woods, virtually overnight, the fledgling town became a melting pot much like Denver, another mineral boomtown half a continent away. Birmingham was overrun by a roiling conglomeration of speculators, whores, gamblers, barkeeps, murderers, adventurers, freed slaves, assorted camp followers, and destitute young men who simply had walked or ridden horses into town looking for any kind of work they could find.

Although it was technically a city, with a core and a discernible "downtown" area, Birmingham was rather more a collection of mining camps strung out over a valley nearly twenty miles long and five miles across. The camps had grown beside the furnaces and the coal mines, shantytowns with names like Coaldale and Blossburg and Dolomite and Blue Creek, hideous clusters of tents and board shacks segregated by four diverse work groups: whites, blacks, immigrants, and convicts being leased to the mines. The raw sewage and generally primitive living conditions invited regular outbreaks of cholera and other diseases swept along by the putrid waters. Men toiled in the dank mines from sunup to sundown, and they owed their souls to the company store, the commissary, which dealt not in cash but in "clackers," imitation money drawn against a man's time, good for enough meal and molasses to get a family through another day. *Harper's Monthly*:

> No man was ever out of debt; he never knew how much he earned. They were a superstitious people with a lurid circuit-rider faith of brimstone and fire. . . . They feared strangers, drank moonshine when they could get it, were given to sudden rages and violence; many could neither read nor write. Some of the towns, patrolled by deputies, were almost impossible to get in or out of. In such cesspools generations were born and died. There was no end to it; cut off from all light or hope, the company town was the whole of life.

The most wretched of the damned were the convicts, leased to the mines by the Jefferson County sheriff, who was raking off as much as eighty thousand dollars a year from the scam as late as 1912. Living in stockades, paid not a cent, dying from tuberculosis, tortured by whipping bosses, unable to strike or complain at all, they were freed to wander crippled into town, or else killed and dumped into shallow holes in the deep woods, gone without a trace.

Since the beginning, zealous promoters had been calling Birmingham "the Pittsburgh of the South," and although it would be a while before there was any truth to such Babbittry, the dim outlines of a real city did begin to appear during the boom-and-bust decades of the eighties and nineties. Downtown, on streets laid out in rigid midwestern grids (avenues running roughly east to west, streets north to south), red brick buildings began to rise: hotels, banks, land offices, retail stores. Little satellite towns, Ensley and Bessemer and Wylam and Irondale, began to grow around the mills. More and more railroads were reaching the city every day, most notably the Louisville & Nashville, connecting Birmingham to the markets in the North. Serious big-time furnaces and mining operations were established—Alice, Oxmoor, Eureka, Red Mountain Iron & Coal Company, Cahaba Iron Works, Pratt Coal and Coke, Birmingham Rolling Mill, McElwain Furnaces—many of them miraculously surviving in times marked by wild speculation, bankruptcy, and the spectacle of companies being born in the morning and swallowed up by larger ones by nightfall. Up on the cool, forested ridge that was Red Mountain, high above the clamor and ugliness, northern entrepreneurs now suddenly swimming in wealth built fanciful "southern" mansions with cheap black labor. Fortunes were being made by bankers and engineers and iron masters and speculators, DeBardeleben and Ramsay and Phillips and Linn and Ensley and Sloss and Hillman—names that would, a century later, adorn schools and parks and municipal edifices everywhere. From the barren farms of the postwar South, eager families of both races kept squeezing into the new city, creating a need for hotels and rooming houses and schools and churches and hospitals and, eventually, city parks and trolley lines. With the poor whites and the freed blacks at each other's throats out there in the mining camps—two races born in fear of each other but now forced to work side by side out of the need to survive —lynchings were occurring with startling regularity; there were twenty-four throughout the state of Alabama in both 1891 and 1892. More humane leaders might have done something besides exploiting those racial animosities to keep the wages down and the unions out, but things were going too well to be concerned with the rabble. The city's drumbeaters preferred to point, instead, to the astonishing growth of what they were now calling "the Magic City." Birmingham's population had ballooned from 4,500 in 1880 to 21,000 in 1885 to 110,000 in 1900. That was a long way from Pittsburgh; but the best—and, in at least one very important way, the worst—was yet to come.

From the start, the healthiest of the monolithic mineral companies in town had been the Tennessee Coal, Iron and Railroad Company, known locally as TCI, with mines and plants throughout Jefferson County. TCI had relentlessly swallowed up smaller operations standing in its way to become the city's largest single employer. There were other huge operations, to be sure, such as Sloss-Sheffield Coal and Iron, and Republic Iron and Steel (both of those also the results of mergers and consolidations and raw takeovers); but by the turn of the century TCI had practically made Birmingham a one-company town. TCI's idea of civic responsibility was to stand firmly behind the new Jim Crow laws that had gone into effect in 1901, stripping black people of the right to vote or to do much of anything except hold the most menial jobs, and to keep a close eye on its own bottom line by using convict labor and crushing union uprisings and pitting the races against each other ("You don't want to work, I know a thousand niggers that do"). Money for expansion was always a problem, but TCI somehow seemed to prevail. TCI was as smugly proud as anyone when Birmingham's exhibit at the 1904 world's fair in St. Louis, a fifty-five-foot-tall cast-iron statue of Vulcan, turned out to be the hit of the show.

But suddenly in 1907, in what would lead to a defining moment in the history of the young city, TCI got into deep trouble. All across the country businesses and banks began to fail, the stock market plummeted, railroads went into receivership, and there were massive layoffs. A panic was on, and TCI had a debt of some five million dollars. A New York City banking firm that held TCI stock as collateral was feeling pressure from the panic, too, and needed to sell the stock in order to save its own neck. Thus, on the night of November 2, there was a meeting of bankers in the library of J. Pierpont Morgan—the one, the only—and after two days of further secret meetings that even brought President Theodore Roosevelt into the picture, the word came down: TCI now was owned by the United States Steel Corporation. U.S. Steel had paid slightly more than thirty-five million dollars for TCI's one billion dollars' worth of assets, less than four cents on the dollar, and had the audacity to call it a "public service" to "prevent a panic and general industrial smash-up." The Birmingham *News* was beside itself with joy: "The U.S. Steel Corporation practically controls the steel trade in the United States. With enlarged and improved plants it can make steel cheaper in this district than anywhere else. Superiority of product and cheapness of manufacture will conspire soon to make the Birmingham district the largest steel manufacturing center in the universe." So great was the elation in Birmingham that few questioned such a brazen violation of the Sherman Antitrust Act. Now the entire city of Birmingham, in a twist, owed its soul to the ultimate company store.

And there was more, all of it traceable to the fact that the

South was still hobbled by the Civil War and Reconstruction, and thus didn't have the bargaining power to stand up against a J. P. Morgan or a U.S. Steel. "This year of 1907 showed clearly that the domination of the absentee landlord was increasing," said *Harper's Monthly*.

> Of the trunk lines entering Birmingham, the Southern had been put together by Morgan in the nineties. The Louisville & Nashville was acquired in 1901 by the Atlantic Coast Line in a Morgan transaction. Now through Morgan the Steel Corporation had annexed the biggest property in Birmingham. In 1907 the Alabama Power Company was organized, which—after many vicissitudes—came to rest as a subsidiary of the Commonwealth and Southern Corporation, reputedly a Morgan company. Ultimate decisions in power, transport, and industry were made at last in a distant banking house.

Promptly, U.S. Steel went about protecting its larger northern investments through such impositions as "Pittsburgh Plus," which artificially raised the price of Birmingham steel and thereby removed its competitive edge, and higher freight rates. The Pittsburgh of the South? Birmingham had become a poor cousin practically overnight, with the stroke of a pen, the shuffle of paper, never again to be master of its own destiny. And the moguls, those hard men who had gotten Birmingham off the ground through sweat and hustle and not a little chicanery, had seen their toys taken away. They were on somebody else's payroll now, emasculated, puppets of the most powerful absentee landlord in the United States. All that work and now this, they must have been thinking as they withdrew to their mansions on the hill, their dreams of creating a great dashing city gone. Never again would the white power elite of Birmingham have the vested interest in their town that inspires men to do noble things for the common good.

.   .   .

In spite of this turn of events, the city began to spread through the gullies and up the hills. Attracted by the promise of work in the coal mines and foundries and steel mills, not to mention a classic cotton-mill village plopped down only two miles from downtown, migrants of both races poured into Jones Valley from all over the South. Now that Reconstruction was over, slavery had resumed in the guise of sharecropping, and the boll weevil was in the process of ravaging the cotton fields and accordingly changing the face of the rural South. Indeed, it was in 1919 that the town of Enterprise, two hundred miles south of Birmingham, erected a monument to the boll weevil in the middle of a downtown street—a backhanded means of thanking the little devil for turning the South away from relying on that single industry. So the sharecroppers said goodbye to the barren fields and the outdoor privies and the aching loneliness of the southern countryside, crowding onto trains or hopping boxcars or cramming themselves into the new Ford automobiles if they had them, leaving to start new lives in Birmingham, "Bad Birmingham," the Magic City.

No matter that the strings were being pulled from afar; the mines and mills were booming like never before. New methods of working with the seemingly endless supply of minerals brought about new products; it was discovered, for example, that tar and ammonia and gas could be made from coal. In due time, Birmingham became the leading producer of cast-iron pipe in the United States. U.S. Steel and the other bosses began to see that allowing the primitive conditions in the mining camps to continue was self-defeating and started cleaning up their acts, even if their reasons were more pragmatic than altruistic. Downtown, at the corner of Twentieth Street and First Avenue, four massive stone office buildings arose, skyscrapers for their time, to create what the ballyhooers were calling "the heaviest corner on earth." When the city was consolidated in 1910, over the protests of mill owners who didn't want to be taxed (the politically powerful ones, like those of TCI's Ensley works, escaped tax-free, of course), the annexation of towns and villages that once had been mining camps swelled Birmingham's population to nearly 133,000.

Not surprisingly, the First World War brought great prosperity to this town of heavy industry. Production tripled, and there was virtually zero unemployment; and when the war ended, Birmingham was on a roll like never before. The factories flamed and belched throughout the night, spur-rail lines backing up to their loading docks to haul the stuff away; and it seemed as though the good times might last forever. Now came movie houses and restaurants and city parks and professional baseball (the Birmingham Barons, after the coal and iron "barons," whose radio announcer was a gravelly-voiced young man up from Selma by the name of "Bull" Connor) and trolley lines throughout the valley and even an unlighted airport, where pilots landed at night by the glow of the adjacent Republic Steel mill. With churchwomen leading the way, a civilizing process came to Birmingham: charity wards, more and better hospitals, temperance unions, summer camps where poor kids could escape the smoke and heat, suffrage movements, scouting organizations, the YMCA and the YWCA, Junior League. In 1921, as the city celebrated its semicentennial, the population figures were 179,000 for the city and 310,000 for the metropolitan area, making Birmingham the third-largest city in the South, behind Atlanta and New Orleans. At Terminal Station, the city's Ellis Island, a huge, lighted Erector Set sign appeared: "Birmingham, the MAGIC CITY."

But lurking deep below the surface, like a latent volcano smoldering and building its strength toward some cataclysmic day of reckoning, there was another Birmingham. Of those 310,000 people in the metropolitan area, 133,000 were black—the highest percentage of blacks in any North American city of 100,000 or more. They were the sons and daughters of slaves and sharecroppers, and even though they were one-half of the work force, they held the most menial jobs, as domestics, yardmen, simple laborers. They lived in a thoroughly segregated society, in scores of shaggy communities dismissed as "Niggertown," and shared not at all in the city's periods of good fortune. In 1910, when there were 19,000 white children in public schools and a like number of blacks, the white schools were valued at $1,374,000, the black schools at only $81,680. To be sure, life was anything but a dream for black people in the other large southern cities, such as Memphis, Atlanta, and New Orleans; but in Birmingham, a gritty town of muscle and very little gentility and grace, segregation was maintained with great vigor.

To make sure it stayed that way, Birmingham boasted of having the largest Ku Klux Klan "klavern" in the nation, the Robert E. Lee Klan No. 1, with 18,000 members. If a white man wanted to get ahead in those days, if he knew what was good for him, he joined the Klan. (Thus a young Birmingham lawyer named Hugo L. Black, the future Supreme Court justice, stepped forward to take the oath.) During the twenties, their annual initiation ceremonies were gala family outings: whole lazy days filled with boating and picnicking and dancing at city parks, drawing crowds as large as 50,000, capped as darkness fell by the sight of as many as 1,750 men stepping forward in hooded white sheets to be publicly welcomed to the Klan in the eerie light of a burning cross. Forty years later, their distant heirs would dynamite a black church, killing four little girls, plunging Birmingham into a nightmare without end.

CHAPTER TWO

The Magic City

Our roots go back to Scotland. Hemphills had left there for Northern Ireland, then crossed the Atlantic to settle for a while in Nova Scotia, wandered halfway across Canada, and from Minnesota floated down the Mississippi as far as the great cotton port of Memphis. There they dispersed, one branch heading southwest to the forbidding pine forests of East Texas known as the Big Thicket (there is a Hemphill, Texas, today), others bushwhacking and following Cherokee trails four hundred miles in the other direction, back into the hills. My great-grandfather, James Eulysses Hemphill, was born in the province of Ontario in 1843, married a woman from Vermont, and sired a son in Chicago in 1867. His name was George Erastus Hemphill, and toward the end of the nineteenth century he had settled in the deep, dark hollows of the Cumberland Mountains in northeastern Tennessee. It was Daniel Boone country, untamed pioneer land better suited for animals than for men, in a swale forty miles west of what would become the first dam of Franklin Delano Roosevelt's vast Tennessee Valley Authority system in the 1930s, sitting beside the L&N railroad tracks in a dirt-road hamlet called Robbins.

This was hard country then, inbred and isolated and dancing to the beat of snake handlers and assorted other fire-and-brimstone Bible thumpers, stuck up there in the barren ridges and hollows not twenty miles below the Kentucky line; and almost all of the traffic was headed the other way from Robbins, following the railroad tracks south and west to Knoxville and Nashville and Chattanooga and even to the new city of Birmingham in Alabama. George Hemphill chose to dig in at Robbins, taking Mary White Lancaster of Sadieville, Kentucky, as his bride, building a frame house right on the road, fencing in a couple of acres behind it to hold some crops and a mule and a gathering of chickens and hogs and cows. By 1900 he had put up a building beside the tracks and opened a country store to serve not only Robbins but other nearby towns, with names like Glenmary, Sunbright, Rugby, and Smoky Junction. Soon he and Mary were raising a family: Helen; then Marie; and finally, when George was forty-three and Mary was thirty-seven, a son. The boy was born in that little house on August 18, 1911, and they named him Paul James Hemphill.

The trading post—and it was exactly that in a part of the country where bartering was the way much business was conducted—did very well because of its location. Mary threw a fit when George abruptly announced that he was becoming a Seventh-Day Adventist, meaning he would close the store on Saturdays, the one big shopping day of the week, but open it on Sundays, when the hardline Pentecostals of the area forbade themselves to go anywhere but church and home. This had come about when George fell under the spell of a group of Seventh-Day evangelists, who had charmed him into letting them use his store right there beside the tracks, rent-free, as a regional warehouse and distribution point for their fervent religious tracts. Even without weekend shoppers, the store survived, and profited to the extent that George and Mary Hemphill were able to buy one of the first Model A Ford automobiles in the county. Thus they were able to join the long caravan of gawkers who, church or no church, cranked up their cars on most Sunday afternoons around 1919 and drove twenty miles over the twisting dirt mountain roads for a glimpse of America's most famous hero of the First World War: Sergeant Alvin York, the sharpshooter, home from the Argonne forest, idling on the front-porch swing of his farmhouse above Jamestown, spitting tobacco over the rail until the grass wouldn't grow in the yard anymore.

But just like that, of a vague "fever," George Hemphill died, barely in his fifties. His elder daughter, Helen, had already gotten married, to a railroad man named Leonard Brown, and moved to Chattanooga to begin a family of her own. His widow, Mary, pondered what to do: stay on the land, such as it was, or follow the army of others who had traced the tracks to the cities? Even at the age of fifty she was already bent, from the poor diet of pork and corn and from the backbreaking work of tending animals and plowing and washing and cleaning, and she could see no future for her children in a world that was being left behind; there were precious few playmates and opportunities for them in Fentress County, Tennessee. She worried most for her son, Paul: a lonesome mountain kid, fatherless now, walking to a stark, puncheon-floored one-room schoolhouse, returning to help out his mother with the chores, his best friend being the mule, Sally—early to bed, early to rise, nowhere to go and nothing to do. And the store: she knew nothing about running a store. She hung on for about five more years, mostly looking for a buyer, since she had made up her mind that leaving was the thing to do; and when she got a decent price for the store and the house, it was time to be moving on. On a morning in 1926, the mother and her two teenage children loaded up the car with all it would hold and, with the fifteen-year-old boy who would be my father at the wheel, lumbered away on a grinding journey of nearly three hundred miles to the city that everybody was talking about.

In Birmingham they first moved in with Leonard and Helen, who had drifted down from Chattanooga, and then rented a house in the neighborhood of Woodlawn, beside a strand of four railroad tracks, four miles east of downtown. Marie soon got married and left. Paul entered nearby Woodlawn High School, one of the largest schools in the state of Alabama, and his mother was so flush that she bought him an upright piano out of Chicago and got him to taking lessons. The money was still there, earning handsome interest in a bank; and there was no struggle to pay the bills. Birmingham might be having its ups and downs due to the nature of its one-industry, one-company economy—"Hard times come here first and stay longest" was already becoming a wry adage—but life was fine. This was, after all, the Roaring Twenties. He was good in school, especially in math and science, and he was growing into a lank young man with a disarming grin and a swaggering independence that made him stand out in a student body of more than one thousand. Being in the city, among crowds, had brought out a gregariousness in him. He was partway through his senior year at Woodlawn High, hearing teachers tell him he should think about going on to college, when the stock market crashed in the fall of '29.

His mother managed to get ten cents on the dollar for her savings, but life would never be the same for them, or for millions of others in America. The Great Depression was on, as severely in Birmingham as anywhere else in the nation, and now everything had changed. They moved in with friends. Mary began to cook and sew and wash clothes again, this time for others, and Paul dropped out of high school to take whatever work he could find: selling newspapers, delivering telegrams, digging coal at speculative "wildcat" mines in the woods, clerking at a grocery store. For one adventurous year, with the help of his railroading brother-in-law, Leonard Brown, he joined the legions of tatterdemalions who rode boxcars and passenger trains with work passes in the pockets of their overalls or in their bindles or stuffed into their work boots—sanctioned hoboes—to repair track and string wires and crush gravel along the Rock Island Line as far away as northern Missouri and southern Iowa, sleeping in makeshift work camps beside the tracks, eating beans, taking money home, going back for more, growing up fast.

Paul came back home to Birmingham for good when he was nearing his twentieth birthday; he lived with his mother again and worked as a stock boy at Hill's Grocery on First Avenue North in Woodlawn. He took to hanging around the steps of the majestic granite First Baptist Church next door to the high school—it was a great place to meet girls, the venue for a mating dance that occurred night after night in the soft Alabama summer evenings. One night during the preening and circling and cooing and strutting he met a demure blonde named Velma Rebecca Nelson. She was one of five daughters (plus one son) of a husky miner and plumber named Charles Nelson and his wife, the former Addie May Caldwell, who lived in a two-story Victorian house, on the main trolley line, only three blocks away from the church and catty-corner from Hill's Grocery. Velma was about to graduate from Woodlawn High, but as with most young women of her time, her dream in life was simply to marry and have children. Paul and Velma locked in on each other immediately, fell in love, vowed they would marry, then realized they couldn't raise enough money even to pay a preacher. That year, 1931, was not the most propitious time to be falling in love.

One afternoon they were panting around the big house when Daddy Nelson, as he insisted on being called, nearly shot up out of the deep, overstuffed hardwood-and-velvet chair from which he ruled the house like a plantation lord (something he had come by honestly, his maternal lineage going back to John Sevier, who became Tennessee's first governor in 1796). Marrying off all of these daughters smack in the middle of the Depression was more than one man could handle; but now, perusing the news of strikes and suicides and bank failings and closed mines and trouble even in the Pacific, he had come across the first promising news he had read in the newspaper in years. "You kids want to get married, here's your chance," he said, thrusting the paper at his third daughter and this hillbilly boy lusting to make her his bride. There was an advertisement announcing that the Ritz Theater, a downtown movie house, was looking for "the perfect couple" to be married right there on its stage between features. Everything would be on the house: rings, preacher, music, honeymoon suite at the Thomas Jefferson Hotel, even passage on the daily excursion train to Chattanooga and a ride up the Incline Railway to see Rock City. It wasn't the church wedding that Velma had envisioned, and she was horrified at the thought of kissing her new husband right in front of all those strangers; but as Paul said—out of earshot of the old man—what the hell! They went downtown to be interviewed, and when the theater manager saw this tall, handsome boy and svelte blond girl he looked no further. Two weeks later, November 19, 1931, on the entertainment pages of the Birmingham *News,* a gaudy Ritz Theater ad in the lower right-hand corner of page 20 served as their wedding announcement.

TONIGHT AT 8:30 P.M.

REAL
STAGE
WEDDING

Miss Velma Nelson and Mr. Paul Hemphill
will be married on the stage.
You are invited to witness
the beautiful ceremony.

Imagine the scene in such a place, in such a town, in such a time. There were a dozen downtown movie houses in Birmingham in those days, charging twenty-five cents in the afternoon and forty cents at night, some of them with live house bands and hoofers and jugglers and magicians between feature movies. During the Depression, that was the best entertainment most blue-collar white people could afford (blacks, of course, had the Carver Theater in *their* downtown), and once a week the newspapers ran glowing summaries of the new picture shows coming to town. But this, now—a real live wedding on the stage of the Ritz—was a promoter's dream. Velma had made her own dress; Paul had borrowed a tuxedo; and her preacher from Woodlawn did the honors. But there were no maid of honor and no best man, because neither bride nor groom could find anybody willing to go up on that stage with them. The only exception (likely because he was pushed or threatened) was a four-year-old nephew named Milton Jones, the ring bearer: decked out in a white satin short-pants suit made by his mother, Velma's oldest sister, Mary, and thrilled by the feel of the satin, he stole the show by rubbing his belly throughout the proceedings. When the couple had said "I do" and swapped rings and kissed and were whisked away to the Thomas Jefferson Hotel, the hoots and cat-calls subsided and the lights went down for the evening's feature movie. (It was titled *Are These Our Children?*) When they returned from their day-long honeymoon in Chattanooga, the newlyweds settled into one side of a duplex in East Lake, a neighborhood three miles farther east from Woodlawn.

The paper that held the wedding announcement told of Birmingham and the world at large in 1931. The Japanese had overrun Manchuria on that very day, November 19. Saturday's Georgia-Tulane football game would be broadcast on WKBC, with Bull Connor at the mike. A runaway "negro" was being extradited from Michigan in the "suspected rape and murder" of a white woman. Single unfurnished rooms were renting for $3.50 a week; women's high-heel shoes sold for $3.65; Pizitz department store ("since 1898") was running a full-page ad promising that soon it would announce a credit plan in these times of woe; and the cigarettes of choice seemed to be Old Golds and Chesterfields and Lucky Strikes. Although the streets teemed with unemployed men and strikers and bloodshed and lynchings, there was none of that in the *News* that day. Rather, the paper carried a series of light diversions: serialized fiction ("The Marriage Racket"); comics ("Mutt and Jeff," "Maggie and Jiggs," "Barney Google," "Toots and Casper"); a column on bridge; horoscopes; radio listings (Paul Whiteman and Bing Crosby aired at prime time); limericks and verse and doggerel on the editorial pages; the "Marry-Go-Round" advice column. No black faces appeared anywhere, of course, except for a caricature of a black woman with her head wrapped in a bandanna à la Aunt Jemima to illustrate the daily "Mammy Sez" feature: "Ole Miss, when er 'Oman wid er PAS [Miss, when a woman with a past] marries er Man wid er FUTURE, dat's every Reason for PRESENT TRUBBLE. Yassum."

Those were grim days, the absolute pits of the Depression, when fifteen dollars a week was considered sufficient income for a couple to get by on, even with a child or two in the house. The trouble was scraping up even fifteen dollars. "Hoover camps" were everywhere throughout Jones Valley. Mines and mills were closed, and huge piles of pig iron lay rusting beside the silent furnaces. Communists and union organizers were working the mining camps, trying to recruit members, but the bosses knew that the way to counteract that was to push the racial button. When an attempt was made to organize the miners in a certain camp in 1931, the bosses spread the rumor that two particular black men who happened to be strong in the movement had raped and murdered two white women, and before the frenzy was over it had resulted in seventy lynchings and cold-blooded murders.

Paul Hemphill wasn't involved in that, never would be, even though he was suffering as much as the rest. When he and his bride had settled in, across the street from Velma's older sister Ethel, now married to an insurance salesman named Forrest Lacey, he continued scraping up money where he could find it:

painting houses, digging for coal in Daddy Nelson's wildcat mine, trying to sell encyclopedias to people who couldn't spell the word. At one point it got so bad that he and Velma had to move in with his brother-in-law Leonard Brown, the railroad man, back in Harriman, Tennessee, on the rail line near Robbins, just to have a roof over their heads. But out of that came a connection with the Southern Railroad, as sort of an unofficial porter on the daily excursion train between Birmingham and Chattanooga. For Velma's sake, to be near her family, they moved back to Birmingham, to a two-bedroom bungalow on the same street as before.

The situation began to ease a bit then, for them and for Birmingham, as Franklin Roosevelt began shaking up the economy. Huge orders for steel rails were being placed with TCI, and there were rumblings of war on two sides of the world, prompting the furnaces and steel mills to reopen. Paul's job on the Chattanooga excursion train opened freelance opportunities for him. When he left the house each day at daybreak to take the trolley that stopped across the street and would deliver him at Terminal Station downtown, his coat pockets would bulge with sandwiches his wife had prepared and wrapped in waxed paper—sandwiches he would sell on the sly, a nickel each, to the passengers. That's where the money was coming from on February 18, 1936, when Velma went into labor and they sped across town in Forrest Lacey's car to the South Highlands Infirmary. At 9:17 p.m. a boy was born: Paul James Hemphill, Jr. It was a new day for everybody: the newborn me, the proud parents who had survived the Depression, and the city of Birmingham, whose mills were beginning to fire up again. Later that same year they dusted off the giant statue of Vulcan, which had been stored at the Alabama Fairgrounds on the western side of town since the St. Louis world's fair of 1904, and carted it to the top of Red Mountain for the whole world to see. I was Vulcan's child.

.   .   .

To pay for my birthing, Daddy painted the house of Dr. R. G. Lovelady, one of those amiable, satchel-toting general practitioners of an era when doctors made house calls. From up on the knobby hill that was Zion City, a little pocket of a black neighborhood that had been virtually hidden there since the close of the Civil War, he recruited a placid, snuff-dipping middle-aged woman known to us only as Louvenia to help Mama with me (at a dollar a day) while he continued on the excursion train. They had been saving their pennies, literally; and as Birmingham recovered and the fires at the mills began to roar through the night to meet new demands for the prewar buildup, he quit the railroad and bought a dump truck and began to deliver coal all over town, from holes he had personally dug, in what amounted to a one-man coal operation. A man with a truck, in a town where heavy stuff needed hauling, was in great demand. At the end of each day he would return, coughing and covered with coal dust and aching all over, but smiling and wisecracking and lighting a cigar as he grandly emptied his pockets of crinkled bills and loose change: "Here's for rent . . . this'll get groceries . . . a dollar for Louvenia . . . and this is for the jar." Life seemed worth living, after all.

Out on the rolling lands to the south of the city, where the plantations had sprawled, there was abject poverty. In the year of my birth, a writer named James Agee and a photographer named Walker Evans had moved in with poor white sharecroppers in a county some fifty miles southwest of Birmingham to document a devastating portrait of that life in a book they would call *Let Us Now Praise Famous Men*. Those who could escape the ravages of the boll weevil and the humiliations of sharecropping, both blacks and whites alike, kept pouring into Birmingham to take jobs in the shadow of the mighty statue of Vulcan. As had happened two decades earlier, with the First World War, the city was on the verge of a boom. The foundries and furnaces and steel mills were going full blast again, trying to keep up with frantic orders from an England that was being drawn into war by Hitler's Germany, and they were keeping another eye on Japan. This meant jobs, and the heavy industries were hiring every available man and woman—especially TCI, which would, on the very eve of the United States' entry into the war, directly employ forty thousand workers (and even have its own one-plane private airline, a daily shuttle service to Pittsburgh for U.S. Steel foremen and executives referred to as "Pennsylvania Airways").

In the early days of 1940, my mother took to the back bedroom of the bungalow that sat right on the sidewalk on Fifth Avenue North in East Lake. I spent entire days under the slippered feet of Louvenia, who would trudge down the hill from Zion City before my father had left; I followed her around as she washed our clothes and cooked our meals and got on her knees to scrub the floors by hand. She was the first black person I had ever known, and I liked the way she smelled and the way she said "I S'wanee" to almost everything and the way she would wink and slip me a penny out of the blue—all mine, to take and hide somewhere—wrapping my fingers around the shiny copper, winking again, making me promise not to tell. I had heard the word "nigger" plenty of times, from my parents and some of my many aunts and uncles, but this was Louvenia.

One of those mornings, Daddy stayed on after Louvenia got to the house, and suddenly there was a flurry. Mama was moaning in the back bedroom and Daddy was on the phone to Dr. Lovelady and Louvenia was put to work boiling towels and I was told to run across the street to the Laceys' house. It was February 6, 1940. For what seemed like an eternity I peered through the Laceys' venetian blinds with my cousins Ed and Jim; but it was probably only a couple of hours later when Dr. Lovelady emerged from the house and paused to wave at the window where he knew I was lurking, and then Louvenia came to the porch, beckoning for me, and I bolted across the street and was led to the darkened back bedroom where I beheld my mother holding a bundle in her arms and smiling weakly. I had a sister now, a playmate, Mary Joyce. I made the public prints for the first time two months later, when I was quoted in the "Baby Mine" feature of the Birmingham *News*: "I want you to take her back [I had told Dr. Lovelady] and bring me a walking one." The *News* paid my parents a dollar for sending it in.

Needing more room, we moved into a three-bedroom rental frame house that was three blocks away on a hill overlooking East Lake Park. My mother was full of herself by now, having survived the Depression and given birth to one boy and one girl, and she became a serious churchgoer for life, beating a regular path to the cozy little Lake Highlands Methodist Church up the street, Sunday mornings and Wednesday nights and half the day on Saturdays, hell or high water, good times or bad. My father never went if he could find an excuse, but these days he seemed to have something big on his mind, something churning inside, plenty to keep him out of church. He was spending a lot of time out front with his dump truck, parked half in the street and half on the sidewalk, peering under the hood and inspecting the mechanism in the rear end that raised the bed in order to dump a load, then standing back for a long look, like an artist sizing up a landscape before painting it. One day when he brought the truck home it had cylindrical fifty-gallon gas tanks strapped to the sides. Another day he arrived and it wasn't even a dump truck anymore; the dump bed was gone, replaced by a fifth wheel he had salvaged from a junkyard. And the next thing we knew, the former dump truck rolled up towing a flatbed trailer he had bought with three hundred dollars he had borrowed somewhere. On a Sunday morning when we walked back home from church we saw him fiercely sawing two-by-fours and bolting them to the trailer to make sideboards. When a neighbor came by to ask him what the hell all the racket was about, Daddy told him, "There's a lot of stuff gonna need haulin', and I thought I'd help 'em out."

What happened next was downright heroic when you weigh all of the circumstances, and it changed our lives forever. In January of '41, with Birmingham's furnaces lighting up the sky all over town on the eve of the war, my father made a deal to haul a load of hatch covers for tanks and ships from a Birmingham foundry to Portland, Oregon, three thousand miles away. He would be pulling the load over the southern Rockies in an untested converted dump truck that had no heater, no radio, no chains, no insurance, certainly no power steering or power brakes. Here was a twenty-nine-year-old whose only experience on the open road had been as a teenager driving a Model A Ford three hundred miles out of the Tennessee hills, and now he was going to strike out across the continent and learn over-the-road trucking in one impossible lesson. All he had when he left one bitterly cold morning was enough cash for gas and oil and occasional snacks, a thermos full of coffee, sandwiches Mama had made and wrapped, a road map, a bill of lading, several army blankets, and a kerosene heater on the floorboard. He would be back, he told us, when he got back. And off he went.

Maybe he called Mama along the way, but probably not, since that generation of Americans who had survived the thirties still squeezed nickels, as they said, "till the buffalo cries." He took the southern route to avoid winter storms, cracking the crank-out windows to keep from becoming asphyxiated by the kerosene heater, driving for twenty of every twenty-four hours, stopping only for coffee and information at roadhouses, napping in the cab and then running around outside to awaken himself before firing up the truck again and moving on. Sweeping out of the South, onward through Dallas and El Paso, he struggled through the mountain passes of New Mexico and Arizona, and when he was clear he hugged the Pacific coast and triumphantly sailed into Portland to deliver the stuff on time. *That's real good, Alabama, now turn around and go get us another one.* He got wind of a return load of crated brussels sprouts in the San Joaquin Valley of California, took it on, and lit out for home. When he got back to Birmingham, exhausted as he was, he could hardly get to sleep. The glory of it all: six thousand miles in ten days, across America and back again! By cutting every corner possible, he had netted one thousand and ten dollars while men with jobs in the mills had earned only sixty dollars in wages. All that he would become, for better and for worse, had been forged on that trip.

CHAPTER THREE

Other Voices:
Surgeons and
Sharecroppers

*Then, as now, there were three distinct Birminghams. We, the
Hemphills and the Nelsons and their progeny, were solidly in the
middle of one. We were part of the white immigrants who had
drifted in from the Appalachian ridges, for the most part, to form
a blue-collar class that in the beginning lived in the coal camps
and the clapboard middle-class neighborhoods and the sooty mill
villages that were strung out through Jones Valley for twenty
miles, from piney woods communities like Clay and Chalkville in
the east to the lusty belching steel towns of Ensley and Fairfield
and Bessemer in the west. Another class, of almost equal size, was
African-American: descendants of slaves and sharecroppers, most
of them having migrated into the city from the farmlands of south
Alabama and east Mississippi, now domestics and laborers,
crowded into an area of only twenty square miles immediately
west of the downtown business section. The third visible class in
Birmingham was formed by the wealthy whites, the doctors and
lawyers and coal and iron barons known collectively (with equal
parts of awe, fear, and distaste) as the Big Mules, people with
breeding and good educations and wherewithal and positions of
power, who literally lived above the fray in mansions on Red
Mountain. The three classes had little in common, seldom spoke,
and did not think kindly of each other.*

While the saga of the Hemphill family played on out there

*in the blue-collar neighborhoods of East Lake and Woodlawn,
two families representing the other major social classes in the city
were going about their lives from entirely different perspectives.
The family of John Thomas Porter, descendants of Alabama
sharecroppers, had arrived in Birmingham in 1926 just as my
father rolled into town as a teenager. The family of Mimi Tynes
(née Emily Symington Wilson) were among the original white
settlers of Jones Valley, later producing surgeons who eventually
became part of the cloistered white elite in what is known as
"over the mountain."*

*Parallel lives. During the summer of 1992, while living in
Birmingham, I spent many hours talking to John Porter and
Mimi Tynes. Porter was born in 1931, the year of my parents'
wedding at the Ritz Theater; the son of a yardman and a domestic, he rose to play a central role in the upheavals of 1963 as
pastor of the largest black church in Birmingham, Sixth Avenue
Baptist. Tynes, born only hours before my sister, on February 5,
1940, lived an isolated life of privilege, devoting much of her
adult life after Smith College to being a wife and mother and
Junior Leaguer, but then experienced an awakening in regard to
race relations and was selected as Birmingham's Woman of the
Year in 1986 as the founder of a program called Youth Leadership
Forum. As I dug through my life during the spring and summer
of my fifty-seventh year, reading and listening and simply riding
around town, the voices of John Porter and Mimi Tynes kept
whispering in my ears, telling me the rest of the story, advising
me of two Birminghams I had barely known.*

Mimi Tynes

The Wilsons were among the original settlers of what would become Birmingham. My father's family came here in the early
1800s. His great-great-grandfather, Allen Wilson, settled in the
Roebuck area. Part of their property became the Roebuck Municipal Golf Course and the old Boys Industrial School, near Wil-

son Chapel Methodist Church. In fact, the family cemetery is behind the original Wilson Chapel. My grandfather, Dr. Cunningham Wilson, a surgeon, was born in 1860 and died in 1949. He grew up in the family home in Roebuck, but he and his wife moved to the Five Points South area, half a block from where the Highlands Bar & Grill is now. The first commercial shops were going up there about that time, and my grandfather sold his lot to early developers of the area. My grandparents were also instrumental in starting the Highlands Methodist Church, which was built across the street from them.

My father's maternal great-grandfather, John Smith, came to Jones Valley in 1816 from the Union District in South Carolina. He settled in Jonesboro, now Bessemer, on a two-thousand-acre cotton plantation. His second child, my father's great-uncle, Dr. Joseph Riley Smith, was born in 1818 and was the second white child born in Jefferson County.

My father, Dr. Frank Cunningham Wilson, was born in 1892. He went to Virginia Military Institute, majored in engineering, and graduated in 1913. He came back to Birmingham and worked in a bank for a few years before deciding he wanted to become a doctor. He went to Tulane Medical School and then did his internship and residency at the Union Memorial Hospital in Baltimore. That's where he met my mother, Emily Bland Symington, a cousin of Stuart Symington, the senator. Her grandfather John Randolph Bland founded USF&G Insurance Company. At one point John Bland purchased Westover, his family's original homestead on the James River in Virginia, but his wife wouldn't move that far away from the life she loved in the city. As a compromise, he bought a large place in Catonsville, Maryland, which was considered far out in the country then. They lived there about eight months of the year and spent the other four in the city. My mother's family lived with them.

Mother started her freshman year at Bryn Mawr College,

but a month later her grandfather died. That was a time when you went into deep mourning. Rather than stay in college in mourning, she left and decided to go to nursing school at Union Memorial Hospital. This was in 1921. Somewhere, we have a newspaper clipping with a headline that says, "Debutante Goes to Nursing School." This is where she met my father, at a time when it was verboten for doctors and nurses to have anything to do with each other socially.

They got married in 1924 and moved to Birmingham. Mother has a lot of good stories about what it was like, coming to visit with his family before they got married. I think there were a lot of people on both sides wondering about this match. For my mother's family in Baltimore it was a long way for their daughter to be going, to this strange young place called Birmingham, and for my father's family it was like having a Yankee come to town.

Their first apartment was in the Hanover Courts Apartments, which are still on Highland Avenue behind the Claridge Apartments. Very early in their marriage, they and four other couples formed a group called the Thursday Gathering. It was like what we would call a supper club, but they met not just once a month but every Thursday night to have drinks and then go out to dinner. They continued this practice until a few years ago, when only four of the ten were still living and they were not quite able to get out at night. It's remarkable to me that they kept on for almost sixty years and that no couple moved out of town or got divorced.

My father was a surgeon, but he was more like a general practitioner to his patients. He always had his black bag in the car, and there was no such thing as not taking calls morning, noon, and night, or on weekends. He played golf and a little gin, but he never really had time for hobbies. If his patients could pay, they paid; if they couldn't, they didn't. Daddy, known to almost everyone as "Dr. Frank," was small of stature, large of character—quite a character—and a much beloved and widely respected doctor in this area. He would have been one hundred years old last March.

My most vivid memories of spending time with Daddy were the times he would take me along when he made rounds at St. Vincent's Hospital. He would introduce me to his patients, the nurses, and the nuns, who wore the old habits like those in "The Flying Nun." Sometimes I would wait for him at the switchboard just inside the main entrance. He always wore a well-known and well-recognized hat, which he left at the switchboard whenever he entered the hospital. If that hat was there, the operator knew Dr. Frank was there, too.

My mother is eighty-nine now. She, too, is small of stature and large of character. She has lived through many stages and transitions, but has happily enjoyed the good and courageously accepted the bad of each. As a young girl she lived in a large, rambling country home run by a large staff of servants and often filled with visiting aunts, uncles, and cousins. Now she lives in a condominium and cherishes the independence of taking care of herself. She is a very resilient woman and was always willing to take steps that took her beyond what was expected of her. I've learned a great deal from her.

John Porter

Both of my parents were born just before 1910 in Russell County, Alabama, in the little town of Pittsview, near Phenix City, across the river from Columbus, Georgia. Their fathers were sharecroppers who worked the cotton fields, had little vegetable gardens for themselves, and raised pigs and cows. My mother may have gone to the fifth or sixth grade, but my father didn't go to school. He could sign his name all right, but I don't think he could read very well, if at all.

They came to Birmingham somewhere around 1926 and rented a three-room shotgun house on the Southside, near where

UAB is today, in Scruggs Alley. My mother has always talked about how clean those little houses were, how the country girls would come to town and get their first house and scrub those floors every day, which was her way of saying that even good folks can come out of an alley. My father worked briefly for Frazer Nursery, a part of Elmwood Cemetery; but just before my sister was born, in '27, he got a job as a yardman at one of the mansions on top of Red Mountain, and he held on to that job for twenty-five years—until I caused him to get fired. I'll get to that later.

The house was owned by Mr. Thomas W. Martin, president of Alabama Power. It was near Key Circle, just east of where they would later put Vulcan, with beautiful views of Birmingham down below, and in the twenties and thirties that's where the very richest white people lived. They had several servants for that one house: yardman, butler, cook, chauffeur, upstairs maid, even a seamstress. Mr. Martin was short in stature, but he was a giant of a man in other ways, a multimillionaire, a tremendous power in this city. He had a traditional southern mentality on race.

Anyway, one of the games that blacks played with whites back then was to borrow money as soon as you got the job. It was sort of a reverse spin on "owe my soul to the company store." If you owed 'em money, they weren't likely to fire you. My father was having to walk nearly two miles uphill just to get to Key Circle every day, so one day he asked Mr. Martin if he could borrow some money to buy a car. Mr. Martin said, "No, you don't need a car, Robert, but I'll lend you the down payment on a house." So, in spite of his traditional racial views, he blessed us in a very special way. They bought a house on Sixteenth Avenue South in what is now Titusville, behind the Birmingham jail, four houses from the railroad tracks—nothing fancy, but it wasn't a three-room shotgun house. I was born in that house in 1931, and my mother still lives there.

My father did manage to buy a car soon after that, but he never let Mr. Martin know about it. Every morning he would drive to the mountain and park the car at Key Circle and then walk up to the mansion. He did that for years, even when I became a teenager and went along to help him in the yard: drive up, hide the car, make Mr. Martin think he'd either walked all the way from Titusville or taken the bus. He was under the impression that Mr. Martin would not be pleased that he was "okay," independent, capable of watching his money, managing his affairs, taking care of business. My mother was the same way about the house. She lived in fear that Mr. Martin might come by the house one day and see how nice it was.

The Martins are dead now, but the mansion is still there, and not long ago I was invited to dinner right across the street from it. I dreamed once of buying it. A house like that, it's almost prohibitive to build one these days, and I can't imagine the upkeep. All of the very rich moved out, farther away over the mountain, and the physicians and contractors who moved in really couldn't afford to have a full-time yardman. The Martins used to have gardens, roses, a fabulous place, but no longer is the beautiful yard there. The mansion is still there, though, overlooking Birmingham, with the same great view. Say what you will about Mr. Martin and his feelings about the servants, that house and the Martins were major factors in our lives.

CHAPTER FOUR

White Bread and Baseball

Turn around and go get another load, Alabama. Daddy couldn't drive hard enough once the Second World War got going. Birmingham went into full-time war production, was being called "the great arsenal of the South," and we were more proud than fearful to learn that the Germans and the Japanese had drawn up secret plans to bomb Pittsburgh first and Birmingham second if they got that far. The factories were running nonstop now, men on swing shifts and women on the production lines, making bombs, rolling steel for warships and tanks, modifying all of the country's B-29 bombers in a plant only a mile or two from our house in East Lake.

FDR's New Deal had been a start toward ending the Depression in Birmingham, and the war finished the job. Now there were traffic jams at the factory gates three times a day when the shifts changed, and anybody who didn't have anything to do with his hands those days was, to quote a southernism, "just plain *sorry*." In due time the old converted dump truck was replaced by a shiny new blood-red four-ton Dodge, and Daddy was hiring himself out from job to job as a "leased operator," a freelance long-haul trucker, busy as a New York cabbie at rush hour—coming home just long enough to hose down the rig and introduce himself to his wife and two young children, collapsing under the covers for deep twelve-hour sleeps while other men across town filled his trailer throughout the night, loading up on roast beef and mashed potatoes while Mama washed his clothes and I crawled all over the exotic behemoth parked outside on the street. Soon he would be roaring off into the night again, to Mobile and Pascagoula and New Orleans and Charleston, wherever ships were waiting. *There's a lot of stuff gonna need haulin', and I thought I'd help 'em out.*

He had found his life's work, a calling that energized him and defined him, and he had a bankroll by the time he was thirty years old. Never again would he make the kind of money he had seen from that quixotic odyssey to Portland, nor would he ever be able to promise Mama a house in the posh new over-the-mountain neighborhood called Mountain Brook; but never again would we be lacking. Money was pouring in, and every time he came in off the road and laid a wad of bills on the kitchen table, he and Mama would count it and record it and buy another fifty-dollar War Bond and then put the rest away in a cigar box they stashed somewhere in the house. A car would be nice to get around in, she said, but they were hard to come by; and besides, he didn't have time to go looking for one right now.

But one day late in 1943, when the war had turned in favor of the Allies and the end was in sight, he did find the time to carry us to the next level. Paying two thousand dollars in cash, and getting a truck-driving buddy known to us only as Wasson to help him transport our meager belongings in one day, he moved us into the house that I would most associate with my childhood. It was a solid frame three-bedroom house on a half-acre corner lot in Woodlawn—6000 Fifth Court South, telephone 9-5509—nearly three miles closer to downtown and only five blocks from where he and his mother and older sister had lived upon their arrival seventeen years earlier. We were situated in the bottoms where Sixtieth Street swooped down from both directions and Fifth Court came down to meet it and form a T; surrounded by Birmingham's ubiquitous railroad tracks, Southern behind us and Seaboard three blocks in the other direction. It was a pure blue-collar neighborhood where every morning the men tromped off to work at physical jobs (bus driver, steel-worker, mechanic, railroad engineer, trucker) while the women stayed home to mind the kids and the house. My new elementary school, Minnie Holman, was a mile away. The business district of Woodlawn was another mile off in the other direction, across the Southern tracks; there we could catch the trolley on First Avenue when we had to go all the way into downtown Birmingham. And up on the hill, beyond a dense stand of trees that served as a no-man's-land between the races, there was a jumbled collection of shanties on stilts jabbed into the rocky red earth, a mysterious place that we called Niggertown.

The end of the war marked the beginning of what seem now, nearly half a century later, the best years of my life: white bread and baseball, adolescent hijinks, bicycles and skates and model airplanes, cowboy movies and radio heroes and playing war between the hedges. The neighborhood had become flooded with kids who were on the tenuous edges of puberty, the off-spring of blue-collar parents who had survived the Depression and the rationing imposed during the war and now were dedicated to giving their children the things they had never had. There were fathers to bring home bacon and mothers to cook it. Automobiles began to appear; on a family trip downtown one night in the truck, in the gleaming showroom at Liberty Motors, Daddy placed an order for a green four-door '46 sedan, which he would proudly call "the seventy-eighth new Dodge sold in Birmingham after the war." And when the first television set showed up on the block a few years later, the houses would empty at dusk on Wednesdays and whole families would take to the sidewalks—"We just happened to be out for a walk. . . . My, my, would you look at that!"—in hopes of being invited into the Hulls' house to take a gander at "The Arthur Godfrey Show." In the wealthy cloisters behind Vulcan's back, over the mountain, children were attending private schools and learning table manners at country clubs and summering at family retreats in the mountains or on the Gulf Coast. Down in the teeming neighborhoods of Tuxedo Junction and Titusville and Pratt City, in the dark continent just west of downtown, black children were wearing homemade clothes and playing with hand-me-down toys and crowding into ramshackle schoolhouses and getting arrested for things white kids did as "childish mischief" on Halloween. But it would be a while before we knew anything of those two other worlds out there.

Our lives were centered at the intersection of Sixtieth Street and Fifth Court South in Woodlawn. We roamed the streets and yards and alleys like a band of ragamuffins, uniformed in Keds sneakers and torn blue jeans and soiled T-shirts, and it's a wonder we survived. From two-by-fours and apple crates and last year's skates we fashioned "skatemobiles" for pell-mell kamikaze runs down the hills. With broomsticks and fishing corks we played "corkball" in the streets. We descended through manhole covers and explored the labyrinthian sewer system. We played sports in season, baseball and football and basketball and a crude southern form of hockey requiring skates and broomsticks and tin cans and towels wrapped around the legs as shin pads. Johnny Sudderth, Wallace Graddick, the Sumners boys, Ed Thorn, Karl Pugh, Earl Freedle, Mickey Robinson. We were all there, gawking, on the day Mickey Rooney came to town in a Chrysler convertible to take another bride: Betty Jean Rase, Miss Birmingham of 1944, who lived at the top of the hill and would be replacing Ava Gardner as the next of the many Mrs. Rooneys. We shot BB guns at birds and threw rocks at streetlights and smoked "rabbit tobacco" in the woods. We peeped into girls' bedrooms and found our fathers' rubbers and carefully monitored Gay Sims's breast development and refused to believe the deck of cards filched from one father's bureau that showed a man and a woman doing amazing things to each other in fifty-two different positions.

One afternoon in October of '46 my father was sitting in the living room, his eyes on the Motorola radio, and he invited me to join him. "You might be interested in this, son," he said. It was the seventh game of the World Series, the Boston Red Sox playing the Cardinals at Sportsman's Park in St. Louis, and when I heard the announcer's breathless description of Enos "Country" Slaughter scoring all the way from first base on a single by Harry "the Hat" Walker (from Leeds, a country town right out the road from Woodlawn) to lock up the Series for the Cardinals, I fell in love with baseball—no, I was consumed by it. The next spring, when an earnest young man from Birmingham-Southern College by the name of Billy Legg came by Minnie Holman to see who wanted to play YMCA baseball, I jumped at the chance. With ten dollars earned from my first job, helping an old truck farmer named Mr. Amberson as he sold vegetables and live chickens on a route stretching from the Avondale Mill Village to Homewood, I bought my first glove at Woodlawn Hardware. Soon I was playing all day and following the Cardinals or the Birmingham Barons of the Class AA Southern Association over the radio at night, in a bedroom virtually wallpapered with color "Sportraits" from *Sport* magazine, with Harry Caray's chatter crackling in and out over the radio from KMOX in St. Louis, and a local announcer named Gabby Bell (Bull Connor, as we shall see, had found other things to do) fancifully re-creating Barons road games with only terse Western Union tickertapes to inform him ("LYONS BAT" would become "Up steps Eddie Lyons, folks, the Barons' dependable little bandy-legged second baseman, with a three-game hitting streak on the line. [*Gabby turns up the crowd machine:*] The fans here at Sulphur Dell in Nashville are booing"). Late in the summer of '47 my father took me out to see a doubleheader between the Barons and the Mobile Bears, starring an angular first baseman named Chuck Connors, and it didn't matter to me that the sec-

ond game was called when irate Birmingham fans tossed their
rental seat cushions onto the playing field. During the 1948 season, as a twelve-year-old boy, sometimes with my father or a pal
but mostly alone, I attended fifty of the Barons' seventy-seven
home games all the way across town at marvelous old Rickwood
Field, built by and named for a steel baron named Rick Wood-
ward, often getting home on the bus past eleven o'clock, which
said as much about the safe passage of a kid in those days as it
did about my love of baseball.

Baseball united my father and me—indeed, the entire family. He had a passion for it that I hadn't known about (his mother
had thought it a game for ruffians and hadn't allowed him to
play), and now I awaited more eagerly than before his triumphal
returns from the road. Until it got so dark that winged bats were
darting for the ball, he would hit towering pop flies to the boys
of the neighborhood in an old cornfield across the street that we
were busy trying to carve into a ball field decades before the
movie *Field of Dreams*. On Saturday mornings, as the Woodlawn
Blues played Roebuck or Huffman in the chatter of a dusty city
sandlot ("Hum-baby, hum-boy, lotsa pepper, lotsa pepper"), I
would look up from my position at second base in the scarred
infield of red-ore dirt and be startled to see him watching intently
from the top row of the bleachers. More than once the whole
family piled into the new car on Sunday at dawn, with a picnic
basket of fried chicken and potato salad made by Mama the
night before, and light out for Memphis or Chattanooga or Atlanta to sit through a doubleheader in box seats, beside the visiting Barons' dugout—the only fans in the park cheering for the
boys in gray road uniforms with "Birmingham" across their
shirts. (This once resulted in my being tossed a new baseball by
a Barons pitcher, later a Red Sox star, Willard Nixon.) Soon I
discovered the free weekly Hot Stove League meetings downtown at the Thomas Jefferson Hotel, where wintering players like

Harry and Dixie Walker would show up and World Series films would be shown, and usually I was the only person younger than twenty-five or thirty in attendance.

That first car had expanded my world considerably beyond Woodlawn and East Lake. Now Mama could haul us around town rather than begging rides or taking trolleys and buses, me to my baseball games and Joyce to her dancing lessons and both of us downtown to the airy department stores just before school reopened in the fall. Sometimes we would just pile into the car and go, the four of us, and I would see a Birmingham I had only heard of or merely glimpsed: the preened stately mansions of the supremely wealthy over the mountain; the dazzling gigantic steel mills, under ominous black clouds of smoke, on the far western end of Jones Valley; the bleak all-black neighborhoods, where anonymous faces stared back at us; the airport at night, where we marveled as twin-engined DC-6 planes, converted C-47 "Gooney Birds" from the war, lumbered in from Atlanta; the First Avenue Viaduct, where we double-parked following a movie and a vaudeville show at the Temple Theater downtown, to look down upon the Sloss Furnace and cheer the awesome showers of sparks and the rivers of slag and the silhouettes of men moving in the glare in an entertainment more dazzling than what we had paid to see at the Temple. We drove to Nashville for the Grand Ole Opry; to Florida for vacations at "Little Birmingham" on what later would come to be called the "Redneck Riviera"; and to Tennessee for visits with the remnants of Daddy's family.

None of this would have been possible, of course, if my father hadn't been a truck-driving man. Even the other kids saw him as something special. Wallace Graddick's father, next door, was a good and gentle man, but he spent his entire working life sitting behind a desk in a branch office of Alabama Power Company. Johnny Sudderth's father, ol' Jake, simply cruised Woodlawn in a car all day, picking up and delivering laundry and dry cleaning, making several stops at saloons to break the monotony. Mickey Robinson's father, Reuben, was the only bona fide steelworker on the block, but he was beat by the end of a shift, and every summer, when TCI went on strike as sure as July, he had to go around begging for odd jobs at other men's houses. All week long as we boys fooled around in the streets, we would see the other men trudge down the hill from the bus line at the end of the day, their lunch pails empty now, their faces drawn from working dull jobs, no one to greet them but a long-tailed dog or a wife standing on the porch wearing an apron and a worried look, and if my chums weren't thinking it, I was: My daddy's better than that. A father who commanded a snarling piece of machinery like mine did, a big old grinding semi truck towing a gleaming trailer—well, a kid could sink his teeth into something like that.

He knew it, too. If these were my best years, so were they his. Never in his life would he be on anybody's payroll or time card, or even belong to the Teamsters, because it wasn't in his constitution. (He began to carry a pistol beneath the driver's seat only after a meeting with a group of Teamsters organizers ended with his telling them to go to hell and their telling him to be careful when he drove under bridges.) He was a freelance trucker, a joyous king of the road who called his own shots, a legend in his time to people in that dim underworld of truck stops and loading docks and weigh stations and other places where men gathered to discuss cops and shortcuts and gas mileage and good coffee. By 1948 he had the closest thing he would ever know to a "regular" Monday–Friday job. He leased out his truck and his services to Alabama Highway Express, leaving out on Sunday nights pulling a trailer loaded with huge spools of cotton twine bound for the tire plants in Cumberland, Maryland, and returning on Fridays with a load of finished tires from there or from Akron, Ohio.

Although I had plenty to occupy my days—school, church, a newspaper route, my Barons, my radio, my chums—I was always looking ahead to late Friday afternoons. Oh, those calamitous homecomings! We would all be out in the street immersed in our scufflings when suddenly we would hear a rumbling at the top of the long hill and stop what we were doing and watch with open mouths as he paused to shift into his lowest gear and yank three long blasts on the air horn and blink his headlights before beginning his descent. Old ladies snapping beans on front-porch swings would crane their necks and dogs would start giving chase and we would edge away from the street to give him a wide berth as the dusty red monster came toward us now with a mighty cacophony of farting and belching and groaning until it finally came to rest with a deep sigh. The instant he had parked the rig on the street beside the house and given one final blast on the air horn—*for me!*—kids would be all over him. He would swing from the cab like a cowboy dismounting from his horse and take the cigar from his mouth and say, like Minnie Pearl at the Opry, "How-*dee,* I'm just so glad to be *hyar,*" pulling my baseball cap down over my eyes and sweeping my cowed little sister off her feet, reaching for a paper sack that we knew held souvenirs ranging from a key to the city of Akron to potholders that said "Kissin' Don't Last but Cookin' Do," briefly addressing the troops ("Soon's I get some sop-sop from Mama I'll see if I can still hit 'em") before barging into the house to hug the love of his life. He would be back outside in the pasture within ten minutes, sleeves rolled up, cigar clenched between his teeth, furiously swatting pop flies to us until the fireflies came out.

And then, over supper, at a Formica table in the little breakfast nook with a picture window that he had added on to the kitchen, audacious tales of the open road: "There was this waitress up in Bristol that had a face so ugly it'd already wore out two bodies. . . ." "They got watermelons that grow so fast the bottoms wear off before they can pick 'em. . . ." "The niggers

in Ohio ain't near as polite as the ones we got down here. . . ."
"Save a lot of gas if you put 'er in neutral going downhill. Call
it 'Jew overdrive.' . . ." "Can't hardly get to Cumberland without going through Tennessee, and I was overloaded, as usual, so
what you do is just wait till the boys on the scales go home at
midnight. They don't take their work near as serious as I
do. . . ." A born liar, refining his art. My mother would endure
these monologues and asides and entertainments, accepting his
playful compliments with a flushed face and a girlish smile I did
not yet understand, while Joyce was so intimidated by his caterwauling presence that she could barely look him in the eye.
"Never seen a truck stop yet that can do pinto beans like your
mama. [*Dramatic pause.*] 'Beans, beans, the musical fruit, the
more you eat 'em the more you toot.' . . ." After five days on
the road, eating what he could when he had time, he would linger
over these white soul-food feasts of pork chops and potatoes and
fried okra for more than an hour, a man who lived to eat rather
than the other way around, and afterwards he and I would retire
to the radio to listen to the Barons or the Cardinals. "We got to
get us one of those TVs, son," he said on one of those evenings.
"They had one at the hotel in Akron, and I saw the Cleveland
Indians playing. Ol' Early Wynn, the one from down there
around Dothan, he was pitching for the Senators. It was really
something, seeing it like that." Soon he would be at the old upright piano, cigar jammed in his mouth, banging through his
repertoire of Hank Williams and Hoagy Carmichael songs.

Then, at long last, the time came for me to go along with
him and see what the fuss was all about. It was the middle of
June in '49, as I recall, and at dusk on a Sunday, after a dinner
of roast beef and mashed potatoes followed by a fitful nap, I
found myself tossing an overnight bag holding a week's worth
of clean socks and underwear into the cab of the truck while he
walked around the rig and ran through what amounted to a

preflight check: tires, turn signals, head and tail and brake lights, gasoline tanks, fan belt, air hoses, trailer hitch. He had already gone to the loading dock and hooked on to a trailer loaded with spools of cotton cord, and brought the rig back to the house. We would be making the regular run to Cumberland and Akron, with a stop he wanted to make in Robbins, Tennessee, if we had enough time, so he could show me the place of his youth. We would cover about two thousand miles between then and Friday afternoon, most of it on old preinterstate asphalt roads twisting northeastward through the long troughs left by retreating glaciers to form the valleys of the Blue Ridge, and my heart was pumping as my parents hugged and cooed on the sidewalk and I surveyed the cab: radio and heater dangling from wires, spare oil cans, toolbox, oily rags, a paper bag holding a thermos of coffee and roast beef sandwiches, and, taped to the roof of the cab (hidden, he foolishly presumed, from Mama), a cheesecake calendar of Rita Hayworth wearing just about nothing. He swung up into the cab and lit a cigar and winked at me and then fired the engine—a mighty explosion, then *barrummppp-bam-bam, brrrmmmm-brrrmmmm,* finally a throaty grumbling and a long purr, *rrrrrrrrr, brrrrrrrrr,* that said we were ready—and he leaned through the window to have a final word with his wife, my mother. "Now Paul," she told him, "I don't want him to grow up being a truck driver." He twirled the cigar in his mouth and fumbled with the other hand to squeeze my knee. "It's good enough for me," he said, "and I notice there ain't nobody starving." With that he gave a blast on the air horn, jammed the gear into low, and we shuddered away from the curb.

Maybe insurance agents, wanting to impress their sons by showing them what they do for a living, dazzle them with amortization tables. Maybe writers' sons sit mesmerized for hours watching their fathers type. Maybe somewhere there is a banker earnestly explaining interest rates to his rapt son. It wasn't necessary for my father to say a word (although he would, of course, you betcha) as we lumbered through the bumpy streets and cleared the choked city until finally, at nightfall, we found old U.S. 11 and he gunned it for the first leg to Gadsden and Chattanooga before he could let it fly on the all-night run through Tennessee. All throughout the long, wonderful night, with a full moon tracking us, I was fully awake, attuned to everything I could see through the bug-spattered windshield of this enormous steed: truck stops sparkling like oases in the misty distance; Daddy and oncoming truckers blinking coded messages with their headlights in an era before citizens-band radio; motorcycle cops hiding behind billboards; "See Rock City" barns. Wind whistled through my hair; tires screamed; air hoses wheezed; all-night truckers' radio shows out of Cincinnati and Chicago and even Mexico kept us entertained ("That's one thousand baby chicks, folks, sex not guaranteed. . . . Now here's Hank Snow with 'Movin' On' "). At a truck stop somewhere in east Tennessee in the middle of the night, advised that I looked just like him, he told a gum-smacking waitress, "Well, the boy can't help it." Soon after, full of coffee and needing to relieve myself as we crawled around a mountain like an aged turtle, I learned the art of standing on the running board and peeing from a moving truck. "Hard work if you can get it," he cracked at some point after a dazzling run through all of his gears, like Gene Krupa on a drum solo, negotiating a tricky zigzag gap in the mountains of western Virginia.

Always overloaded or otherwise illegal, he slept all day and ran all night to dodge the weigh stations and checkpoints that littered his path like land mines. One time, in a particularly mean-spirited county, he shut down and left me in the darkened cab to walk half a mile for a look at a favorite ambush point in the valley, and soon trotted back with a grin and the news that "the boys must've got their quota and gone home." We rolled into Cumberland in time for them to unload the trailer on Tuesday afternoon, got a few hours' sleep at a motel run by a Pennsylvania Dutch family, and spent Wednesday night in the musty lobby of a hotel in the dingy armpit side of Akron. We might have run over to Cleveland that night so I could see my first major league baseball game; but since Daddy had to wait by the pay phone in the lobby for the call saying the trailer was loaded with tires and ready for the return trip, I had to settle for scrunching down on a sprung sofa in the lobby and watching the Indians play the St. Louis Browns. (Pitching for the Indians was Satchel Paige, the first black man I had ever seen playing base-ball, and curious to me now is the fact that I thought nothing of it either way.) Daddy shook me awake around midnight and we bobtailed along the brick streets of Akron, slick and eerie in a misty rain, coupling to the trailer once more and pointing south toward home. We would have to save Robbins for another trip, he said, thanks to the lazy-assed union dockworkers who had taken their sweet time loading the tires; and so we sailed home. This time, I was the one being hailed as a returning warrior by the kids on the block.

The sliced bread on the table wasn't the only thing in our world that was white, of course, and only now was I beginning to have vague questions about that. There was our world, and there was a black world. "They" lived in their own neighbor-hoods, went to their own schools and churches and theaters and restaurants, rode in the rear of buses and trolleys, couldn't try on clothes at the department stores, used "colored" fountains and restrooms, and were, in spite of making up forty percent of the city's population, an acquiescent shadow society. The only person with black skin that I had ever known was Louvenia, who now had to walk two miles and ride the trolley for three more every day just to reach our new house in Woodlawn, and I was puzzled that my mother had become sharp with her and made her take her share of the lunch she had prepared for us to the concrete-floored back room off the kitchen. There she sat and ate in silence at a folding card table, a blessed respite from a morning of standing on swollen feet beside the ironing board and semi-automatic washing machine. One Saturday during the grade-school years, for no reason that we could discern, our gang picked a rock fight with the black kids our age who lived on the hill in Niggertown and who now scurried for protection behind the rickety steps of the stilted homes. It raged all day, and ended only when one of ours fetched his pump pellet gun and winged one of theirs in the leg, and two little girls braved the fire to drag him to safety beneath the house. Not a week later, as we were gathering on the corner to make our morning trek to Minnie Holman, we were paralyzed by a confrontation that took place right in my front yard: the same kid we had shot came running down the hill, this time fleeing his father, who caught him and tore a low limb from a spruce in the yard and began to thrash him on the spot ("Charles, you get yo' black ass to school or I'll kill you, boy"). He was a large kid, jet black and menacing, and from then on we knew him as Nigger Charles and gave him plenty of room when he defiantly walked through our neighborhood on the way to or from his.

It would have been perfectly all right for me to casually use the word "nigger" around the house—practically everyone I knew did—and I might even have been rewarded with a smile and a pat on the head from my father as an acknowledgment that I was growing up just fine. We kids would speak of the black nuts in our Christmas stockings as "nigger toes"; would yell "nigger soccer" as a way of announcing that all formal rules like no tackling and no running with the ball were being suspended; would refer to the uncovered concrete grandstand in right field at Rickwood as the "nigger bleachers" (unaware that during games played by the Birmingham Black Barons of the Negro American League, featuring a local teenager named Willie Mays, the seating was reversed and whites got what might then have been called, for all I know, the "honky seats"); and when we skipped rope on the sidewalk we chanted a rhyme that went "Eeeny, meeny, miney, moe / Catch a nigger by the toe / If he hollers make him pay / Fifty dollars every day . . ." but I wouldn't dare use the word in the presence of the benign Louvenia. It was baffling. My parents, like most of my aunts and uncles and the other adults in that white blue-collar world in which I was growing up, had always said "nigger" as effortlessly, as matter-of-factly, as they would use the word "trucker" to describe my father. Then, on Christmas afternoons, after we had stuffed ourselves with the white meat and the rest of the good stuff, my mother would wrap a plate of leftover turkey and dressing and we would get into the car and drive over to the ragged hill village of Zion City and honk the horn, and presently Louvenia would come out and walk across the bare dirt yard in frayed slippers and the only dress I had ever seen her wear, her relatives waching in silence from the porch. And she would fall into ingratiating exultations of joy over this wonderful gift ("I S'wanee, Miz Hemphill, y'all so good to us") as my mother passed the plate to her through the window and wished Louvenia and hers a merry Christmas and reminded her to bring the plate back on Monday. My sister and I would watch all of this from the backseat, nervously regarding the rundown houses and the chickens in the yard and the gaggle of mute black people who had come outside to observe the exchange, sometimes holding up to the window our favorite Christmas presents so Louvenia could see, and not once did any of us step out of the car. Presently, Daddy would wave to the crowd on the porch and crank the car and we would spin away, trailing dust, feeling good.

But then, almost imperceptibly at first, my father's glib references to "niggers," as well as to Jews and Catholics, began to take on a meaner edge. Unknown to me, the South had just heard the first shoe drop. My father at first had championed Harry Truman as the workingman's friend, when he succeeded the despised FDR and dropped the bombs on Japan to end the war; but not anymore. Truman had struck fear in the hearts of white southerners like Daddy by bluntly saying that it was time to end racial discrimination in America: he had desegregated the armed forces, and now he was saying that lynching and Jim Crow were out, fair employment and voting rights were in. Now politics was being spoken around the supper table, not food and baseball and last week's run to Cumberland, and my father began to change in ways that made me nervous. No matter how I would try to change the subject as we tore into Mama's meat loaf and cornbread, he would always manage to swing it back around to race and politics. If I talked about Gabby Bell's clever broadcasts of Barons games, Daddy would say that's how Bull Connor got his start and look at ol' Bull now: commissioner of public safety, keeping the niggers in their place, leading the Dixiecrat revolt against Truman and the Democratic party. If we talked about my sister's tap-dancing, it easily spun off into a diatribe about how niggers were born to dance. Mama's mention of a sale at the Pizitz department store downtown would give him a chance to kill two birds with one stone: rich Jews and the pushy niggers dumb enough to buy from them. I held my breath in hopes that he wouldn't look through the picture window and notice the bedsheets that Louvenia had washed and hung on the clothesline earlier in the day, now flapping in the breeze and flashing in the moonlight, like Klansmen dancing in the glow of a burning cross.

CHAPTER FIVE

Other Voices: Mountain Brook and Titusville

Mimi Tynes

From the apartments on Highland Avenue, my parents moved to a house on what was called the Old Atlanta Highway, actually Country Club Road right before it becomes Montclair Road at Ramsay Park. A railroad ran behind the house. It went to warehouses in English Village and on beyond to mines on Red Mountain. One day my brother Bland, who was about five at the time, put on his cowboy outfit and went out and "held up" the train. The engineer stopped the train and got out and gave him a spanking and brought him back to the house.

There were four boys, the oldest being fifteen and the youngest seven when I was born in 1940. My oldest brother, Frank, Jr., is a surgeon. He initially practiced with Daddy and continued on his own when Daddy died. My second brother, who died in 1986, was an artist and portrait painter. He signed his paintings William W. S. Wilson or W. W. S. Wilson but was known to all as Billy or Watlo. The third, Bland, graduated from Virginia Military Institute, served in the Air Force, and is in the mortgage business. The youngest, Tommy, is a heart surgeon who was in the last year or so of his residency at the University of Alabama Medical Center when Dr. John Kirklin, the famous heart surgeon, came to Birmingham. The group of doctors Tommy joined started open-heart surgery at Baptist Montclair and performed the first such operation done in the Birmingham area outside University Hospital.

By the time I was born, the family was living on Mountain Brook Parkway, in the original part of Mountain Brook laid out by Mr. Robert Jemison, Jr. It was big news when the Wilsons had a girl after all of these boys. My now husband happened to be a student at Mountain Brook Elementary School, where two of my brothers were, and when you ask him how long he's known me he can say literally that he remembers the day I was born. He also says he remembers seeing me in a baby buggy, and that's probably true, too. I was premature and weighed only three pounds and thirteen ounces. Mother says one of the things that brought me on early is that she went sledding in the big snow of February 1940. The doctor told her, "Don't get your hopes up, I don't think this baby can make it." They had to make an incubator for me at the Children's Hospital, and my father would go by the Salvation Army Home for Unwed Mothers and get milk to feed me. They had to struggle just to get me to eat for the first week or so, and I joke that I've had a struggle *not* to eat almost ever since.

Mother did a good job making sure I wasn't spoiled, as the only girl. I was pretty much a tomboy, though, playing cowboys and Indians, and I loved most sports, particularly baseball, when I was between seven and twelve years old. Judge Clarence Allgood lived in our neighborhood, and he used to take me to Barons games at Rickwood Field when they had the great team in '48 with Walt Dropo. My best friend's father was a big Auburn fan, and I remember going to the Gator Bowl in Jacksonville when Auburn lost to Vanderbilt, around 1955. We were introduced to Joe Childress, one of the Auburn stars, by Bob Phillips, sports editor of the *Post-Herald,* but we were so shy that we could hardly say hello. Bland played football at VMI, and Mother and Daddy took me with them to Atlanta for the VMI–Georgia Tech game his senior year, in 1950. Bland didn't get into the game until the fourth quarter, but he recovered a fumble to help preserve an upset win for the VMI Cadets, and I was about as excited as anyone in the stands that day. Bob Phillips mentioned that game in his column and quoted me as saying, "Oh, quit worrying. Bland's not going to let them make another touchdown."

The first school I went to was called Miss Ward's, a one-room school, first grade through fourth or fifth, in an upstairs room of her house behind Ramsay High School. The first grade was in the first row, the second grade in the second row, and so on. She was an excellent teacher, and a lot of people would stay there four or five years before going on somewhere else. I stayed only one year, then moved on to Mountain Brook Elementary from the second through the fifth grade, riding to school with my father and then walking home in the afternoons. Then I went to Brooke Hill, a private girls' day school that later merged with Birmingham University School and was renamed Altamont.

Brooke Hill was a wonderful place. It was founded in 1939 or 1940 by a group of parents who wanted a college preparatory school for their daughters. When I started, there were something like eighty students in the fifth through twelfth grades, and when I finished there were more like a hundred and twenty. It was in an old house on Rhodes Circle, off of Highland Avenue, near the Altamont Apartments. I grew up always wanting to be involved in a variety of activities, and you certainly could do that at Brooke Hill. The whole school was divided into two teams, the Greens and the Whites, and they competed with each other in sports and academics. Your team got points for making the honor roll, for wins in basketball, volleyball, and softball, and for participating in extracurricular activities. I was involved in sports, the school magazine and annual, the National Honor Society, even in building stage sets. Most of us went on to college, quite a few in Virginia and some in the East.

There are so many memories of growing up in Birmingham.

As a much younger child, seven or eight years old, I was one of several junior ladies-in-waiting to the Queen of the Christmas Carnival. The Queen was the daughter of some of my parents' best friends. I think the carnival was over Thanksgiving weekend, and it involved riding on a float in a Christmas parade downtown as well as a big presentation event at the Municipal Auditorium. I remember other years of watching that parade from my uncle's office window in the Frank Nelson Building on Twentieth Street, but I don't think it continued much beyond the early fifties, if that long.

I was introduced to opera at the Starlight Theater, an outdoor theater on the campus of Birmingham-Southern, and at performances of the Metropolitan Opera at the Municipal Auditorium. I can also remember attending performances of the Birmingham Symphony at the Temple Theater and its youth concerts at the auditorium as well as Junior Program productions at Phillips High School. Saturdays were often spent at the movies. When I was old enough to ride the bus by myself, several of us would ride from Mountain Brook to the Homewood Theater for the Saturday matinee. Finally, when I was a little older, we were allowed to go all the way downtown on the bus. There we would often have lunch at Loveman's or Pizitz and then have a choice of movies at the Alabama, the Melba, the Ritz, the Empire, or the Lyric Theater. Most of our shopping was done downtown at Burger-Phillips and Blach's as well as Loveman's and Pizitz.

My first date, I think, when I was a teenager, was to a movie, also downtown, and then all the way to Howard Johnson's next door to the Motel Birmingham, just beyond what is now Eastwood Mall, for an ice cream sundae. Other occasions were high school sorority and fraternity leadouts at the Pickwick in Five Points. I particularly remember a fraternity dance at the Tutwiler Hotel close to Christmas. For a break we went window shopping around a good part of the major downtown area.

But as much as any of this I remember how my mother was always involved in a variety of community activities, and how that was passed so easily from mother to daughter. The one that always comes to mind first was when she was trying to get what became known as the Junior League Speech and Hearing School off the ground just after the Second World War. A friend whose son was deaf started a speech and hearing school in Atlanta. There was not anything like that in Birmingham, so Mother thought this was something we needed. It took a lot of work for her to get the Junior League to approve this as its primary project. I was just six or seven years old, but I remember the committee meetings at our house to make flash cards to be used in classrooms for deaf children; participating in the area-wide Christmas-caroling fund-raiser, then going to collection point at the Church of the Advent downtown and counting the money on Christmas Eve night after the caroling was done. Public school superintendents at the time told Mother that classes for speech- and hearing-impaired children would never be a part of the public school system. Only ten years or so later, those same classes were taken over by the Birmingham public schools.

Another thing Mother had been involved with for years was the Children's Hospital. She worked as a volunteer in many capacities and was first elected to its board in 1930. Daddy was involved with Children's, too, of course, and I remember a lot of dinner-table conversations about what was going on there. Mother was also involved with the women's organization at the church. So there were always things going on, and as the youngest of the clan I tended to be taken along with her when she had something to do. I remember the Lenten noonday preaching services at the Advent, a program that continues today. A visiting bishop or clergyman would give a sermon, and then those attending could get a quick soup-and-sandwich lunch and be back at work in an hour. The units of the Women of the Church took turns preparing and serving the lunches. If I was on vacation from school, I went along and helped, whether it was making sandwiches at the church, making up beds before St. Martin's Nursing Home opened, or manning a booth at the garden club's Easter sale. So I was exposed to the idea of community involvement and taking part in a variety of activities long before I went to college.

John Porter

In the late thirties we had these coal trains that sort of curved around Titusville, headed for places south of Birmingham on the L&N tracks. You would find fifty open carloads of coal coming out of Birmingham, those steam engines chugging uphill out of the valley, all day long. We lived nearby and we'd hear that whistle blow and we'd run toward the tracks. Big crowds would turn out, and as the train started up the incline, going its slowest rate, the community would invade that train. The young boys would get on top of the boxcars and begin to throw coal off the train and the rest of the family would run along with sacks and pick up the coal. It was a lot of fun for the kids, but for the parents it meant coal to heat the houses, and they'd get enough to last a long time. My mother wouldn't allow us to get coal, but my brother would get up there and throw coal anyway, until the diesels came in and you couldn't catch 'em anymore because they were too fast. The railroad detectives caught him a time or two. Being the youngest, I guess, I didn't get into much trouble as a kid. My brother got into enough for both of us.

The most secure people in Titusville were the domestics. The steel mill workers and the coal miners were in the soup lines during the Depression, but the domestics fared better. There was some income, little as it was, and you could supplement it with things you would be given from around the house where you worked: clothing, food, even toys for the kids. Many of the white people who hired domestics were so very rich, anyway.

So it was a stable neighborhood, mostly homeowners, kids

everywhere. I had a very happy childhood in that it was safe, almost like an extended family, on a dead-end street with little traffic. There was no trick-or-treating in those days, but on Halloween we would all gather around the schoolhouse just to be there. Big crowds would gather, and sooner or later the police cars would arrive and everybody would scatter, running and laughing. Then on Christmas we'd gather again, this time with our new skates. We had a slight hill, and there would be hundreds of kids in a one-block area, trying to skate, and you could hardly move. That was just super. We had a few bold guys, and if a car came along going slow enough they'd catch the end of the car and soon we'd have maybe ten kids behind the car, like in a conga line. All in all, my childhood was rather uneventful, smooth and even, and now I realize that coming home to the same house every day was a tremendous blessing. There were some other kids who would have to move at the end of every month. If you couldn't pay your rent, you'd move to another house for a month, and so on. But not us.

Early on, the contact with whites happened so seldom. I had very little of that during all of my growing-up years. I used to wonder, as early as when I was about five, whether white people went to the bathroom or not, had these natural functions like we did. It sounds dumb, but they were so foreign to us. I knew nothing about them except that they were white and they literally lived on the other side of the tracks. I remember, Anthony Marino was the son of the Italian family who ran the neighborhood store. Their home and the store were attached, not a block away from our house, and I would see Anthony in the store all the time; but although he was my age, I never got to know him at all. There was this awe about them, even this white boy the same age as me.

It must have been when I got into high school, first at Ullman and then at Parker High, said to be the largest high school in the world, that I began to see the differences. It happened so very early, so slowly, that I really can't pinpoint when it became a full-blown realization. My father never uttered a word about race, never spoke a negative word about anybody, really, he was such a mild spirit. It was innate with him and my uncles. He would tell me about respect, and the kinds of things you had to do when you met white people, like take off your hat or step aside on the sidewalk or say "Yes, sir" and "No, sir" to them. So that became a way of life for me, just like it had been for my father.

After a while, though, when I started getting out a little bit, I began to see that anybody who said he didn't have feelings of inferiority was either retarded or dumb. Everything was structured to make you feel less than equal. "Colored" signs on the buses, elevators, fountains, restrooms. If there were whites on the bus, you had to reach from the ground and hand the busman your money and then go around to the back door to get on. Those were big reminders that we were together and yet very, very separated; the constant reminders that you were inferior were always there. And with white women, white girls, I don't think I ever looked at one with any kind of sexual observance or appreciation. Sometimes I'll read the paper and wonder, How in the world could so-and-so rape that white girl? It was so ingrained that even the thought of looking with any kind of erotic ideas was just absolutely not done, and so you didn't.

I was in high school before I began to react. You could go to Vulcan, but it had to be Saturday and it had to be before noon. This friend of mine and I, Charles Harrell, decided we were going to go up there one Saturday afternoon. We were adventurous, lived outside of our world, liked to walk around talking about Chopin and Beethoven and the opera when we'd never seen an opera in our lives. We knew we weren't supposed to be at Vulcan on a Saturday afternoon, but we went, anyway. The moment we walked into that park a white policeman stepped out from the bushes and said, "What are you niggers doing up here?'' We turned and ran all the way down the hill to Five Points South without stopping. It had scared us to death. We were bold, but not bullies, and in those days we had no recourse, nobody to go to and say, "I was mistreated." Another time, on VE Day, rather than go to Fourth Avenue where blacks were allowed to celebrate, Charles and I went to Twentieth Street. White people were shouting, singing, dancing in the streets, and I was looking back at something, just walking along on Twentieth Street, when suddenly a hand hit me in the face. I was startled, trying to collect myself, when I saw this white man coming back to give me another blow. Then a white sailor came up and pushed him off of me. I'm sure the man was half-drunk, because everybody was drinking, but we were just in a place where we should not have been. We knew it, and they knew it.

What happened the day I caused my father to lose his job at the Martins' mansion wasn't really a racial matter, just sticking up for what I thought was fair. I was twenty, home from college in the summer of '51, and I had begun going up there to work beside my father in the yard, and one of my duties was to water Mr. Martin's English boxwoods. He wanted them watered late in the afternoon, not in the heat of the day, so I always had to stay over late to water the boxwoods. When payday came one Saturday, I went up to him with my hat in my hand, just like my father had always taught me, and in a proper southern way I asked for my overtime. Mr. Martin just got furious, so mad he was shaking. He could not stand the idea that I was correcting him. He couldn't even speak, he was so upset. The servants were the wife's, not the husband's, so he turned and ran into the house and told Mrs. Martin to take care of it. She came out and said, "John, you don't appreciate what we've done for you and your father, so go and get your things and leave." Then she turned to my father and said, "And you, Robert, you've been sassing me lately, so you can get your things and leave, too." I thought the world had come to an end, but to the day my daddy died he never ever mentioned that day. Well, by about Tuesday Mr. Martin began to call and say my father could have his job back if he would come and apologize to Mrs. Martin; but it was too late, because he had already gotten a job taking care of the grounds at Ingalls Iron Works. You were who you worked for, and when he told them he had worked for Mr. Thomas W. Martin of Alabama Power Company for twenty-five years they hired him on the spot. It turned out to be the best thing that ever happened to my daddy, because now he got Social Security and Medicare and retirement. He worked for Ingalls Iron until he retired, and then at the Ingalls family's private home, since work was all he knew, and he lived to be eighty-three.

CHAPTER SIX

School Daze

There were only ten of us in the graduating class of January 1950 at Minnie Holman, seven boys and three girls, and every time I see Woody Allen's movie *Radio Days*, with its evocation of childhood long ago in America, I'm carried back to the last years of the Second World War and those immediately following: spitball fights; oily floors; pigtails and crewcuts; lunches of war-surplus Spam and cabbage; the delectable Sara Frances Woodrow wearing bobby sox and lipstick; corporal punishment from the tight-lipped Miss Long (five to ten raps across an open palm, in front of the class, with two vibrating wooden rulers); the coal furnace roaring from the basement in the winter like a hobbled elephant; an old, overalled black janitor wandering the halls with a wrench and a claw hammer (and one kid always inquiring, "How's your hammer hanging, Henry?"). Although a few kids from better circumstances had begun enrolling there in the late forties, their parents having built sleek brick houses in a subdivision called Crestwood that was sprouting around the school, for the most part we were the children of the laboring class. I happened to be selected as class valedictorian, certainly not because of any academic excellence, charged with delivering a brief message of hope from the stage of the school's cramped little auditorium. I have no recollection whatsoever of what I might have said that morning, while my parents beamed from the audience (Daddy shifting nervously in his metal folding chair, tugging at the collar of a starched white shirt). Mainly, I remember my first suit: a coarse wool double-breasted number bought on a trip downtown to Blach's department store, where I got a glimpse of Fred Hatfield, the Barons' nifty third baseman, on his off-season job in the men's department.

On the following Monday we trooped off to Woodlawn High School, the fierce dark brick fortress on First Avenue where most of our parents had gone in the twenties when the building was new and where many of the same teachers still held forth. Woodlawn was the biggest white high school in Alabama, we were told, and it had two traditions to uphold: football, which had produced many championships and all-Americans, most notably Harry Gilmer of the University of Alabama's '46 Rose Bowl team; and an annual blackface production called *The Warblers Minstrel*, which drew sellout crowds from all over the city every night for its week-long run. A boy either played football or joined the Warblers, a well-intentioned group that was more of a fraternity than a place where it was okay to speak in black dialect, and I was too frail for the former and too shy for the latter. It's quite possible that I was the smallest person in the entire school, weighing in at ninety-seven pounds when I turned fourteen that February; and that, coupled with my mother's seemingly far greater interest in my sister's doings than in mine during my father's absences, had suddenly made a loner of me. (Years later I would strike up a correspondence with a woman who had been a classmate; she, as a poor kid from the projects, had been a bit of an outsider herself. "One day I saw you standing on the landing," she recalled, "gazing out the window like a lost soul while everybody else was talking and laughing and rushing to class, and I thought then that you just might grow up to be a writer or something a little different.")

Woodlawn High was filled with burly, raucous all-state football players and refined, Ivory-scrubbed girls who seemed unattainable, plenty of kids whose fathers were engineers and bosses and civic leaders; and for the first time in my life I began to develop a notion that my old man was "tacky," just a truck driver, and that this made me inferior. I had no way of knowing that many of those kids whom I perceived as being superior to me—who I thought would perhaps become leaders of the city and the world—would reach the apex of their lives in the next four years, when they made the National Honor Society or the Birmingham *News*'s all-state football team, never to excel again. I'm not sure that it would have been of any consolation to me at that point, anyway. Like the city itself, big bad Birmingham, I had already developed an inferiority complex and begun to crawl into my own shell.

College? Forget it. Two or three of my older cousins had gone on to Alabama Polytechnic Institute (now Auburn) to study engineering, as part of the wave of lower- and middle-class kids all across America to become the first in their family to study beyond high school; but college was something that never came up at 6000 Fifth Court South. Trucking may have been good enough for my father, who had been forced to drop out of high school because of the Depression, but I had seen enough on those adventures with him to know that it was damned hard physical work and thus not for me. There was none of this sitting around the supper table at our place discussing literature, world affairs, music, or anything remotely connected with the abstract (unless we count Daddy's discourses on "niggers" and Hank Williams and Communists and memorable truck-stop meals he had known). Except for my mother's Bible and a dusty collection of Frank Merriwells and Bobbsey Twins that had piled up as my sister and I grew, there were no books lying around. The only reading anyone did was from *Life, Reader's Digest,* the *Upper Room, Boys' Life, The Sporting News,* and the Birmingham newspapers. My father was a committed anti-intellectual with an almost violent reaction to anyone who represented any world other than his. It's possible that he despised wealthy educated whites even more than he did Jews and Catholics and blacks. "I hate *wa-wah*," he would begin a devastating impersonation of FDR doing a "fireside chat" during the war, "my wife *Elah-noah* hates *wa-wah*, even my dog Fala hates *wa-wah*." If by chance, while trying to find Gillette's Friday-night fights on the television set, he came across a barrel-bosomed soprano booming forth from the Metropolitan Opera, he would bellow, "Lord, honey, where's it hurt at?" Where he came from, getting decent pay for an honest day's work was all that counted; this other stuff—ideas and anything else you couldn't actually see and hold in your hand—was fool's play. He had lured an adoring son into this world, and there would be hell to pay, for both of us, when I finally began the long struggle to break free.

High school daze. Woodlawn was one of five white public high schools in the city limits, each with a distinctive student body. The largest, of course, was Woodlawn, on the eastern side of town, mainly stocked with the children of working-class families with middle-class aspirations. Not five blocks from City Hall was Phillips, an eclectic mix of kids from the downtown projects and the fringes of over-the-mountain. On the sooty, steel-making western side of Birmingham were Ensley and West End, whose students were primarily from families connected to the mills. Finally, there was Ramsay High, at Vulcan's feet in Southside, a relatively small school which served a polyglot of ethnic neighborhoods packed solid with people named Mizerany and Schilleci and David, descendants of the Greeks, Lebanese, Syrians, and Italians who had initially come to work in the mills and foundries. It would be 1957 before the first attempt to integrate any of these schools was made, even though the *Brown* v. *Board of Education* ruling made segregated schools illegal in '54. During my high school years Parker High was just a rumor, some great dark force somewhere in the hills above Legion Field, the giant skeletal stadium where Big Five football games were played on smoky Friday nights. Parker was where all black children of our age got their schooling. Its football games were barely mentioned on the sports pages of the *News* and the *Post-Herald,* and white Birmingham knew of the school mostly from its band's electric appearances at parades on the downtown streets (always at the end of the line), which gave people like my father ample opportunity to speak of the black propensity for rhythm and dance.

Life at Woodlawn High centered on the football season, which culminated with a city championship playoff match, the Crippled Children's Clinic Game, before crowds of twenty thousand on Thanksgiving Day at Legion Field. Since each school had a distinctive makeup, tending to balkanize the whole high school system, the rivalries were so fierce that cops were everywhere on Friday nights when the postgame Big Five Dance was held at the Municipal Auditorium. No matter who had squared off at Legion Field that night, supporters from all of the schools would show up in their letter sweaters and jackets, ostensibly to mingle and dance but in reality, as it invariably turned out, to strut and flirt and agitate until fistfights and shoving matches broke out like little brushfires and the dance had to be cut short. Poor Ramsay High, with all of those ''foreigners'' in an Anglo-Saxon Protestant town: Baumgartners and Salems and Pharos made the Ramsay Rams a feared football team, year in and year out, and I cannot remember a single Woodlawn-Ramsay game during my four years at Woodlawn that did not involve an all-out brawl on the field.

The Woodlawn High Colonels band, more than one hundred strong, was the largest in the state except for Parker's, and I played trumpet with them. This went back to the nights when our family would drive into town to attend movies at the Temple Theater, where between features starring Edward G. Robinson or Joan Crawford or Deanna Durbin there would be a half-hour vaudeville show, and I would beg that we sit near the orchestra pit. I was mesmerized by the dandies who played trumpet, handsome devils with thin mustaches and slick hair (reminding me of

Harry James, who had married the luscious Betty Grable), and before I left Minnie Holman I was being groomed for the Woodlawn High band by the music teacher there, who was the wife of the Woodlawn band director, Gerald Smith. She had taught me to "triple-tongue" a note before I left, and had passed me on to her husband as a prime prospect for Woodlawn's famed Trumpet Trio: three gallant trumpeters who stood beneath the mammoth American flag at Legion Field during the halftime show and echoed, in chilling harmony, the stanzas of the Woodlawn school song (which happened to be a variation on the Russian national anthem, we were reminded in those Cold War years). The members of the Trumpet Trio were stars in their own right, guys the girls went for, and I practiced mightily to attain my goal, memorizing "Carnival of Venice" and Harry James's "Ciribiribin," gladly agreeing to play before my mother's church functions as "the entertainment," working toward the day when I would be tapped for the trio. I finally had found something that I was good at, something to set me apart, and I was beginning to come out of my shell—until one nippy spring morning in my sophomore year. My parents had given me a beautiful new Conn trumpet for Christmas, and we were on the football field behind the school practicing our routines for the coming season when I saw one of the football coaches eyeing me from the sidelines. It was a bony man named John Blaine, who was always overmatching me in boxing sessions during gym class, exhorting me to "be a man" during my weekly pummelings, and wasn't called "Bloody" Blaine for nothing. "Well, well, *well*," he said when we had finished and I was putting my horn in its case, "if it isn't little Hemphill. A *trumpet* player." The sonofabitch. I looked around and realized that I was the only boy in the band who also fancied himself a jock of any sort, although I hadn't even gone out for the baseball team. So I quit that same day, and never played the trumpet again.

Now my full attention turned to baseball. Either classes

were easy at Woodlawn in those days or I had enough innate intelligence to get B's without trying (my father, after all, never forgot a word once he saw it, and arrogantly worked crossword puzzles with a fountain pen); whatever, I seldom opened a book during my four years there. We weren't so flush that I didn't have to work to earn my own money; I had a newspaper route first, then began delivering Western Union telegrams all over downtown Birmingham; and during my senior year I was a bicycle messenger for the advertising department of the Birmingham *News*. And when I wasn't working I was earnestly preparing myself to become a professional baseball player. I read about it in *The Sporting News* and *Sport* magazine; I missed few Barons games at Rickwood; I burrowed beneath my covers to catch Harry Caray's broadcasts of Cardinals games; I memorized the Official Rules of Baseball, including the tricky Infield Fly Rule, and studied every diagram of the only book I owned, Johnny Mize's *How to Hit*; I bought a pair of Charles Atlas handgrips to build up my forearms like Stan Musial said; I stuffed myself with proteins and half-and-half milk in a futile attempt to fill out my stringy frame; I went to the playground at Minnie Holman on winter days to run wind sprints alone in the new spikes I had gotten for Christmas; when the weather turned, on Saturdays my next-door pal, Wallace Graddick, and I would bicycle the three miles to Stockham Park, in the shadow of one of the mills, taking sack lunches and a bag of refurbished balls we had snagged at Rickwood so we could hit ground balls to each other and then hold two-man batting practice; I drilled a shaft in the barrel of a thick-handled Jackie Robinson bat (similar to the model used by my hero Nellie Fox, the little White Sox second baseman), filled it with molten lead, and swung it outdoors during the daytime and in front of a full-sized mirror in my room at night. There was a slip of a girl I dated for a few months during my senior year (*she* kissed *me,* out of some exasperation, on our thirteenth date); but my passions were kept under the covers.

In what would turn out to be a serious mistake, I chose not to compete with the high school team but rather to study the game and train on my own during the spring and then spend summers at a place in southeastern Missouri called Ozark Baseball Camp. I had found an advertisement for the camp in *The Sporting News* ("Major League Instructors . . . Promising players will be evaluated"), and my parents drove me up there in our new '51 Dodge Coronet when I had turned fifteen. The owner and operator of the place was a farmer and a New York Giants "bird dog" scout, Carl Bolin, who set this city boy to baling hay and slopping hogs on his farm, to pay my way, until the rest of nearly one hundred boys from ten to eighteen years of age arrived. In a valley beside a sparkling trout stream there were four baseball diamonds laid out back to back, like at the complexes I had seen that spring, when my father had taken me on a tour of the camps in Florida, and a series of rustic cabins and a big house on the hill that held a cafeteria-style dining hall. The "major league instructors" were a couple of local men—Elmer Brown, who had pitched briefly for the St. Louis Browns and Brooklyn Dodgers during the *First* World War, and Goldie Howard, a hairy, barrel-chested fellow who had been a prodigious power hitter in Triple A but had never made it to the big time —plus a gnarled old Yankees catcher named Wally Schang, who had been a roommate of Babe Ruth's during the twenties. Throughout the long hot Ozark summer we drilled and saw instructional films and played camp games and drilled some more, even rode up to St. Louis to watch my first major league game (Satchel Paige, now with the Browns, threw a looping "hesitation" pitch that the Yankees' Mickey Mantle hit into orbit). It seemed to be an invaluable experience for me, although I was left with something to think about when, in August, Goldie Howard told me that practicing was one thing and playing truly competitive games was another: "It's like life. Situations come up, stuff happens, and no amount of practicin' and studyin' and talkin' is going to prepare you for it." Although Goldie wasn't intellectually inclined, more of an amiable country philosopher, I do believe he was trying to tell me that baseball is a metaphor for life.

All of this was fine with my father. He was doing his share of grumbling as more and more black players followed Jackie Robinson into the major leagues, meaning that soon, because of Birmingham's ironclad segregation ordinances, no more big-league clubs would be coming through town to play the Barons on their way north to open the season; but he figured that was the North's problem. We were united in baseball now more than ever before, and the household seemed to be split along gender lines: mother and daughter, father and son. While they were involved in church doings and Joyce's dance rehearsals and recitals, we were listening to the Barons or going out to Rickwood to see them in person (their big star in the early fifties was center fielder Jimmy Piersall, who would go nuts before our very eyes during the '52 season), making more tours of the spring training camps in Florida, both of us conspiring toward the day when I myself would be cited in the *The Sporting News* as a rising young second baseman in the minor leagues. I made a few more trips with him, including one that took us through Robbins so I could finally see the graves of my ancestors and the shack where he had grown up; and now he would work out an itinerary so we could catch a game in Chattanooga or Atlanta or Nashville. My mother was still crestfallen over my having given up music ("I S'wanee, and we'd just bought you that pretty new trumpet") and regarded baseball as something I would outgrow. She was on a mission toward respectability those days, anyway. One of her sisters and several of her friends from Woodlawn

RIGHT: Author's maternal great-grandfather, Cicero Alexander Caldwell, at his print shop in downtown Birmingham, ca. 1890.

BELOW: Paul Hemphill, Sr., in foreground, wearing gloves, in southern Iowa with work gang on the Rock Island Line, stringing lines and laying track, ca. 1929.

Author's parents, Velma Rebecca Nelson
and Paul James Hemphill, before their
marriage. Photo ca. 1930, in Birmingham.

Paul Hemphill, Jr., at age four, during freak snowstorm of 1940. Dumptruck in background is the Dodge that would be converted less than a year later into a road-worthy "semi" tractor for pulling a trailer—Paul Hemphill, Sr.'s over-the-road truck.

Studio portrait, 1942, of Paul Hemphill, Jr., aged six, and Mary Joyce Hemphill, aged two.

Paul Hemphill, Jr., at age twelve, riding a homemade "skatemobile" in front of the house in Woodlawn in 1948. Passenger is his cousin Jim Stewart, at age two—later also a Nieman Fellow at Harvard and currently covering the Pentagon for CBS Television News.

Brother and sister, Christmas 1948, Paul, aged twelve, and Mary Joyce, aged eight.

OPPOSITE: Class of 1950, Minnie Holman Elementary School, Birmingham. Third from left, front row, is Paul Hemphill. Far right, front row, is Earl Freedle, only one of the class the author could locate forty-two years later, for a discomfiting lunch described in this book.

Paul Hemphill, Sr., right, in about 1946 (around age thirty-five), and a driver known only as Wasson. Hemphill chose to drive the 1940 Dodge, the same one he had converted from a dumptruck in '41, while Wasson drove the 1946 Dodge at left. Hemphill owned both trucks and flatbed trailers, leased first to Eagle Motor Lines and later to Alabama Highway Express.

ABOVE: Paul Hemphill, Jr., next to Ty Cobb, summer 1952, at the Ozark Baseball Camp in Darien, Missouri. Boy on far left unidentified. Photo was published in *The Sporting News* with no credit.

LEFT: Author, at right, with best boyhood friend, Wallace Graddick, summer 1952, Ozark Baseball Camp. The two were reunited when the author returned to Birmingham in 1992.

ABOVE: Author at Ozark
Baseball Camp, summer
1952.

RIGHT: Author, aged nine-
teen, with semipro baseball
club in Oswego, Kansas,
summer 1955.

Only known snapshot of
Hemphill family maid, Louvenia,
in backyard of Hemphill house in
Woodlawn neighborhood of
Birmingham, ca. 1944.

BELOW: First college graduate in
Hemphill family, Auburn University, March 1959. From left: Paul
Hemphill, Jr., sister Joyce, Paul
Hemphill, Sr., Velma Hemphill.

Methodist had managed to move up the social ladder to Crestwood, the subdivision across the Seaboard tracks, and she was pressuring Daddy to give up trucking and take a more secure job—like, say, driving a Greyhound bus—so we could move there, too. She also was dropping remarks almost daily about the growing numbers of my cousins and acquaintances who were going on to college after graduating from Woodlawn High. Daddy treated the idea of becoming a bus driver as blasphemy ("I ain't made to work for nobody else"), said the houses in Crestwood were "built flimsy," and told her that college would just delay my baseball career.

School was something to do between summers. I returned to Ozark Baseball Camp for the summer of '52, this time with my buddy Wallace Graddick. That was the year Ty Cobb, arguably the greatest player of all time, spent two weeks with us as a "guest instructor." Carl Bolin had brought us all together in the dining hall on the night before Cobb's arrival and cautioned us about asking "Mr. Cobb" if he really had purposely spiked opposing players, on the grounds that he had aged and mellowed. Naturally, that was the very first question asked of him the next day, and Cobb narrowed his eyes and slammed his fist on a Ping-Pong table: "You're goddamn right, and I'd do it again to the sonsabitches." Off on a roll, Cobb proceeded to cite names, dates, ballparks, and offenses. He was sixty-six years old, but still a sight to behold. One day, wearing Hush Puppies and khakis and an Ozark Baseball Camp T-shirt, he personally showed me how to execute a hook slide, tearing into third base with such vigor that he ripped the bag from its mooring.

I would spend part of the next summer near Waco, Texas, at the Big State Baseball School, coming home on crutches before the Fourth of July after being seriously spiked. There was one more semester of high school to endure, the fall of '53, and I faked it as I had done all along: never did manage to fight my way through *Wuthering Heights*, just interviewed the survivors.

No mentors had presented themselves to me during my time at Woodlawn High, and why should they? I was in the school but not of it. What lessons I had learned about the real world had come not from books, which I read only to survive tests, but from those adventures on the road with my father and from being away at those camps in the company of kids of all shapes and backgrounds (except black)—guys from Chicago and Texas, even Alaska and the Panama Canal Zone. On the last day of classes, when our homeroom teacher asked everybody to stand and tell their plans for the future, I got up and blurted, "To play professional baseball," startling classmates who weren't aware that I played. At the graduation ceremony that night, when I would become the first Hemphill to get a diploma, my mother cried—not out of joy but because the crowd was still wildly celebrating George Grubbs, the football star and Warbler, and she never heard them call my name.

The baseball dream crashed on takeoff. Two weeks after graduation my father dropped me off at Cocoa, Florida, on his way to Miami with a load of steel (advising me, sometime during that long, anxious night, to "always use a rubber"), depositing me at dawn in front of the seedy Seminole Hotel. I would bite the bullet now, see how I stacked up, meet baseball head-on. With about a hundred and twenty other hopefuls from all parts of the country, I would show my stuff at the Jack Rossiter Baseball School. Minor-league scouts hovered around the little ballpark like breeders at a cattle auction, and every day word would spread that another one of us had been signed to a contract. During the last week a fellow representing the Panama City Fliers of the Class D Alabama-Florida League stocked his entire spring training roster by signing forty of us to "conditional" contracts that would pay $150 a month if we made it. I lasted three days at Panama City, one of eight second basemen to be let go, and hitched a ride to the little peanut-farming town of Graceville, in the same league, when I got word that the Oilers didn't even have a second baseman in camp. I was great in practice, turning nifty double plays with a little veteran Mexican shortstop named Joaquin Toyo; but when we played our one exhibition game, against a powerhouse post–Korean War team from Fort Benning, I struck out all four times I came to bat against a rocket-launching left-hander who would be pitching for the Birmingham Barons the next year when he got out of the military. The next morning, while giving me my dollar-and-a-half lunch money, a grizzled old manager named Holt "Cat" Milner said there wouldn't be any more. "Got a boy coming in on the bus right now from Corpus Christi, Class C," he said. And then, an echo of Goldie Howard: "You wadn't bad in practice, son, but a game's different. How you gon' hit ol' Onion Davis up in Dothan on opening night if you can't even get a foul off this damned private?"

Talk about life's sobering moments. The one skill I thought I possessed had been judged lacking at the lowest level of organized baseball, by a ragged unaffiliated club in the smallest town in one of the weakest Class D leagues in the game; and although I would play here and there for three more years, I knew it was over. My father didn't quite know what to say about this turn of events, except to clip stories he would come across about others who had overcome early failures ("If at first you don't succeed, keep on suckin' "); but my mother certainly did. She began to pound away about college now, even went to work outside of the house for the first time in her life, as a clerk at the Social Security offices downtown, to show that she was willing to help finance the start of a college education for me. But what would I study, and where, and why? In April and May, while baseball seasons opened all across America, I banged around the house on Fifth Court South like a wounded soldier whose war had ended. To get her off my back as much as anything, I agreed to enroll at Auburn in the fall to study engineering like almost everybody else I knew. And then, at loose ends and unable to let go of baseball entirely, I hitchhiked first to Ozark Baseball Camp and finally, with a disgusted push from Goldie Howard, to a little town in southeastern Kansas called Oswego, where I would spend that summer and the next playing semipro ball without much result. Except, *except:* On the team was a swift little outfielder named Hank Scott, a local *black* kid, the first I had ever spoken to, and it stunned us both when we became the best friends on the team.

Auburn was known as the state's ''cow college,'' much like Texas A&M and Mississippi State and South Carolina's Clemson; it was considered a poor cousin to the University of Alabama on the other side of Birmingham. Auburn turned out engineers and county extension agents, while Alabama produced doctors and lawyers. I didn't plan to be any of those things, of course: I just bought myself a slide rule and T square and all of the other accouterments of the engineer-in-training and aimlessly followed the crowd into classrooms where the basics of engineering were being taught. I got a job slinging hash; shared a double-bunk room with my cousin Melvin Sims (who was already a ''co-op'' student with a job as a trainee with Chicago Bridge & Iron in Birmingham); wore my orange-and-blue freshman beanie while trudging the dirt paths connecting the buildings on the rustic campus stuck down there on the high farm-pond plains near Columbus, Georgia; discovered beer at rowdy roadhouses on the edge of town; signed up to play freshman baseball in the spring. More than once I lay awake wondering what the hell I was doing there, a worldly boy with a major failure in his past at the age of eighteen, intimidated by rosy-cheeked fraternity boys and lissome blondes who could recite Shakespeare. But a promise was a promise, even if I was barely dodging F's in every class that had anything to do with engineering.

Then, for the first time in my life, a mentor stepped forward.

I had scored high on the English portion of a pre-enrollment classification test, meaning that rather than taking the basic freshman English courses in grammar and the like I would be placed in "special" classes where we would spend our days writing instead of parsing sentences. In each of those three quarters I was placed in the care of Walter D. Jones, a precise man who cared deeply for the language but was saddled with the chore of teaching freshman English to football players and future farmers and engineers who devoutly prayed they would never see another semicolon after they got through this ordeal. I felt the same way in the beginning, but the joke was on me. I began getting A's on my little essays, with promising notations scribbled across the bottom page ("Fine analogy" or "Apt metaphor," Professor Jones would write, sending me to the dictionary). At some point late in the spring quarter I went by his office to explain why I was making a D in his course on Chaucer and Shakespeare. (It was because I was bathed in calamine lotion from an overdose of penicillin and was having to mumble through a contraption of wires and rubber bands, the result of a broken jaw from playing freshman baseball.) "What's really important to me," he said, "is that you have the makings of a writer." *What? Me? A writer?* "You aren't 'academic' in the truest sense, so I don't know where it comes from. But I think you should think about that."

That's all he said, and that's all it took. I sold my slide rule and T square and engineering textbooks, bought myself a portable typewriter, and became a writing fool. Like most failed jocks who had turned to writing by accident (I would discover in time that there was a very long and distinguished list), I would learn by writing about sports. I gingerly picked my way through the student catalogue, avoiding any classes that might take me away from my private scribblings (it was back to the dictionary again when someone said I was an "autodidact"), looking for the soft spots like speech and all six of the courses taught in the one-man journalism department. In exchange for serving meals in the athletic dining hall and pitching batting practice for the varsity baseball team (well, actually, I led the Southeastern Conference in batting during the '56 season by going one-for-one in a blowout against Kentucky), I got my room and board the rest of the way. My fraternity brothers became the boys at Graves Center, the scholarship athletes who lived in a gathering of cottages meandering through the pines in the shadow of the stadium, and my textbooks were the sports pages. Shamelessly copying the styles of Benny Marshall of the Birmingham *News* and Furman Bisher of the Atlanta *Journal* and Red Smith of the New York *Herald-Tribune,* I began to fancy a career as a sportswriter. Had I gone to Alabama I might have washed out (Gay Talese had been the latest writer to come out of there), but at Auburn I was a big frog in a little pond. In 1957 I was sports editor of the school paper, the *Plainsman,* the year Auburn won the national collegiate football championship in spite of being on probation for buying players, and before I graduated I was tapped to the national honorary called Blue Key along with a future astronaut named Thomas ("Ken") Mattingly and an all-American football player named Jimmy ("Red") Phillips.

CHAPTER SEVEN

Other Voices: Leaving Home

Mimi Tynes

For years, Mother wanted me to go to Merestead, a summer camp in Maine. Two of its directors had been the head counselors there when she attended. Finally, when I was fifteen, I went. It was a small camp, with only about ninety campers. At first, even though I had a connection with the directors and one of my cousins was also there, I wondered what I had gotten myself into. After a few days I really loved it, because I liked all the people so much: the directors, the counselors, and the campers. Most of them were from the Baltimore-Philadelphia-Boston area, with a few from Virginia, but no one else from even close to Alabama.

When I went back the next year, the summer before my senior year in high school, six counselors were either students at Smith College or entering freshmen. I had already decided to apply to Randolph-Macon and Sweet Briar in Virginia. Even before that summer, Smith was the only one of the Seven Sisters colleges that was somehow in the back of my mind. Becoming quite good friends with several of those already at Smith led me to apply there, too. After spending a weekend with them on the campus early in December, I loved everything about Smith and decided that was definitely where I wanted to go. I didn't have enough sense to realize that I might not get in.

I was fortunate enough to be accepted by all three. When Mother called me at school to tell me I'd been accepted, I whooped and hollered and everybody came in fussing at me because there was all of this noise and Brooke Hill was such a small place. I became the first person from Birmingham in ten years to go to Smith.

I'm sure going to college in a very different part of the country and with few people I knew or had any connection with helped give me confidence, in later years, in my ability to enter new and challenging situations. The enrollment at Smith was only twenty-two hundred when I started in the fall of '57, but after Brooke Hill that seemed huge. I truly enjoyed the experience of Smith: the people, the activities, the homelike atmosphere of the house system, the town of Northampton, and the academics, too.

Sometimes I may have felt somewhat defensive about being from the South, especially when the subject of segregation or discrimination came up. Thanksgiving weekend of my sophomore year, I was appalled at someone else's prejudice. I went home with my roommate to the south shore of Long Island, and on Thanksgiving Day we went to the service at a small Episcopal church there. I was shocked when, in his sermon, the rector denounced the Jewish community for commercializing Christmas so much that he had to appeal to merchants to take down their Christmas decorations before Easter. I have to add that my roommate was rather appalled at his attitude, too. For the first time I truly understood that every community or area has its own prejudices, and I no longer felt as defensive about ours in the South.

There were no more than five black students in my class of almost six hundred at Smith, and I never knew any of them beyond knowing their names and saying hello occasionally. I did learn later that one of them became the first black woman from Africa to become a doctor. But during my sophomore year Smith had its first black faculty member: Mr. Banner, a visiting professor from Howard University. I first noticed him in the academic procession at the opening convocation. One of my courses was a fairly large entry-level comparative religion course. Everyone met together once a week for a lecture; then we were divided into small sections for the other two classes per week. He was among the faculty at the first lecture, and he was also the teacher in my smaller section. It was a strange feeling at first, but Mr. Banner was a warm and congenial person as well as a good teacher. I don't remember where he was from, but I think he was from the South, and he seemed to enjoy having a southerner in his class. Daddy was not too pleased about my having a black professor, but he didn't make any fuss about it, either.

My greatest challenge and most rewarding experience came when I decided to write a thesis my senior year and have Alice Dickinson as my thesis advisor. In the math department at the time, the thesis did not have to be an original paper. It was more like doing an independent study. It was challenging, because I was doing something somewhat on my own; rewarding, because it gave me an opportunity, through weekly meetings and discussions, to share a unique experience with a rare person. Alice was a gifted mathematician, but she also had that rare talent of getting her subject across in a special way in the classroom. Often that senior year, I would enter our session with the feeling that I had no idea of what I was doing. Invariably, after a good dose of her patience and encouragement, I left with renewed confidence in my own ability and a sense that I could accomplish the task at hand. That entire experience, more than anything else, continues to make me feel that if and when I am called upon, I do have a certain amount of ability to bring to a given situation. Alice Dickinson did her task so well that I was elected to Sigma Xi and Phi Beta Kappa, and graduated summa cum laude.

Often another part of my weekly sessions with Alice Dickinson was conversations about Birmingham, the South, and my feelings and reactions to what was happening in 1960–61. I must admit that I was not nearly as tuned in or concerned about what was going on as she was, and I don't remember the specifics of those conversations, probably due to my own somewhat apathetic feeling at the time. She herself was quite interested. Later, she was instrumental in having Smith students involved in exchange programs with predominantly black colleges and volunteer activities in the summer. She came through Birmingham one summer in the late sixties on her way to visit some students working somewhere in Mississippi. She may have been disappointed that I didn't follow a teaching career, but I have always felt that she would have been very proud of my efforts later on.

Since I didn't do a lot of dating in high school or college, I didn't expect to graduate from Smith and immediately get married; but that was before I really got to know Bill Tynes. Our families knew each other but weren't close friends. He had known my brothers at Mountain Brook Elementary, and I mentioned that he probably saw me being pushed around in a baby carriage. He went to Ramsay High, graduated from the University of the South, Sewanee, in 1954, and then spent three years in the Air Force as a navigator with the Strategic Air Command. Though not as an Air Force pilot, he had learned to fly a small plane, and he bought a single-engine plane of his own. While I was at Smith I kept hearing about dates he would have with girls I knew, about this attractive bachelor with an airplane and how he would fly them to Sewanee or to his family's place in Highlands, North Carolina, for the weekend or just for a Sunday afternoon.

In July of 1960, the night that John Kennedy was nominated for President, a neighbor of my parents had a cousin visiting and she had a small group over to her house to watch the Democratic convention on television. My mother's cousin Stuart Symington was running for President that year, so I was more interested in him than in John Kennedy on that particular night. Bill was at the party, too, but with someone else. At some point during the evening he decided that I was an interesting person and he wanted to have a date with me. I was making my debut that year, my senior year in college. We began dating then, and we had a wonderful time going to all of the debut parties together.

Bill's father was born in Shuqualak, a small town in eastern Mississippi. After graduating from Millsaps College he came to Birmingham and worked for his uncle, who owned Hardie-Tynes Manufacturing Company. Ever since Bill got out of the Air Force he has worked as a manufacturer's representative selling iron and steel castings—sort of a middleman between foundries and companies that need particular parts made from castings. For about ten years he shared an office with his father and uncle.

During spring vacation in '61, Bill and I went to visit his mother's aunt Lula in Church Hill, Mississippi, near Natchez, where his mother's family was from. Aunt Lula was ninety-six, had never married, was still living alone in the house where she was born. After I met her and had gotten her approval, Bill formally proposed to me right there on Aunt Lula's front porch. I had thought about going to Boston or New York, getting some kind of a job for a while. Then I had an interview here with IBM; but you had to go to Atlanta for training, and that wouldn't work if I was going to get married. Much to my surprise, I became one of those people who graduated from college with an engagement ring on her finger.

John Porter

There was never any encouragement for me to go to college, because there was no history of it in our family. You know, "Do you want to go to college, son?" I knew my parents would support us as far as we wanted to go. My brother probably broke the record of F's you could make in school, because his heart and mind just weren't there. But somehow it happened in high school that my buddies were from families where they had gone to college or they were economically higher than I was, so when I looked up and saw that they were on their way to college I grabbed my bags to go, too.

Parker High was located in the black neighborhood called Smithfield not far from Dynamite Hill, and there would be nearly five hundred graduates in both the January and June classes. Everybody in Birmingham wound up there their last two years, and you had to study for a vocation in your senior year, "learn a trade," even if you were in the college preparatory class.

There were some great teachers there, and they taught us to talk proper, to use the correct grammar, what we called "putting on airs." For oratorical contests we would spend a whole month on gestures, pronunciation, the whole package of delivery— emoting, overemphasizing everything—and it didn't take long to see that the people who put on airs were the ones who were sort of "up there." If you wanted to get up there with 'em, you'd begin to put on airs.

But it was the guys I ran with who really got me into college. I was ambitious, president of the student body my senior year, president of my section of our graduating class. I graduated in January of '48, but I didn't make it to college for a year and a half. One of the guys told me later, "Man, I admired you so. But one day I was on the streetcar on First Avenue and I looked up and there you were, washing windows at a jewelry store." He had just known I was going to college and everything. The truth is, it took me a while to get my stuff together.

Except for helping my father in Mr. Martin's yard, I didn't have a job, had never been out in the workplace, until after I finished high school. During that year and a half I worked at a jewelry store and in a printing shop and as an interoffice messenger at Protective Life downtown. The experience at Protective Life really drove it home, that the races were together and yet very much apart. It was always there. We blacks had our separate restroom, elevator, and drinking fountain, and I brown-bagged it because there was no place for me to go for lunch. There was little interaction. You performed your job and then you went home.

I developed two private protests that I never told anybody about. One of them was that I would never say "Yes, sir" to a white man like my father had taught me. Around the office my name was "John" and everybody else was "Mister," and I was expected to say "Yes, sir" or "No, sir." That was easy enough to get around. My boss would say, "John, have you seen that book on such-and-such?" and I would say, "I believe . . . I believe it's over there . . . let me go get it," and I'd be off. Interestingly, years later the guy I had worked for told me I hadn't fooled him for a minute. The other vow I made was that no white man would ever outwalk me on the streets of Birmingham. I would walk up to that curb like it was a track meet, tense as a sprinter, waiting for the light to change, and when it turned green I'd be off to the races. It was my silent protest. I was saying, "I'm somebody."

In September of '49 I enrolled at Alabama State in Montgomery, with no idea about what I wanted to do. Doctor, lawyer, Indian chief. I'd developed a stammering problem, something you pick up like slang or an accent, and it cost me a girlfriend, because by the time I would finish saying "I-I-I l-l-love y-y-you" she'd be gone. I broke the habit by holding a mirror to my mouth, something they had taught me in drama class, watching the movement of my lips while speaking, to remind me that I was stammering. At any rate, I was majoring in history, president of my classes, into extracurricular activities, sailing along, at the peak of my college career, just about to graduate, when I got sick. It was diagnosed as TB of the lymphatic gland, or something of the sort, not contagious, but I was losing weight. I was the big man on campus, but when I left for a weekend of rest I didn't get back for two and a half years.

It was while I was confined, locked up, with plenty of time to think about what I should do in life, that I got the call to preach. We had always been regulars at Sixth Avenue Baptist, but now I was giving some serious thought to the ministry. When

I recovered sufficiently, I took a job as a civilian employee with the Department of the Navy in Washington, D.C., using the typing skills they had taught me at Parker High, and when I had saved enough money I called my mother to tell her I was ready to go back home and finish college, and she said, "You're not coming *south* again, are you?" I told her the only difference between Washington and Birmingham was that they didn't actually have signs that spelled out "colored," that they had their own ways. So in the fall of '54 I returned for my senior year at Alabama State in Montgomery, determined now to be a preacher, and when I went to the Dexter Avenue Baptist Church I met the new pastor there, Dr. Martin Luther King, Jr.

Part Two

BOMBINGHAM

CHAPTER EIGHT

Prelude to Terror

Maybe in other parts of the country the fifties belonged to the silent generation, epitomized by the placid presidency of Dwight Eisenhower—the years of big-finned automobiles and Elvis and postwar prosperity—but that was not so in the Deep South. Harry Truman had given the old Confederacy its first wake-up call in 1948 when he said the time had come to recognize the Negro as a human being, which seemed like a dangerous and altogether radical proposition to most whites in Dixie, and the second warning came like a thunderclap with the *Brown* v. *Board of Education* ruling in '54, which outlawed school segregation. For too long the South had been left to its own devices, virtually ignored by the national press and by presidential candidates who would rather have the vote of the Solid South than get it riled up, in effect allowing the Klan to have its way under the cover of darkness. But now there was a new agenda building in the nation: equal rights for all citizens; and when the media began to focus on the South, it was as though they had stumbled upon an ancient civilization.

In Mississippi and Alabama and all across the steamy southern outback of tarpaper shacks and fallow cotton fields and dying towns with billboards at the city limits reading "Nigger Don't Let the Sun Set on Your Head," everything was separate and nothing was equal: drinking fountains, restrooms, public transportation, housing, schools, churches, hospitals, justice, job opportunities. Jim Crow law ruled, no matter what the federal laws

said, and most black people in the South knew that their choices
were to stay and endure or pack up and follow so many Dixie
Highways to the urban ghettos of Chicago and Philadelphia and
New York, where, they too often would discover, white north-
erners had their ways, too. Other parts of the country had pol-
ished more discreet forms of keeping black people in their place,
such as redlining neighborhoods and denying credit, genteel dis-
criminations that maintained de facto segregation.

But our racists were inherently more brazen, more violent,
more Neanderthal than those found anywhere else in the nation;
and now, in the fifties, fearing the imminent heat of the federal
government and the glare of the national press, the woolhats and
peckerwoods and various yahoos began to salivate as embold-
ened blacks dared to begin stirring. In 1954 my beloved Birmingham Barons began to wear a Rebel flag, like a chevron, on
their uniform shirts. In '55 a black teenager named Emmett Till
was lynched in Mississippi for allegedly allowing his eyes to linger too long on a white woman; a black domestic named Rosa
Parks refused to move to the rear of a city bus in Montgomery,
Alabama; and explosions began to rend the night air in Birmingham as black churches and homes were dynamited (the
total came to thirty-one during the decade). A full-fledged bus
boycott was under way in Montgomery; riots erupted when a
black woman named Autherine Lucy tried to enroll at the University of Alabama, bad enough to bring in the National Guard;
Birmingham unilaterally outlawed the National Association for
the Advancement of Colored People, even made it against the
law for whites and blacks to gather together; and civic "leaders"
uncomfortable with the Klan's violent image formed the White
Citizens' Council to "protect states' rights."

And there was the autumn of 1957, when I, as sports editor
of the Auburn *Plainsman* and a "chowboy" waiting tables at
Graves Center, spent most of my hours learning how to put
words together as I tracked the team that would win the national

football championship. In early September, federal troops had to protect black students during the desegregation of Central High in Little Rock, Arkansas; when a black preacher named Fred Shuttlesworth tried to enroll his daughter at Phillips, the high school in downtown Birmingham, he was badly beaten with brass knucks and his wife was stabbed, and for that he was called a "troublemaker" by the Birmingham *News*. And then, on Labor Day night, after a weekend that had seen the murder of six black males in Birmingham and half a dozen cross-burnings at schools targeted for desegregation, a black man named "Judge" Aaron was kidnapped by Klansmen, blind-folded, taken to an abandoned house, beaten and stabbed and emasculated with straight razors, and left to die. ("Investigators," said the Birmingham *Post-Herald*, "are seeking to establish a motive for the assault." The *News* commented that it was not known whether Aaron was a member of a Communist organization.) Ike, before leaving on a golfing vacation, said he wished everybody would calm down.

These developments were not altogether lost on us at Auburn, "Loveliest Village of the Plain," although most of us were still walking to the rhythms set by our parents. Auburn was the more conservative and Christian of the two major white state universities, a homogeneous WASP outpost, a friendly little place of only eight thousand students, future engineers and county extension agents and pro football players and "homemakers" angling for their "M.R.S. degree," insulated from a broader society that soon would demand tolerance toward people who were different from us. As we sat in the Student Union Building's cafeteria—Elvis yowling on the jukebox, bobby-soxed sorority temptresses at one long table, the football players at another—we read the newspapers and, for the most part, made bold predictions about what might happen if a "coon" tried to get into Auburn. On slow nights we would go out to the local high school football stadium to watch the black school play—Lee County

Training School had to play its games in the middle of the week—howling at the demeaning Amos-'n'-Andy play-by-play account offered over the public address system by none other than the school's principal: "Oh, Lawd, eighteen and a half yards fo' talkin' in da huddle. Things is lookin' *baaaad* fo' da home team." There were, of course, exceptions to the perceived wisdom. A *Plainsman* columnist, Anne Rivers, daughter of an Atlanta lawyer, was fired for writing a fairly mild essay merely suggesting tolerance in the wake of the Autherine Lucy affair. Let the University of Alabama have the Jews, Catholics, Yankees, and Autherine Lucys, we were saying; we'll take an ol' boy from Talladega anytime, teach him how to build bigger bridges or grow taller corn, get him married to a Tri-Delt, and the supply of War Eagles will never run out.

In the fall of '58, after a summer internship in the sports department of the Atlanta *Constitution,* I hired on as a sportswriter with the Birmingham *News.* My beat was the Big Five and I was in heaven. With my sister at Auburn, I moved back into my old bedroom at the folks' house in Woodlawn, hoping to build a bankroll from my salary of seventy-five dollars a week; and every morning at daybreak I would be hunched over a clattery Royal typewriter in the turn-of-the-century ambience of the *News* sports department, batting out the latest from the camps of the West End Lions and the Ramsay Rams and, yes, the Woodlawn Colonels. (This time, by God, *I* would be the one in control of any conversations with Coach John Blaine of Woodlawn.) Most of the people I had known at Auburn were back home, too, settling into jobs in the front offices of plants where their fathers had merely labored, and to them I was "Scoop"— actually paid to sit up there in the press box at Legion Field during Big Five games with binoculars, tracking the games, keeping the statistics, being called "sir" by fullbacks and tackles

I now realized were mere teenagers with an overdose of testosterone.

This was the real world to me, where I would learn my craft and join the company of men. My boss was Benny Marshall, whose breezy column style I had blatantly imitated in the Auburn *Plainsman,* and he had taken me under his wing. A merry little gnome, a confidant of Bear Bryant, who had just come aboard at Alabama, Benny was there laying out that day's paper when the sun came up and he was there writing his column for the next day when the sun went down. The staff included Alf Van Hoose, who wrote a column and covered the Barons and, for loose change, served as official scorer for the Black Barons when they got Rickwood for Sunday doubleheaders; George "Ace" Kabase, the dour "slot man"; Ronald Weathers, who tromped the sidelines at county football games with a notebook and a bulky Speed Graphic camera; Neal Ellis, main man on the college beat; and me, the kid, in a flattop crew cut and, emulating Benny and Van Hoose, clip-on bow tie. In that forgotten corner of the newsroom known as "Toys and Games" we wrestled with a daunting headline type that could be stretched to a maximum of four and a half counts per column (thus, a 10–2 win by the Little Rock Travelers over the New Orleans Pelicans became "Pebs Pop Pels"); rushed stories and headlines and photos to the pressroom by way of pneumatic tubes; ripped copy from clattering wire-service printers; and mumbled inanities among ourselves to keep things interesting: "What would you have if a couple of Barons took three Mobile players to lunch?—Goldy, Locke, and the three Bears." Ronald Weathers's commentary on a baseball All-Star Game featuring a large number of black Dodgers and Giants: "Every time the National League came to bat, it looked like the jig was up."

If we buried news of the Birmingham Black Barons and Parker High School deep in the sports section, we were merely

following company policy. Calling the fearless Fred Shuttlesworth a "troublemaker" and hiding the story of Judge Aaron's
emasculation (on page six of the *Post-Herald,* September 4, 1957,
under a one-column, two-line headline, "Hunt Continues for
Night Riders") were in accordance with unwritten laws. As the
city's major industry was controlled by absentee owners, so
were the newspapers. The morning *Post-Herald* was part of the
Scripps-Howard chain, the afternoon *News* a chattel of New-
house, although each was given local autonomy to cover the city
as local mores dictated. Both papers had their moments during
the late fifties when they helped uncover underworld doings at
Phenix City, Alabama—"Sin City U.S.A."—near Auburn on the
Chattahoochee River; the *Post-Herald* won a Pulitzer for its
work. For the most part, though, they aimed their news and
editorial pages at the white population, which made up only sixty
percent of the 340,000 people in the city at that time, putting all
news of the black community on what editors around the city
desk referred to as "the nigger pages." Blacks who wanted to
know what was going on in Smithfield or any of the other black
neighborhoods could find it only in the conservative Birmingham
World or in the succession of black weeklies that came and went,
or, for a larger view of the gigantic struggle that was soon to
come, in the Atlanta *Daily World,* available on the streets in
black areas of town.

By contrast, Atlanta had Ralph McGill. Every day of the
week on the front page of the *Constitution,* McGill, a native of
small-town Tennessee who had been a sportswriter, represented
the major voice of reason to be found on a large newspaper
in the Deep South. He was a sensitive writer who preferred
being called a "reporter" rather than a "columnist," and he
showed why when he was penning lyrical 750-word dispatches
from the southern countryside about tenant farmers and quail
hunts and baptisms and barn raisings. But what really set him
apart in those tumultuous times was his conscience. He was an

old-fashioned moralist, an FDR New Dealer, a dyed-in-the-wool "yellow-dog Democrat," a friend of kings and presidents and dirt farmers and Carl Sandburg alike, an avowed enemy of the Ku Klux Klan and the White Citizens' Councils that had taken its place. All of this, of course, made McGill a "liberal," and people like my father, now getting himself lathered up over the coming civil rights movement, dismissed him as "Rastus" McGill. He would win a Pulitzer for a column he wrote following the dynamiting of the Temple, Atlanta's largest synagogue, in October of 1958: "Let us face the facts. This is a harvest. It is the crop of things sown. It is the harvest of defiance of courts and the encouragement of citizens to defy law on the part of many Southern politicians. . . . When the wolves of hate are loosed on one people, then no one is safe. . . ."

Meanwhile, in Birmingham, the voice of the two big dailies was John Temple Graves of the *Post-Herald,* who also wrote a free-ranging daily column. But unlike McGill, who had to endure bomb threats and sidewalk tongue-lashings and vituperative late-night telephone calls and was a marked man even in the relatively moderate atmosphere of Atlanta, Graves was perfectly in tune with his audience. He knew what was on the minds of Birmingham's whites, knew which buttons to push to rouse both the blue-collar workingman in the valley and the Big Mule over the mountain, and every morning he continued a running diatribe against the usual suspects: the NAACP, the United Nations, the Supreme Court, liberals and "integrationists," Atlanta and Moscow, even Ralph McGill. The column would open each day with a quote from Shakespeare, set in italics, an embarrassing exercise in pseudointellectualism in a city of coal and iron, and off he would go. Answering an anti-Birmingham article in the Atlanta *Daily World:* "You wonder why they [blacks] don't all move away. But in my travels over the United States I have found Birmingham looked on as a favorite place for colored people, one where they are considerably happier than in, say,

Atlanta, or in Detroit, Chicago, or Los Angeles.'' He celebrated the Girl Scouts, ''whose Handbook contains 60 changes made mostly in response to criticism for too much emphasis on the United Nations as against the United States and too feverish a social-mindedness in an essentially individual-building organization.'' Willie Mays couldn't even come home and bury an aunt in peace: ''If Mr. Mays yearned to play ball with some of our white boys and felt frustrated, he should blame the Supreme Court, whose decision provoked the Birmingham [segregation] vote.'' On integration: ''Whom God has put asunder let no man join together!'' Championing the new White Citizens' Councils, which were little more than Klansmen in coats and ties: ''Their literature is well printed and chosen. . . . Correspondence is on good paper, beautifully typed. . . . Sensibly, 'racial integrity' rather than 'white supremacy' is stressed.'' It was this sort of leadership that had made Birmingham safe for Bull Connor.

Theophilus Eugene Connor was born in 1897 at Selma, in Alabama's lush Black Belt, so named not only for its soil but for its overwhelmingly black population, to a railroad dispatcher and a farm girl from nearby Plantersville. One of five sons, his first name taken from that of a notorious bank robber of the time, Eugene was left motherless at the age of eight when Molly Connor died of tuberculosis. He was a scruffy ragamuffin, the runt of the litter, who would peak out at five-eight and learned early on that he had to jump and shout to be noticed. His sense of worth wasn't helped when he had an eye shot out with a BB pellet during a period when he lived with an aunt and uncle in North Birmingham. He never completed high school, due to a boyhood largely spent traveling around the country with his nomadic father.

When he married a girl from Plantersville in 1920, he was already a railroad telegrapher like his father; he lived in hotels and boardinghouses in seven states during his first year of marriage. In the course of his wanderings he stumbled into a career as a sports announcer. "One day in Dallas," writes William A. Nunnelley in his excellent biography, *Bull Connor*, "he attended what was known as a baseball 'matinee,' a re-creation of a game by an announcer using telegraph reports [wherein] fans unable to attend an actual game could follow the progress of their team at a matinee in a downtown storefront studio." Connor was there as just another baseball fan, but he wound up pinch-hitting when the regular announcer showed up sick, getting five dollars for dramatizing the simple information as it came across the Western Union ticker, and the crowd loved him. Soon he became a regular, earning ten dollars a game, and by 1922 he had moved back to the closest thing he had ever known as home: Birmingham.

During the twenties, first as operator of his own baseball matinee (charging thirty-five cents admission to hear him call Birmingham Barons games) and then as a full-time sports announcer for WKBC, he became a popular figure. He would broadcast college football games and professional boxing matches, and would sometimes announce election results to audiences at downtown theaters; but baseball was his big ticket. Barons baseball was an affordable entertainment, a relief from drudgery for the men of the mines and plants and mills in the Pittsburgh of the South. Their heroes were men with names like Yam Yaryan and Buttermilk Smith. Soon the man who recorded their exploits from the wood-and-steel Rickwood Field became known as "Bull," for his booming voice and his bulldog appearance and his ability to "shoot the bull" during lulls in the action. Even *The Sporting News* (the one publication he revered more than the *Saturday Evening Post*) acknowledged that he had "earned a following second to none throughout the Southern Association." Everybody knew ol' Bull; he was a good old boy, a friend of the workingman, and as he strutted along the downtown streets, exchanging sports banter with his fans, he knew he was home for good.

Full of himself, urged on by his fans, Connor decided to run for a seat in the Alabama House of Representatives in 1934. It may be true that he knew nothing about politics and was running on a whim and to test his popularity, but he was no dummy. This was during the depths of the Depression, a desperate time for Birmingham, and his was a purely populist platform: no higher taxes in any form; reductions of gasoline and oil taxes and the cost of automobile tags; legalization of beer sales; authorization for county "local options" on the sale of hard liquor; and strict civil service laws that would eliminate patronage and open up jobs for state, county, and city employees. He won as one of Jefferson County's seven representatives, as the Birmingham *News* pointed out, "without the support of a political organization." Clearly, as a poor boy up from poverty, a common man who eschewed "uppity talk" and spouted a mistrust for the wealthy and educated ruling class, he had all the makings of a southern populist along the lines of Georgia's Tom Watson and Louisiana's Huey Long. Sadly, as with Watson, he would become ensnared by the race issue and resort to demagoguery.

Connor served only one two-year term as a state representative in Montgomery, standing by his platform promises and receiving high marks for his performance. He opposed pay raises and paid holidays for legislators, fought the legalization of horse racing and any form of gambling, and came out against an anti-sedition law (ironically, as it would turn out years later, when he would rebel against federal integration rulings). He led the way in a fight for a civil service system that would do away with political spoils in Jefferson County, wherein winning candidates routinely cleaned house and filled city and county jobs with their friends and supporters, and he was always on the side of the workingman. In his time he helped create a state Department of Labor, supported the Workmen's Compensation Act and legislative reapportionment to give Birmingham a stronger voice in Montgomery. He enjoyed taking part in a floor fight, strutting around and ridiculing his opponents. But in his gut, he didn't care that much for the legislative life in the state capital—particularly the part about having to go behind closed doors, where his clowning and outrageous pandering to the public had no audience, to haggle and make concessions with bankers and lawyers whose backgrounds and educations were intimidating to him. In short, he missed the limelight.

In those days, Birmingham was ruled by a three-man commission: a mayor, a commissioner of public improvements, and a commissioner of public safety. In 1937 Connor was among nine candidates for the two commission posts. In a time of unemployment, which had deepened the antagonism toward TCI and the Big Mules, Connor positioned himself as one who had "no entangling alliances," which was about as fanciful as his rhetoric got. Cashing in on his popularity from the sportscasting days and his record as a loyal and honest representative of Birmingham interests while a state legislator, he led the field in the general election and won the runoff in a landslide. When asked, as was the custom, which of the two commission posts he wanted, he quickly chose public safety commissioner. He would be in charge of the police and fire departments, the board of education, the parks and the libraries. One of his first actions was to literally take the doors to his office off their hinges. He would be a man of the people.

During his first four-year term, Connor was a reformer. He named new chiefs for the police and fire departments, which had been shot through with dissension and graft, and even outfitted the cops with radios and high-speed cars. He proclaimed war on dice games, numbers runners, "whiskey houses," and prostitution. He voided all special parking tags that allowed holders to park anywhere they wanted downtown. He ended kickbacks in city purchases, made the city's municipal court judges work full days instead of part-time, even appointed a liberal social activist preacher to oversee the parole board. Barely forty years old, Bull had found his calling. Forget the mayor, Jimmie Jones, who had been in office for a dozen listless years; the most popular public figure in Birmingham was Bull Connor, who spent his days hailing admirers on Twentieth Street, playing bridge and dominoes with his friends at the fire stations and police precincts, and swapping "nigger jokes" and baseball stories with the boys in the press room at City Hall. Little wonder, then, that he was swept back into office without a runoff in the spring of 1941.

The black community of Birmingham could only stand by and watch helplessly as the reign of Bull Connor unfolded. Blacks formed nearly forty percent of the city's population at this time, but because of poll taxes and other restrictions not five percent were registered to vote. They remained as always: a shadowy underclass of domestics and laborers scratching out an existence under utter segregation in the forgotten corners of the city. Since there was no visible leadership to speak in their behalf, they could only smolder and keep their grievances to themselves. Sporadic visits from the Klan were all it took to keep them in the place prescribed for them by the white man.

But in 1948, when it became clear what Harry Truman was up to, Connor was among the delegates leading the southern walkout at the Democratic convention and forming the Dixiecrat party. Then came the first of the bombings of black homes near designated white neighborhoods that caused the city to be dubbed "Bombingham" by the eastern press. Led in the streets by Shuttlesworth and in the courts by an elegant Birmingham civil rights attorney named Arthur Shores, the first black to practice law in Alabama, blacks began to stir and question the city's segregation practices for the first time. Connor didn't like this, and began to link integration with communism: "These Communist rattlesnakes, they're like the Negro Youth Congress. . . . It may be unfair to fleas, but fleas and Communists are a lot alike. It doesn't take a whole hide-full of 'em to make you mighty uncomfortable.'' Using these tactics, he was reelected in 1949 with his highest plurality ever.

It looked like ol' Bull would go on forever—until four days before Christmas of 1952, when he was caught by a disgruntled police detective and a *Post-Herald* photographer, shacked up with his secretary at noon in the downtown Tutwiler Hotel. He got off the hook when a deadlocked jury led to a ''mistrial,'' but the detailed coverage of the story had damaged him badly in a city so relentlessly Christian as Birmingham. And so, in 1953, he wisely chose not to run again. He slinked away to run his service station in Avondale, about halfway between my parents' house in Woodlawn and downtown, where he sat around playing grab-ass and cussing ''niggers and Commies.'' One of his best customers was my father.

Life went on in the *News* sports department; I put in a second year covering the preps. And then one day in August of 1960 Benny Marshall drove me down the road to Tuscaloosa to formally introduce me to Paul ''Bear'' Bryant. Alabama had lost to Auburn's national champions, 40–0, in 1957, and hired Bryant to come back to his alma mater. His first team, minus most of the best athletes from the thrashing of the year before (whom he had run off, calling them ''prima donnas''), managed to lose to Auburn by only 14 to 8; and now that he had the house in order he was on a roll. The '59 team had thrown what would be the first of four straight shutouts against the addled Auburn, and I was being promoted to covering practices at both schools and writing locker room stories on Saturdays just as the Bryant legend began. After Benny introduced me to Bryant that day, we three sat down for a chat in the coach's office. ''Looks like you've got some pretty good horses this year, Coach,'' Benny said, for openers. ''Aw, shit, Benny,'' said Bryant, ''they ain't nothing but a bunch of goddamn little pissants.'' Benny laughed nervously and nudged me, the Kid, and I glowed. This was going to be fun.

Maybe Bryant knew I was an Auburn boy and took it as a challenge to win me over; or maybe, as Benny had hoped, I would become the young sportswriter that Bryant had always seemed to single out as a confidant wherever he had coached. Whatever, at dawn on alternate days of the week (the other days I drove to Auburn) I would find myself eating breakfast with the Bear at a diner adjacent to the campus in Tuscaloosa, where he would grumble and nod at startled students and poor-mouth the "little bitty country boys" who clearly were on their way to a national championship. I would hang around for practice in the afternoon, and often wind up drinking beer at the house of an assistant coach. Several of the assistants, like Gene Stallings, the current coach at Alabama, had been among Bryant's famous "Junction Boys" at Texas A&M during the mid-fifties, survivors of the hellish preseason camp he had held at a dot in the road called Junction, in southwest Texas. Now they were a rabid band of true believers, and there was a lot of beer drunk on those late afternoons. "Lord, Pat, how're you going to explain this when you get home?" the wife of the host asked one of the young assistants, his face flushed, his knees beginning to buckle. "Aw, hell," he said, "I'll fuck my way out of it." The next day, at Auburn, Coach Ralph "Shug" Jordan, whose habit was to go home at lunchtime for tea and a nap, was not amused when I reported how things were going in Tuscaloosa.

As cloistered as I was back there in Toys and Games, I couldn't avoid the tension that lay over Birmingham as thickly as the pall of smoke from the mills. Bull was back now as commissioner of public safety, having won by only 103 votes in '57 on a blatantly racist platform, and he was turning the screws on "niggers, integrationists, and Communists." The bombings of black homes in the hills above Legion Field had continued, to the extent that the area now was being referred to as Dynamite

Hill. There had been the Nat Cole incident, the Judge Aaron emasculation, and the sporadic attempts to integrate schools and neighborhoods and buses (usually led by Fred Shuttlesworth, who had formed the Alabama Christian Movement for Human Rights when the NAACP was banned).

As tension escalated, Bull lost interest in all facets of his job except the one that enabled him to be the de facto police chief of Birmingham. By dint of his bellicose personality and the tacit support of the white electorate, Bull had always been able to intimidate the various police chiefs and mayors and even fellow commissioners he had served with. And now he had surrounded himself with a cadre of loyalists, cops he could trust, creating a virtual police state all his very own. It was a well-drilled police force, and they were everywhere: tapping phones of ACMHR members and other suspected "subversives," breaking up civil rights meetings, hassling black people on the streets, generally keeping a high profile.

When the tactics of lunch-counter sit-ins finally reached Birmingham early in 1960, just as Bull was preparing to send forty-five of his cops off to a Dale Carnegie course on "How to Win Friends and Influence People," the police were ready. On the last day of March, in a movement synchronized by Shuttlesworth, five two-man teams of black students from Miles College sat down at lunch counters in five separate department stores in downtown Birmingham precisely at 10:30 A.M. It was over by 10:35, and there to see that the ten were slammed into waiting paddy wagons was Bull Connor himself. "Give 'em hell, Bull, give 'em hell!" came shouts from white office workers who had gathered on the sidewalks to watch the show.

Although Birminghamians these days still claim that their city was neck-and-neck with Atlanta in the race to be the dominant city of the South until the sixties, the war was lost long before that. During the fifties Atlanta's population grew by forty-seven percent while Birmingham's grew by less than five percent.

The basic difference between the two neighboring cities, separated by only 150 miles, was that Atlanta was a diversified city looking to the future while Birmingham was a closed society clinging to the past. Modernization in the steel and iron industries had caused the number of TCI employees to drop from its peak of forty thousand workers in 1940 to some sixteen thousand in the late fifties; and virtually no new industry, blue-collar or otherwise, had filled in the gap, mainly because U.S. Steel and the local barons didn't want the competition. The feeling was that Birmingham was a steel town, by God, the Pittsburgh of the South, and it would be back. Atlanta had always had a broader-based economy and a more enlightened civic leadership and more moderate newspapers, the principal factors in its getting the Southeast's airport hub before that idea even occurred to Birmingham. Both cities were tightly segregated, of course, although Atlanta, instead of having a Bull Connor, was home to the black Atlanta University complex and headquarters for Dr. Martin Luther King, Jr., and most other leaders in the civil rights movement.

Birmingham's leaders got a fair warning around this time, in the form of a Metropolitan Audit. In 1958 a business-oriented group calling itself the Southern Institute of Management came to town with the idea of conducting extensive surveys to find out what Birminghamians thought of their city. It was not sanctioned by city hall, and many business and church leaders at first looked upon the idea as more meddling by outsiders; but a modest budget of $30,000 was raised, and soon the survey began. Questionnaires went out to forty thousand people—blacks excluded, as usual—and over the next year and a half the results began to trickle in. "What Makes Birmingham Tick?" read the heading in one company house organ, imploring its employees to fill out the questionnaire. "You'll have fun reading the answers!" Well, as they say in Irondale, *au contraire*. What emerged was a four-hundred-page report, the Metropolitan

Audit of 1960, loaded with omens of Birmingham's future: "Defensive . . . sense of inferiority . . . people do not speak well of their city . . . dates to the Civil War and belittling by the North. . . . Not bold enough, not planning for the future. . . . Industries fight new industries . . . absentee owners . . . unions versus industry. . . . Conservative and reactionary in religion, business, education, government and social life. . . . Lacks ambition and aspiration, shuns newcomers. . . . Moral prudishness. . . . Censure of Birmingham's [racial] actions and policies serves only to incite defensive measures rather than positive action to solve them. . . . No dreamers or visionaries. . . . Even the architecture affirms conformity and order. . . ."

The report wasn't well written, and it waffled a bit on the racial issue; but even so, it was too much for City Hall to swallow. The *News*'s editors slapped it on the desk of a reporter and asked for a series based on the report, and the negative responses came out with a positive spin—"We Are a City of Churches" was the headline on the report's observation that Birmingham religion was conservative and reactionary. City Hall ignored the findings of the survey, sending its copy over to the Birmingham Public Library to be filed in the archives.

For a long time Birmingham had been keeping a low profile; but now, as the civil rights movement edged closer and closer to Bull Connor's turf in narrowing concentric circles, the city could hide no more. In April of 1960 the New York *Times* published a lengthy two-part series by one of its Pulitzer Prize–winning reporters, Harrison Salisbury—"Fear and Hatred Grip Birmingham"—which introduced the city and Bull Connor to the outside world: "Fear stalks the streets of Birmingham . . . fragmented by the emotional dynamite of racism, enforced by the whip, the razor, the gun, the bomb, the torch, the club, the knife, the mob, the police and many branches of the state's apparatus. . . ." Salisbury pointed out that of the city's 135,000 voters, only 8,000 were black. The Chamber of Commerce and public officials reacted with disbelief and then with anger. The *News* reprinted the articles under a headline that read, "Can This Be Birmingham? New York *Times* Slanders Our City," and thundered in its editorials: Salisbury's report was "an amazing recital of untruths and semi-truths . . . maliciously bigoted, noxiously false, viciously distorted." On the heels of the *Times* came the Washington *Post* with a similar report, headlined "Birmingham Brims with Race Bias." The *News,* again: "This Birmingham of ours is a lovely place. It is a city in which fear does not abide. What Harrison Salisbury reported, we all should know, is in substance untrue." Connor filed a lawsuit, but the *Times* was upheld by the United States Supreme Court. Now Birmingham was giving the world twenty-four hours to get out of town.

"Out of town" for me, in the second week of May in 1961, was Auburn, where I was reporting on the Southeastern Conference track championships for the *News*. I had just turned twenty-five and I figured I had reached a dead end in Birmingham. With Alf Van Hoose in charge of covering the Barons for life, should he choose, there wasn't much of interest for me to do between football seasons except for spring football practices at Auburn and Alabama, the "Bowling Beat," a grab-bag three-dot column I called "File Thirteen," a Sunday roundup of the Alabama-Florida League, and occasional telephone interviews with personalities such as Ted Williams. I had moved out of my parents' house and taken an efficiency apartment on Southside, not far from Vulcan, and was seeing a girl I thought I would marry. There had been a feeler from the athletic director at Florida State University in Tallahassee about my becoming FSU's sports information director; I wasn't so sure I wanted to make a career out of that, but my ninety-dollar-a-week salary at the *News* wasn't going to make it if I married.

Track and field meets were new to me, but I made do. At the end of each day's events I would go into the basement of the field house, where once I had worked as a student assistant in the sports information department, to gather the results and write my story and arrange to wire the package to the *News*. Elsewhere in the newspapers, the big story was about the Freedom Riders, an integrated group organized by CORE (Congress of Racial Equality) that was traveling through the South on buses to test the Supreme Court's recent ruling outlawing segregation on buses and trains used in interstate commerce. They were due to arrive in Birmingham on Sunday, Mother's Day, just two weeks after Bull Connor had received his strongest mandate ever with a sixty-one percent vote. But, as usual, that was somebody else's beat.

My plan was to take my mother to church on Mother's Day. As soon as the track meet ended on Saturday afternoon and I filed my story, I would drive the two and a half hours back to my apartment in Birmingham. There was a thrilling finish to the meet, a mano-a-mano duel in the gloaming between two ex-hausted high jumpers, one from Auburn and one from Louisiana State University, which would determine the SEC championship; and during the drive home I was already envisioning a "Monday follow" story about the drama. I had been smitten by the literary sports journalism I had seen in *Sports Illustrated* magazine, which Benny dismissed as "Sports Elevated," and since nobody seemed to be paying much attention to these spring sports I figured I could try a new voice in an empty hall.

I got home, slept, arose on Mother's Day, drove to Wood-lawn and picked up my mother, and we went to Woodlawn Methodist Church. It was just another Mother's Day, no special sermon from the feisty little preacher, Brother John Rutland, al-though I had heard my mother's complaints that he was on the liberal side. Bull Connor was a parishioner who sometimes came to Sunday services, but he wasn't there that morning. After tak-ing my mother to lunch I went home to change clothes and then drove to the *News* building, where I had the sports department all to myself for a glorious afternoon of trying to create some literature out of a high-jump competition.

That's where I was when, not four blocks away at the bus station, the shock troops in the war for racial justice in America came rumbling into Birmingham. Unknown to me, sublimely pecking away at my typewriter in the serenity of the sports department, a Greyhound bus full of black and white Freedom Riders had already been jumped by one hundred white thugs and was in flames sixty miles east of Birmingham in Anniston. About four o'clock in the afternoon, while I was still writing about how the Auburn guy had finally prevailed in the high-jump pit, another mob of one hundred boarded a second bus of Freedom Riders at the Birmingham bus station and began to drag them off and beat them with chains, clubs, and pipes. I had noticed a commotion in the main newsroom of the paper, unusual for late on a Sunday afternoon; but I was in my own world and didn't pay any particular attention. Satisfied with my story, I left it in the basket for Benny and Ace Kabase and went home to my apartment. The war had begun, and I didn't even know it.

Shameful to admit now, I didn't hear about the beatings at the bus station until Monday morning as I drove to work. It was difficult to find Perry Como or Hank Williams anywhere on the dial of my car radio. Instead, the airwaves were reverberating with news of the Freedom Riders: straight reports, interviews, editorials, Klansmen and shocked moderates alike clamoring to get onto call-in shows to shout their views. Indeed, ''shock'' was the word of the day. Until then, I had looked at the civil rights movement as just some distant rumbling that was somebody else's problem in a far-off land—the way we can't really fathom reports that thousands have died in a volcano on the other side of the world in a country whose name we can't pronounce. But there would be no more looking away for Birmingham, for me, for anyone I knew, no matter whose side they were on. The battle was engaged: it was *here*, it was *now*. As I raced toward the

News building, I felt like a fool. Covering a goddamn track meet!

The story of the Freedom Riders was everywhere in the papers, getting top play over a number of events that also had large ramifications: Alan Shepard's becoming the first American in space; the announcement by the new President, John F. Kennedy, that he was willing to send troops to a country called Vietnam; and, of lesser importance, the death by cancer of the actor Gary Cooper. The front page of the *News* was splashed with photographs of the burning bus near Anniston and of the mob attacking Freedom Riders at the station in Birmingham, topped by a two-line streamer all-caps head, "Integrationist Group Continuing Trip After Brutal Beatings Here," and an over-the-masthead editorial that trumpeted, "Where Were the Police?" Bull Connor was denying that he had promised the Klan fifteen minutes of batting practice before sending his cops to the scene, adding that it was, after all, Mother's Day. The *News*'s editors were outraged, having just given Connor strong support for reelection, and it showed. "Fear and hatred did stalk Birmingham streets yesterday," the editorial began, in reference to Harrison Salisbury's report of the previous year, deeming the massacre a "rotten day for Birmingham and Alabama." Bull Connor stood his ground, calling the Freedom Riders "out-of-town meddlers" and promising he would "fill the jails" the next time "people come into our city looking for trouble." His opportunity would come soon enough.

CHAPTER NINE

Other Voices: Into the Fire

Mimi Tynes

Bill and I got married in September 1961, after I graduated from college in May, and the next year I went back to Brooke Hill and taught there for two years. I thoroughly enjoyed teaching, but I stopped when my first child was on the way. I always thought that sooner or later I would go back to teaching, but I never quite made it back. All three of my children went to Altamont, Brooke Hill's successor, with the last one graduating just two years ago. I served on the board at Brooke Hill and then Altamont from soon after I stopped teaching until a year before my last child graduated.

The Birmingham I had returned to was, of course, going through its most difficult times. In May of that year, Mother's Day, the day of the attack on the Freedom Riders at the bus station, I had been at Smith studying for my comprehensive exams. I remember knowing about it, hearing about it, reading about it, but I can pinpoint Alan Shepard's space flight that month much more easily. It may be that I didn't know about the bombing of the Sixteenth Street Baptist Church in 1963 until I saw it in the paper the next morning. I associate that date with the next day, the sixteenth of September, which is our wedding anniversary and my mother's birthday.

The morning after the bombing, Bill went to his office in the old Stonewall Building downtown, which still had manually operated elevators. He was alone in the elevator with Catherine, the operator, a black woman. She turned to him and in a plaintive voice said, "Mr. Tynes, what are we going to do? We can't go on living like this. What are we going to do?" Bill said, "I don't know, I just don't know." He felt ashamed and helpless but pleased that she had come to him with her plea and concern. He also felt that the bombing was the turning point in Birmingham and that those children did not die in vain. Bill's concern and criticism now is that so many don't realize how much progress has been made since then; that there is impatience, of course, but it needs to be in the perspective of where we are in relation to where we've come from.

What disturbs me now is that I wasn't very disturbed about all of those things going on then. I was over the mountain and I was teaching school and newly married and more involved in day-to-day doings. Intellectually, I knew that what was going on was wrong, segregation and all of that, but I wasn't motivated at that time to have any personal involvement. I was glad that people were working together to bring about changes that did come about. I may have been a little more strongly influenced by the opinions around me that Martin Luther King had come to Birmingham because he knew he could stir up trouble here, that he knew Bull Connor would react the way he did, and that this would be an event that would help the movement.

I grew up in an era and a community where segregation was the norm. There had always been domestic help in the house, frequently one or two who lived in. I had a "baby nurse," Bernice, who was my personal nurse from the time I was a baby until I was about five, and in the days before washers and dryers we had a laundress. They were the only black people I had any personal contact with, growing up. The first time I remember being aware of someone's race was when at about eight years old I was surprised to find out that Joe Louis was black. I'm not sure why that was such a surprise to me, but it was probably because I expected anyone in a prominent position to be white.

In 1963 I didn't feel that what was happening in Birmingham was that much worse than what was happening in other parts of the country. The events—the dogs, beatings, firehoses, bombings—were terrible, and the attitude of Bull Connor and some others in power was deplorable, but I didn't feel it was fair for Birmingham to be portrayed as the only place where that kind of racism and poor leadership existed.

On the other hand, it probably did take dramatic events like those here to make decent people everywhere wake up and say, "This isn't right, things need to be different." Still, I had no sense of a need or desire to be directly involved. I wouldn't reach that point until twenty years later, when—finally—I got to know black people personally.

John Porter

Martin Luther King, Jr., was in his first year at Dexter Avenue in Montgomery when I went back to finish up at Alabama State in 1954, and he invited me down to be his pulpit assistant. I'd been going to a church near the campus and I needed a new image of what a preacher was supposed to be. Reverend Johnson was a good man, but he was from the old school: lack of style, little training, slow-talking, no sense of order. Before King, the pew was growing but the pulpit was standing still. In King I saw another kind of preacher. He was just John Doe then, but he had life, zeal, fervor, style, and his greatest gift was his humility. I would be involved with him for the rest of his life.

In 1955, then, more than seven years after getting out of high school, I finally graduated from Alabama State, with a major in history and a minor in English. My master plan was to move on to Morehouse College in Atlanta, where I could get a master of divinity in the graduate program of religion and at the same time work at Ebenezer Baptist Church with Martin Luther King, Sr. The scheme was that when I finished the seminary work I would have the benefit of the old man's national contacts and he would help me get a church. Well, my whole plan went down the drain.

A lot happened in my three years at Morehouse and Ebenezer, and I had about as good a relationship with King, Sr., as one could have. I became interested in Christine, the daughter; but with the old man you had to come under his umbrella, and I just couldn't do that. I could never call him "Daddy King," because he was at times cruel, a bitter pill to swallow, although I guess if you could get him down he'd do you good. He would take you and shape you, but if you didn't get away from him he would break you. I was janitor, pulpit assistant, and a whole lot of things at Ebenezer, but I didn't preach very much. By the time I finished up there, Martin, Jr., had gone into orbit, but Martin, Sr., did not suggest one church for me.

I wrote letters and letters and letters to churches all over the place; very few of them bothered to write back. But then my aunt in Detroit called and said there was a vacancy up there. It was a big church, a black Baptist church right in the middle of a Polish Catholic neighborhood, and I didn't have much hope they would take me. But they invited me up to preach at Christmastime, and again at Easter; and finally, one week before graduation, I got a telegram saying I'd been called. I remember Old Man King saying, "Porter, don't you go up there. Them's mean folks up there. Don't you go. I know that church. That's a tough church. I know you, Porter, you won't fight." I'm really mild, like my father, and I never liked that in myself. King, Sr., had a way of motivating you negatively like that. "You won't fight, Porter." I was convinced to make him a liar if it was the last thing I'd do.

It seems like the Martins were destined to be a part of our lives forever, even if they did fire my father and me for my being "uppity." Before I left for Detroit, I wrote Mrs. Martin a letter telling her that I had graduated from seminary and had my first church and I needed a pulpit robe. She wrote me back a nice letter, saying she was proud of me, and sent a check big enough to buy one of the best robes you could find in those days. The only thing she wanted was for me to promise I wouldn't read the King James Revised Standard Version of the Bible, the more enlightened one. I don't remember promising her I wouldn't.

Sometimes I wondered, "Lord, why did you send me to Detroit?" It was a strange phenomenon up there. There were close to eight hundred people in the church, in a beautiful building, a very stable congregation, pretty much an all-black situation, and in ways I felt blessed to be called up there. What had happened was, they had built the church in an area of town they thought would be a black neighborhood, but before the blacks could get there the Poles moved in. A black church in the middle of a Polish neighborhood, and they are very Catholic. Every time I would have a problem at church and start thinking I had to get out of there, I could hear Old Man King saying, "Porter, I know you. You won't fight." All in all, it was a good four and a half years.

But I wanted to give what little talent I had to the South. One day I was driving down the street and I almost had an accident with a white lady, and when I got to the next corner she pulled up beside me and rolled her window down and told me, "Get over, nigger." And suddenly, for the first time, it didn't bother me. I looked at her and I smiled. I had matured to the point that I felt that if that was good for her, it was okay. I remember thinking to myself, "Now I'm ready to go South again." I had grown. I was ready to go back; to be cursed, to be called a "nigger." She needed to call me that, and now I realized it didn't take from me. I had finally learned, as a Christian and as a moral person, to appreciate the dilemma that some people are in.

CHAPTER TEN

Moving On

The sixties would be as pivotal for me as for most Americans who were in their twenties going in. The decade would begin with my being a neophyte prep sportswriter who lived with his parents in the old neighborhood, and end with the writing of my first book while a Nieman fellow at Harvard. There were many odd stops in between, all a part of living and learning by the seat of the pants, and the images zipped past like telephone poles on a mad high-speed drive without a map: a bad marriage; an ill-advised stab at public relations; a year in France; two children; leaving sports to become a general columnist; a racial awakening in the shadow of Ralph McGill; estrangement from my parents; discovering whiskey and women; covering the Vietnam War; finally beginning to take shape when I turned thirty-three at Harvard. Almost everybody I grew up with had done their time in college, mostly at Auburn, returning to Birmingham four years later as though they had never left: marrying childhood sweethearts, buying houses in the neighborhoods where they had grown up, taking jobs in the same general work as their fathers, venturing from Birmingham only for shopping expeditions or football weekends or vacations. Some ran into a ditch, like the good friend who chose to methodically drink himself to death just when his life seemed to have come together; but the overwhelming majority opted for safe lives that allowed no room for surprises.

When the phone call came from Florida State, formally offering me the sports information job, I was on my knees in front of a garish orange sofa in my cramped efficiency apartment, formally proposing marriage to a girl I barely knew. She had listlessly attended Auburn for two or three months, never returning after the Christmas break, and was working as a bank teller until a husband came through the drive-up window. Her mother happened to work next to mine, as a clerk in the Social Security office downtown, and her stepfather operated a small offset printing shop. I thought I wanted marriage, and I knew damned well I wanted sanctioned sex on a regular basis. She wanted babies and a white picket fence, very little else, so we had a deal. Having grown up in a happy fifties household where Daddy worked and Mama stayed home, all happiness and light, just like in "Father Knows Best," I thought I wanted that, too, and figured it just happened that way: you find a mate and promise to love, honor, and obey, and everything falls into place. What I failed to recognize was that my parents' marriage had been forged and strengthened in the crucible that was the Depression. And here I was, at the beginning of another cataclysmic decade in American history, a virginal babe still in the embryo stage.

No sooner had I taken the job at FSU than I got called to active duty with the Air Force. The joke was on me and scores of others, including several players on Auburn's national championship team, all of us having finagled appointments in the Alabama Air National Guard to avoid the draft after college graduation in the late fifties. John Kennedy was in the White House now, fending off "Communist aggression" in Berlin and Cuba and Southeast Asia, and a military buildup had begun. The 7117th Tactical Reconnaissance Wing of the Alabama Air Guard seemed a safe place to be, based at the Birmingham airport with twenty RF-84 photo reconnaissance jets that held cameras rather than guns, even though we would later learn that eighty of our men had been secretly recruited for the futile Bay of Pigs invasion of Cuba, and five of those had never come back. I had put in my three months of basic training in Texas, come back to my job at the *News,* begun spending one weekend a month attending Air Guard "drill" at the airport, then taken the FSU job and begun house hunting in Tallahassee in anticipation of the wedding. Then I got the word that we had been called to active duty and would go to France as Kennedy's response to the Soviets' putting up the Berlin Wall.

Following Florida State's opening game of the '61 football season I drove back to Birmingham, got married in an elaborate church wedding, and six weeks later was on an old four-engine C-118 transport plane lumbering across the Atlantic. There were nearly a thousand of us, all white southern "weekend warriors" being sent to an air base about sixty miles west of Paris that had lain all but abandoned since the Second World War. The only good thing about the situation, as far as I could see at that point, was that I had been made an instant second lieutenant when it was discovered that we had to have a commissioned officer in the Public Information Office. When we landed at Dreux Air Base, empty except for a couple of hundred U.S. Army caretakers, we chased the cows and sheep off the runway and made the barracks livable and then bunked down and wondered what next for a thousand accidental soldiers from Alabama.

This was a long, long way from Birmingham and from the comforting cycle of the sports seasons that had orchestrated my life to date. Sports wasn't there to keep me occupied anymore, and when I looked around I discovered that a lot more had happened in 1946 than Country Slaughter's scoring the winning run in the World Series. During the winter, on a train trip through Bavaria to some sort of indoctrination for the newly activated reserve officers in Europe, I was startled to see rusty tracks veer from the main line to the stark remains of Dachau. I was reading the *International Herald-Tribune* now, rather than *The Sporting News.* As I sipped espresso at an outdoor cafe one evening in Paris, Algerian nationalists gutted the lobby of a hotel a block

away with a *plastique* bomb. When my bride came over a few
months later, we moved into a stone building in a courtyard in
a little village with quite another history: Jewish deportations,
Vichy control, hangings in the square, Nazi occupation. With my
best friend, Dave Langford, a reporter for the *News* who was
older and worldlier, I explored the literary hangouts and jazz
clubs in Paris. As part of my job, I had to make the acquaintance
of local police and mayors and ordinary citizens. And now, beginning with the works of Ernest Hemingway, who had killed
himself that summer, I started to read serious literature for the
first time in my twenty-five years. In the dead of winter, typing
beside a kerosene lamp in that dank stone cottage, I even tried
a short story having to do with postwar France in a village much
like my Maillebois; it finished second in a contest sponsored by
the air base librarian, the winner being an elementary school
teacher from North Birmingham, but at least I had gotten myself
on a new track.

We got the *News* and the *Post-Herald* by way of slow mail,
and once we had clipped all of the photos and news releases they
had used ("Brave Airmen," "Freedom Fighters," " '*Parlez-
Vous* Y'all?' ") we caught up on the news from home. It wasn't
good. The editorial pages rankled with columns and letters to the
editor obsessed with Birmingham's tarnished image since the
Freedom Riders incident (not the fact that what had happened
was morally wrong), and the basis of almost every commentary
was the argument that it was a local problem and none of Washington's business—the same old "states' rights" posture that
had been the South's justification for slavery. Bull Connor was
carrying on a running shouting match with the federal government over that issue, in fact, and it seemed like every day he
was arresting the new young manager of the Greyhound bus
station for allowing blacks and whites to eat together. "What
Negroes Are Doing" continued to occupy a single page buried

deep in the Sunday paper. In November it was abruptly announced that the entire system of city parks would be closed rather than integrated; and that included Rickwood Field, home of the Barons, since some teams in the Southern Association intended to have black players during the '62 season. In the wake of the Freedom Riders and the closing of the parks and a black boycott of downtown stores, there was a movement led by the relatively progressive Young Men's Business Club to change Birmingham's form of government from the three-man commission to a mayor and council—meaning, Get Bull out of there. Finally, in the spring, a young rural politician named George Corley Wallace, who had been moderate in the past, came snorting into the gubernatorial primary with a vow that he would not be "out-segged" as he had been four years earlier.

I had heard and read it all before, but now I had begun to change my interpretation. An ocean away, and in a neutral environment, I found myself taking an entirely different look at my hometown. Frankly, what really did it for me was reading that they were willing to give up the Barons—just like that, no more Rickwood, no more Barons—all over the issue of integration. Christ, I thought, they're serious. Bull just cut off his nose. I remembered the summer in Kansas when I was a teammate of Hank Scott, the speedy little hometown outfielder, and how easy our relationship had been from the first handshake; that he wasn't at all what my father had said "niggers" were; that Hank Scott, in fact, seemed startled that I would even ask him, as I did one day during batting practice, how it was to be a black man. "I'm just black, that's all," he said. Word was passed to me later that Hank had left Oswego, Kansas, like most young people had to do to find work, and had been found floating face-down in a YMCA pool in Kansas City. Foul play? Suicide? Nobody knew.

As I pondered the fate of the first black person I had really known to any extent, using all of this enforced leisure to consider a larger world, I had found a woman named Denise Rydeng to rush me along. My office was authorized to have a civilian interpreter, and since Denise knew of our coming and was practically waiting on the tarmac when we landed, I hired her for the job. She was middle-aged and married now, living in a village near the base, but she had been in the French Resistance during the war and had stories to tell about the Nazis and the Jews and the coming of the Allies. Since one of my duties was to befriend the locals before they petitioned against the roar of our jets, she took me around for visits with mayors and gendarmes and farmers in the area (even finding the little stone "apartment" for me and my wife), and as a consequence we spent a lot of time together. As we swapped stories, rattling along in her little Deux Chevaux for, say, lunch with the mayor of Brezolles, Denise Rydeng was appalled at what she heard about Birmingham. "It is a master race, the white people, just like the Germans," she would say; and "This Connor, he sounds like the Gestapo. It is the same thing." The concept of separate everything for blacks and whites was by no means new to her, remembering the castigation of Jews even in France, but she was amazed to find that it was going on in the invincible America. "Perhaps you should have stayed home to fight this Bull Connor rather than come here to fight the Russians."

We returned to Birmingham late in the summer of 1962, bearing trinkets and stories. A couple of the guys, having fallen in love, didn't come back at all. There had been too much loose talk at the NCO and officers' clubs in France about the covert involvement of the 7117th in the Bay of Pigs disaster, and Dave Langford and I were among those who would be angrily discharged for that by the commander of the Alabama Air Guard, a Patton wannabe named General George Reid Doster, the moment we landed in the States. At the airport—expanded while we were gone, and now dressed up with a chirpy Chamber of

Commerce billboard saying, "It's Nice to Have You in Birmingham"—I was met by my parents and my sister (who had been married by Brother John Rutland at Woodlawn Methodist Church on Mother's Day) and my wife, who had returned ahead of me and was now beginning to swell with our first child.

In the few days I had at home before having to move back to Tallahassee and resume my duties in the athletic department at FSU, I assessed the damage that had been done to Birmingham in our absence. The final rounds of golf on public courses had been played on the last day of '61, and Connor's response to Washington's orders to integrate the city parks had been to fill with dirt the pool at East Lake Park where I had learned to swim. Connor, in a particularly spiteful move, had tried to shut down Jefferson County's surplus food program, whose ten thousand recipients were ninety percent black. The Barons were a memory, Rickwood Field like a graveyard. George Wallace had won the Democratic gubernatorial runoff in a blowout, meaning his reign as a rabble-rousing racist ("Segregation now, segregation forever!") was about to begin. The one black leader in town, the unsinkable Fred Shuttlesworth, had left for a church in Cincinnati. The black boycott of downtown stores had put the Jewish merchants in a quandary—should they empathize with these other victims of racism when their businesses were hurting badly?—but without strong leadership the boycott had dried up and gone away by the middle of the summer. Those businesses that showed a willingness to give in to integration, especially the restaurants, were being hounded by city inspectors, who were suddenly writing them up for shortcomings ("fire hazard" and "insufficient elevator") that had never before been noticed. It was revealed that Birmingham had suffered a ten percent decline in jobs during the past four years, just at a time when the despised "liberal" Atlanta was on the verge of taking off on a rocket trip to prosperity. "It's Nice to Have You in Birmingham" indeed. The only positive signs were that a biracial panel called the Senior Citizens Committee had begun to meet, that a group of whites led by liberal lawyers Charles "Chuck" Morgan and David Vann appeared to be succeeding in putting together a referendum to change the city's form of government (i.e., dump Bull and his cronies), and that the failed boycott at least had given Birmingham's down-so-long black community its first taste of organized mass protest.

The mood had changed at home, too. On a soft summer evening in the backyard of the house in Woodlawn, on the terraced patio my father had made from flagstone wrenched from streams along his route through the Blue Ridge, I wanted to tell my parents and my sister and her husband about what I had seen and felt in Europe, but they wouldn't listen. The whole situation of Bull Connor and blacks and John Kennedy and integration had made them, in view of what I had seen and read and heard over there, almost strangers to me now. My father was especially inflamed by it all, and as he basted the chickens he sounded like a Klansman. "NiggersJewsandCatholics" was one word now, spat out of his mouth like a loose strand of cigar leaf, and his vision of a worldwide conspiracy of liberals had grown considerably: Roosevelts, Rockefellers, Kennedys, Communists, Jews, "this nigger Martin Luther Coon," Earl Warren of the Supreme Court, and on and on through the roster of enemies compiled by the White Citizens' Council and George Wallace.

My mother was firing black maids almost monthly now, it seemed (Louvenia had gotten too poorly in the feet to continue the long trek from Zion City), on the grounds that they were all "lazy and getting pregnant all the time." She was terrified that it wouldn't be long before they "let niggers work at Social Security," which brought my father back into the conversation with the news that my cousin Charles had joined the John Birch Society *and* the Citizens' Council. This prompted my mother to confide that once when she was a child she came across a Ku

Klux Klan robe in Daddy Nelson's closet. That led my father to say he didn't exactly approve of the Klan, but their hearts were in the right place. My new brother-in-law, an Auburn engineer now in the construction business, said with a straight face that the closing of the city parks was hurting a lot of golf games.

"Daddy," I said, trying for common ground, "I can't believe there won't be any more Barons."

He poked at the chickens he was barbecuing. "There's always the Nigger Barons."

"The Black Barons. They're gone, too."

"Damned shame, ain't it? Guess they'll have to go back to eatin' watermelon."

"Really," I said. "You and I loved baseball when I was a boy. Bull's messing with it, and I thought that would kinda hack you off."

"Naw, naw, that ain't what he's doing at all, son." He took the cigar out of his mouth and spat a stream of juice on the flagstone. "He's sending the damn niggers and Kennedy and Coon and the whole bunch of 'em a message, is what he's doing."

The others sat quietly on aluminum lawn chairs, clucking and nodding, as dusk settled over the backyard. The conspiracy was here in my own parents' backyard, not just in Washington. I felt the blame was being directed toward me, the only son, and that I was being replaced by a toady. A reality sank to the pit of my stomach: my brother-in-law had become my father's surrogate son. And so it was on that note that I left Birmingham the very next morning, fairly certain that I would never return.

Even before I had been called to active duty and forced to leave the job at FSU after the first football game of the '61 season, I knew I had made a mistake. It wasn't Tallahassee and it wasn't Florida State, both the town and the school being agreeable places; it was public relations. In a cramped little office at the gymnasium, with a view of the baseball park and the football stadium through my window, I was swamped with work I found to be unfulfilling and distasteful: batting out press releases; updating mailing lists; arranging accommodations for writers and broadcasters; assigning seats in the press box; smoothing the egos of coaches in the "minor," nonrevenue sports like swimming and golf and tennis, who were getting short-shrifted now that FSU had chosen to go all out in football; spending most of Sundays figuring the official statistics of Saturday's game and then wiring them to NCAA headquarters; flying ahead of the team to, say, Lexington, Kentucky, to mingle with the media and drum up interest for the FSU-Kentucky game. That year's football team created considerable angst at three SEC schools that had always used FSU as a breather, playing Georgia, Kentucky, and Auburn to ties on the road, but even that wasn't enough to hold my interest.

I knew almost from the start that I wasn't long for that sort of job. Our first child, a daughter we named Lisa, was born just before Christmas in Tallahassee, and I was looking for a new job not for the money but because I wanted to get back to writing for a living. In the living room of our little duplex on a hill above the football stadium, I typed late into the night on Hemingway-esque vignettes—simply copying the man himself, sometimes, in order to find his rhythms—writing not for publication but to continue my self-education as a writer. It was back down the hill the next day to appease Bim Stoltz, the swimming coach, trying to explain why he was getting little space in the St. Petersburg *Times* these days. At night I would be back at my desk at home, now dissecting Steinbeck's interchapters in *The Grapes of Wrath*, which I had not even heard of until then. Back down the hill the next morning, this time to unscramble the syntax of the football coach, Bill Peterson ("Gentlemen, when they play that Star-Spangled Anthem, I want you to stand on those helmets and take off your sidelines. . . ."). Home again at night, discovering Faulk-

ner and Dos Passos and Irwin Shaw and scores of other writers
I had missed on my sashay through high school and college. It
occurred to me that I was learning to write in much the same
way my father had learned to become a long-haul trucker on
that fateful odyssey to Portland and return in the dead of winter
some two decades earlier. I was feeling my way, by the seat of
my pants.

Going back to the Birmingham *News* sports department was
never an option, mainly because I had already done that and
there seemed to be no future for me there. I had also begun to
look upon Birmingham as the place of my childhood, filing it
away, closing the book on it, much as we store snapshots in
family albums and then put them away somewhere and forget
where we hid them. I didn't know at the time that what I really
wanted was to get out of sports, at least on a full-time basis, and
try my wings in the "real" world. But I lacked the confidence
to try that, and the camaraderie of sportswriting was still comforting, so I let it be known in the jock network that I wanted
back in. When an offer came to take over as sports editor of the
Augusta *Chronicle,* in Georgia, I jumped at it. I would be the
boss, write a daily column, cover college football, and, most ap-
petizing of all, record the fortunes of the Augusta Yankees of the
Class A South Atlantic ("Sally") League.

Augusta was a scruffy military town of fewer than fifty
thousand people on the Savannah River, hard by an atomic plant
on the South Carolina side, best known as the home of the Masters golf tournament and as the locale for Erskine Caldwell's
Tobacco Road. This was going to be just fine. I had just turned
twenty-seven when we moved into a little rental bungalow there
in March of 1963, and the first week I found myself buying lunch
for Rube Walker, the old major league catcher who would manage the Augusta Yankees that year. There would be plenty to
keep me interested—the Masters in April, the Yankees throughout the summer, four major college football teams (Clemson,

South Carolina, Georgia Tech, Georgia) during the fall—and I would begin learning to use the English language the surest way of all: writing a one-thousand-word column, six days a week, in sickness or in health.

Birmingham was three hundred miles away, even farther in my mind; and except for phone calls and letters to apprise my parents of the progress of their baby granddaughter, I had about quit thinking about my hometown, until the first week of May. On May 3, as I was looking ahead to the column I would write before heading out to the ballpark, I heard Birmingham scream. After all of those years of living under the strictest segregation in America, after Bull Connor and the dynamitings and the Freedom Riders and nearly a century of grinding daily degradations, the black people of Birmingham were fighting back. Dr. Martin Luther King, Jr., of the Southern Christian Leadership Conference, had come to town and rallied them. I was sitting in our little house in Augusta, half-dressed and leaning forward to catch the images on our black-and-white television set, showing mayhem in the streets of Birmingham, and I couldn't speak. There was Bull Connor, in baggy pants and a straw hat, running back and forth on the streets of my hometown shrieking orders to his policemen and firemen. Hundreds of black kids, mostly elementary and high school students, were screaming and running from police dogs and from high-powered water cannons. Paddy wagons were being filled with students and preachers, including Dr. King himself, while crowds of white spectators laughed and cheered for the dogs as they tore into buttocks and for the firemen as they sent teenagers cartwheeling like tumbleweeds. The place had finally erupted, for all the world to see, and my emotions ranged from disbelief to outrage to shame. Mesmerized, I watched rerun after rerun on the news, searching for familiar faces, hoping I wouldn't see a cousin or a buddy from my childhood. And I thought, Oh, Daddy, just look here now, look what it's come to.

CHAPTER ELEVEN

1963

It could be said in retrospect that the seeds for the eruption in 1963 had been planted nearly a century earlier, even before Birmingham was chartered as a city, when Jones Valley was stocked with a mix of two races that knew nothing of each other: barely literate white miners following the vast beds of coal and ore, and recently freed slaves who had known whites only as their masters. Surely personal one-on-one friendships of a sort must have developed over the years between blacks and whites relegated to the most menial jobs, but just as surely they were based on the tacit understanding that the white man, simply by the color of his skin, called the shots. "That boy," my father would say of a swarthy black dock worker ten years his senior, "works harder than any white man I ever saw." Then, almost solemnly, intending a compliment, "He's a good nigger." But on an institutional basis, forget it. As the black population expanded over the decades, creating competition between the lower-class blacks and whites for jobs and housing and respectability, tensions inevitably worsened. In a sense, the whites got whiter and the blacks got blacker, until Birmingham, by the forties, had become almost as rigidly segregated as South Africa. And the presence of rabble-rousers like Bull Connor and the Klan, doing the dirty work for the Big Mules and U.S. Steel, two groups whose only vested interest in the city was in keeping costs at a minimum, made sure that it stayed that way. "Who Speaks for Birmingham?" the *News* had asked in the anxious days following Har-

rison Salisbury's reports in the New York *Times* and the
bloodshed at the bus station on Mother's Day and the certainty
that the worst was yet to come. Bull Connor, that's who: the
spokesman, a century later, for those unlettered Appalachian
miners who had pioneered the valley in the first place.

Until the attack on the Freedom Riders and the resulting
bad press that Birmingham received all over the world, Connor
had also spoken for the city's white elite. Unlike their counter-
parts in Atlanta, a coterie of patriarchal old-line millionaire businessmen led by Robert W. Woodruff of the Coca-Cola Company
who directed their city's affairs with Boy Scout fervor ("The
City Too Busy to Hate" and "What's Good for Atlanta Is Good
for Business" were their mottoes), Birmingham's white elite
seemed to have very little vested interest in the city's affairs. The
Big Mules had been born into wealth and gone to college in the
East and had come back home to preserve the status quo. Insulated in their over-the-mountain enclaves and their executive
suites high above the Heaviest Corner on Earth, the real power
belonging not to them but to U.S. Steel in Pittsburgh, they chose
not to participate in the gritty business of civic affairs. Most of
them didn't even pay taxes to the city or vote in Birmingham
elections, in fact, since they lived in the incorporated bedroom
villages of Homewood and Mountain Brook and Vestavia Hills.
They had a good life over there, behind Vulcan's back, where
the air was always clear, where there were no poor people, where
they devoted their efforts to charity balls and beautification projects and zoning ordinances, where they could enjoy being rich
together at their country clubs or at the exclusive haven beside
Vulcan known as The Club. Throughout the century, spanning
two world wars and a severe depression, they had left the city
of Birmingham to its own devices. They had little in common
with Bull Connor, this unseemly little martinet down at City
Hall, but by their silence they had conferred power on him and
thereby allowed a monster to flourish.

In a case of better late than not at all, the Big Mules finally had been roused to action by the donnybrook at the bus station. The story of Sidney Smyer's awakening would become legendary. A strong segregationist and a Dixiecrat from 1948, a major downtown realtor and incoming president of the Birmingham Chamber of Commerce, Smyer was in Tokyo as head of the city's business delegation at the International Rotary Convention when the story of the Freedom Riders broke. He couldn't read a word of the Japanese writing in the newspapers, but he certainly could make out the photographs of whites clubbing Freedom Riders to the floor. "As a result," writes Taylor Branch in his remarkable *Parting the Waters: America in the King Years, 1954–63,* "Smyer found himself the object of cold stares and perplexed questions from his Japanese hosts and the assembled international businessmen, who had suddenly lost interest in Birmingham's climate for investment. Words failed Smyer and his Birmingham friends as they tried to explain that the incident was grossly unrepresentative of their city. They felt like zoo specimens on display. . . ." Smyer left Tokyo earlier than he had planned, telling his colleagues as they flew across the Pacific that Bull Connor had to go; and when they got home he went to work. Astonished to learn that blacks had to ride the freight elevators at the Brown Marx Building, one of his properties, on the corner of Twentieth Street and First Avenue, he personally took down the "Colored Only" signs; and then, in a more far-reaching move, he became a major force on the Senior Citizens Committee, a coalition whose main purpose would be to change the form of city government that had allowed Connor to do as he pleased.

During the two years following the Freedom Riders incident, it seemed that Birmingham might be on its way toward reaching some sort of racial harmony. There was an ongoing poker game between the forces of Connor on the one hand, and on the other, the whites who had changed their minds and now saw integration as an inevitability that must be dealt with if the city was to survive. At long last, for the first time in the city's history, blacks and whites were sitting down at conference tables to talk with each other: black preachers; Episcopal priests; liberal lawyers; the aging black entrepreneur A. G. Gaston (worth millions from an empire including funeral homes, real estate, communications, and insurance); white businessmen like Smyer; black and white academics; Jewish retailers like Isadore Pizitz. There were the Senior Citizens Committee, Fred Shuttlesworth's Alabama Christian Movement for Human Rights, the Young Men's Business Club, the Downtown Action Committee—no end to the number of groups feverishly working to overthrow Connor and get on with the business of saving Birmingham before it went up in flames.

It was parry and thrust, win some, lose some; and a perfect example occurred in September of 1962 when Shuttlesworth, who had taken his new pastorate in Cincinnati but still spent half of his days in Birmingham, talked Dr. Martin Luther King, Jr.'s SCLC into holding its convention in Birmingham. As a part of the deal, many of the Jim Crow signs in downtown stores were painted over or quietly removed. Local leaders of both races held their breath as such forceful black personalities as New York Congressman Adam Clayton Powell and Jackie Robinson came to town to address a coalition of most of the organizations involved in the nationwide civil rights movement. Everything went fine until the final day, when a member of the American Nazi party, who had come down from Virginia, leaped to the podium and began punching Dr. King in the face as he spoke. King refused to press charges; the man was convicted and chased out of town; and even Mayor Art Hanes, the latest of Connor's lackeys at City Hall, acted outraged over the incident. But then, when SCLC had left town, Connor came charging back: Get those ''Colored Only'' signs back up, he said, or you're going to jail.

The forces of tolerance won the big one, though, when, in a special election called in November of '62, the electorate rejected the three-man-commission form of government that had persevered for half a century. Now if Bull wanted to retain his power, he would have to run for mayor in an election called for the first week of March. He entered the race with three others: Albert Boutwell, a moderate former state lieutenant governor; a crew-cut drinking buddy and fellow commissioner named Jabo Waggoner; and a relatively liberal lawyer by the name of Tom King. In a record turnout, so inflamed was the issue, Boutwell got thirty-nine percent to Connor's thirty percent. That forced a run-off, held the first week of April, and when the votes were counted it was clear that Connor's days were numbered: although he won big on both ends of the valley, in the blue-collar bastions of East Lake and Ensley, he lost to Boutwell citywide by a margin of 29,000 to 21,000. There would ensue a period bordering on slap-stick (the Three Stooges came to mind) when Connor and Waggoner and Hanes literally refused to give up the keys to their offices, the result of some legal shufflings that allowed the three to linger a while longer as the Alabama Supreme Court acted upon an appeal. But for the most part Birmingham's blacks and white moderates were elated. They had done it. Without having to call in help from outside, by appealing to the good people of Birmingham themselves in a bona fide election, they had broken Bull Connor's rule. Now, if only they could make it to the end of May, when due process had run its course, they would be home free.

Dr. Martin Luther King, Jr., had spent the better part of the past two years in a futile attempt to bring down segregation in the medium-sized city of Albany, two hundred and fifty miles from Birmingham on the undulating plains of the Black Belt in southwestern Georgia. The success of King's strategy of "non-violent protest" depended on massive arrests and the filling of jails by brutish cops, followed by dramatic television coverage, culminating with national outrage directed at the city in question.

King had been stymied in Albany because the police chief there, Laurie Pritchett, wouldn't cooperate. Pritchett had bothered to study Gandhi's demonstrations against the British in India, the source of King's plan, and he chose to meet nonviolence with nonviolence. As King sent his disciplined SCLC troops to battle in Albany, whose segregation was every bit as time-honored as Birmingham's, he fully expected a rowdy reception that would fill the jails and then the evening news every night until Albany was broken. What he got, though, was a cool police chief who ordered courteous arrests and dispersal of the protesters to nearby cities and counties so there would be no untidy scenes for the television cameras to feast upon. King withdrew the SCLC from Albany in frustration.

The Reverend Fred Lee Shuttlesworth, Jr., had been a one-man civil rights movement in Birmingham since before the *Brown* v. *Board of Education* decision in 1954. Taut, jaunty, combative, weighing in at a wiry 140 pounds, he was forty years old and in his fighting prime when the showdown neared in '63. None could refute his credentials as a civil rights activist over the years. He had been raised in Rosedale, one of the traditional black neighborhoods on Birmingham's west side, gotten degrees from Selma University and Alabama State College; and then, from his base as pastor of Bethel Baptist Church in North Birmingham, he had proceeded to barge in where all other blacks feared to tread. The black elite had always favored taking the cautious path (even ridiculing Shuttlesworth's dialect and his soul-stirring sermons), and the rank-and-file laborers and domestics simply lacked the courage to follow his lead in standing up against Connorism. Shuttlesworth had spearheaded the NAACP in Birmingham, had been present at the formation of the SCLC, had tried to enroll his daughter and two other black children at Phillips High. His reputation reached mythical heights on Christmas night of 1956. In the wake of the Supreme Court decision that affirmed the year-long bus boycott in Montgomery, he had announced that the ACMHR would launch a bus boycott of its own in Birmingham on the twenty-sixth of December. On Christmas night a bomb blew his house down, with him in it, but he escaped without a scratch. The only lights still working when firemen arrived were on the Christmas tree, and Shuttlesworth made sure everybody understood the message, that "God saved me to lead the fight." For days the house stood as it had when the smoke had cleared, Shuttlesworth and his wife refusing to clean up the rubble so crowds of anxious gawkers could cruise past to see what hate had wrought.

The words "patience" and "compromise" were not in Shuttlesworth's vocabulary. For too long he had heard the black elite and the handful of white moderates and liberals make their pleas for sitting down at the negotiating tables, for letting the courts decide, for putting it in the hands of the Lord. His first entreaties for Martin Luther King, Jr., to forget Albany and come on over to Birmingham had come during the SCLC convention in September '62, and by the following January King was sending his advance scouts to lay the groundwork for what would become his most massive nonviolent demonstration. They studied city ordinances, checked out bail bond situations, and set up workshops on methods in nonviolence. Connor's spies, who attended one such workshop, heard King himself define the strategy and its larger purpose: "We are not out to defeat the white man but to save him. We are struggling to set twenty million Negroes free, and in so doing we will set eighty million whites free." Now, with Bull Connor staggering, Shuttlesworth felt the time had come to thrust the dagger to the heart.

King and his aides called it Project C, for "Confrontation," and it officially began on the third day of April 1963, the day after Bull Connor's loss in the mayoral runoff with Albert Boutwell. First there was a series of sporadic sit-ins at downtown lunch counters that led to routine arrests and jailings. (At one

point, Connor invited Chief Pritchett of Albany to come over as
a consultant on how to handle King; but Pritchett turned around
and went back home when he saw that Bull wasn't going to
listen to anybody.) King kept sending out demonstrators; Connor
had his police put them in jail. The number of protesters being
held at the Birmingham jail grew to three hundred by the end
of the first week. At nightly meetings in the Gaston Motel, King
considered a massive march in the streets. From his bunker at
City Hall, Connor countered with an injunction against "marching without a permit." King's top-ranking aides, among them
Ralph Abernathy and Andrew Young, implored him to concen-
trate on raising funds for bail money rather than risk his own
arrest. Finally, on Good Friday, unable to contain himself in that
motel room any longer, needing to force Connor's hand and bring
the national press onto the scene, King got himself arrested and
hauled off to jail. While there, refusing bail for eight days, he
composed his famous "Letter from Birmingham Jail," addressed
to moderates of both races and even to a Kennedy White House
that was, to him, dragging its heels:

> . . . When you have seen vicious mobs lynch your mothers and
> fathers at will and drown your sisters and brothers at whim;
> when you have seen hate-filled policemen curse, kick, brutalize
> and even kill your black brothers and sisters with impunity;
> when you see the vast majority of your twenty million Negro
> brothers smothering in an air-tight cage of poverty in the midst
> of an affluent society; when you suddenly find your tongue
> twisted and your speech stammering as you seek to explain to
> your six-year-old daughter why she can't go to the public
> amusement park that has just been advertised on television,
> and see tears welling up in her little eyes when she is told that
> Funtown is closed to colored children, and see the depressing
> clouds of inferiority begin to form in her little mental sky, and
> see her begin to distort her little personality by unconsciously
> developing a bitterness toward white people; when you have to

concoct an answer for a five-year-old son asking in agonizing
pathos: "Daddy, why do white people treat colored people so
mean?"; when you take a cross-country drive and find it necessary to sleep night after night in the uncomfortable corners
of your automobile because no motel will accept you; when you
are humiliated day in and day out by nagging signs reading
"white" and "colored"; when your first name becomes "nigger" and your middle name becomes "boy" (however old you
are) and your last name becomes "John," and when your wife
and mother are never given the respected title "Mrs."; when
you are harried by day and haunted by night by the fact that
you are a Negro, living constantly at a tip-toe stance, never
quite knowing what to expect next, and plagued with inner
fears and outer resentments; when you are forever fighting a
degenerating sense of "nobodiness"; then you will understand
why we find it difficult to wait. . . .

It was a remarkable document, scribbled on scraps of paper
and smuggled out of jail for King's lieutenants to decipher and
have typed out, but it languished for a month, seen, in the beginning, only by the SCLC's inner circle. The movement had
been checkmated. The Birmingham *News* and *Post-Herald* were
keeping the stories of the stirring in the street on their inside
pages, and the black Birmingham *World* was blandly editorial-
izing that a "certain degree of restraint [should] be shown on the
part of all responsible citizens." Even the city's most liberal
white ministers were criticizing King for coming to town just
when the new Boutwell administration needed support, needed
a "period of grace," urging blacks to give up the demonstrations
in favor of further negotiations. Toward the end of his letter,
King struck strongly at the group that he felt was as guilty as
Connor for the deadlock in Birmingham:

. . . I have been gravely disappointed with the white moderate.
I have almost reached the regrettable conclusion that the Negro's great stumblingblock is not the White Citizen's Council-

er or the Ku Klux Klanner, but the white moderate who is more devoted to "order" than to justice, who prefers a negative peace which is the absence of tension to a positive peace which is the presence of justice, who constantly says "I agree with you in the goal you seek, but I can't agree with your methods of direct action," who paternalistically believes that he can set the timetable for another man's freedom. . . .

Clearly, what King needed when he got out of jail toward the end of April was a dramatic confrontation. Money was rolling in from all over the nation, as a response to reports of the stand-off in Birmingham by the networks and papers like the New York *Times;* so the bankroll was there for bail money. And now, with King back at the Gaston Motel to confer with his men, not unlike a general working from a battlefield tent, it appeared that they had found the answer. What had begun as a simple call for black students to join the demonstrations in order to "fill the jails"—as both King and Connor had threatened, albeit for crossed purposes—had mushroomed. Black children of all ages, some of them first-graders, with or without their parents' and teachers' permission, were committing themselves to what would later be called the Children's Crusade. A popular black rock 'n' roll disc jockey known as Tall Paul was broadcasting word about the "big party" to be held on Thursday, May 2, at Kelly Ingram Park, and he didn't have to explain what it was about. "For King," writes Taylor Branch,

the moment brimmed with tension. Eight years after the bus boycott, he was on the brink of holding nothing back. Eight long months after the SCLC convention in Birmingham, he was contemplating an action of more drastic, lasting impact than jumping off the roof of city hall or assassinating Bull Connor. Having submitted his prestige and his body to jail, and having hurled his innermost passions against the aloof respectability of white American clergymen, all without noticeable effect, King committed his cause to the witness of schoolchildren.

For Birmingham police assigned to the daily roadblock cutting off the route from the Sixteenth Street Baptist Church to City Hall, three blocks east, what they saw shortly after one o'clock that Thursday afternoon must have been as startling as the sight that greeted German soldiers when they peered through the slits of their pillboxes at Normandy on the dawn of D-day and saw the horizon filled with warships headed straight toward them. The officers were keeping their eyes on the usual crowd of blacks who were milling about in Kelly Ingram Park; both factions heard the faint sounds of freedom songs filtering through the brick walls and stained-glass windows of the church. But then the doors burst open and fifty black teenagers emerged, two abreast, singing "We Shall Overcome," not in the usual solemn dirge but to a spirited ragtime beat. The cops quickly jumped to their duties, reciting city ordinances and then filling the waiting paddy wagons. But when they looked up they saw another double line of kids spilling from the church—and another, and another, and another. "Hey, Fred," one of them shouted to Shuttlesworth, according to Branch, "how many more have you got?" "At least a thousand," said Shuttlesworth. "God almighty," said the cop. One child, as she passively climbed into a paddy wagon, allowed that she was six years old. One group panicked and ran at the sight of city firemen beginning to lay high-pressure water hoses across Fourth Avenue. Crowds now pulsating in the park cheered lustily as the police began calling in school buses to haul the students away. It was all over by four o'clock; and at a spirited hymn-singing gathering at the church that night, King told the two thousand assembled that the number of arrests that day had come to six hundred. "If they think today is the end of this," he said, "they will be badly mistaken."

The events that would transpire in and around Kelly Ingram Park on the second day of the confrontation—Friday, May 3, 1963—would echo throughout the world and change Birmingham forever. That was the day of the dogs and the hoses. Thursday had been a prelude, a mere feeling-out, like the first round of a heavyweight championship fight. By noon on the second day, an air of expectancy shimmered among the three thousand or so who had crowded around the park. The battle lines had been drawn. Inside Sixteenth Street Baptist, more than a thousand young blacks were being given their marching orders; across the way, blocking the route to City Hall, was a bristling armada of policemen, firemen, school buses, ambulances, and police cars. Milling around the park, jockeying for ringside seats, were anxious parents and a corps of national media that had hurried into Birmingham. With the city and county jails bulging, Connor's strategy this day was to scatter the demonstrators rather than to make arrests. Nervous firemen, reluctant to use their frightening high-powered hoses on children, stood by.

At first, when the lead group of singing students was warned by the fire chief to disperse "or you're going to get wet," they retreated when sprayed with fogging nozzles. Everything seemed to be in hand. The fire chief next took up his bullhorn and ordered the demonstrators and the onlookers alike to clear out, evacuate the park; and they were in the process of doing just that when everyone noticed that about ten of the original sixty marchers in that day's first wave had stood their ground and were chanting "Freedom, freedom, freedom!" Defiant, already soaked to the skin, they were showing no signs of backing off. *Parting the Waters*: "It was a moment of baptism for the civil rights movement, and Birmingham's last effort to wash away the stain of dissent against segregation." That's when the firemen moved on them, turning on the full power of their hoses, forcing them to sit down and cling to curbings or bushes or whatever they could find to give them some stability against the laserlike streams of water. Finally, unable to dislodge the students with ordinary firehoses, the chief called for the special "monitor guns," single-nozzle cannons mounted on tripods, and the horrors began. Two little girls had their dresses simply shredded away. Arms and legs began jerking like those of puppets on a string, bodies cartwheeling across the grass like scraps of paper caught in the wind; and soon bricks and stones and bottles began to fly toward the firemen from bystanders on the perimeter. There was bedlam everywhere—and the worst lay ahead.

Just as on the day before, the waves of singing children continued to spill from the church, and as they were directed away from the maelstrom in the park by King's men, heading for City Hall, the maneuver spread the ranks of the police and firemen. The plan to make no further arrests that day was abandoned in the heat of battle as policemen began rounding up the demonstrators they could catch and shoving them onto the school buses in a futile attempt to disperse a crowd that was swelling by the minute. Finally, hauling out their ultimate "weapon," they got the command from Connor to bring on the dogs. There were eight of them—"K-9 units" of one policeman and one German shepherd each—and there were shouts of fright and outrage as the beasts were queued up on the corner of the park farthest from the church, snarling and baring their fangs and straining at their leashes. In the pandemonium, many fled immediately for the safety of the church; some stood their ground and threw rocks at the dogs and their handlers; and a few bold teenaged boys flapped their water-soaked shirts and taunted the dogs, like so many bullfighters. Suddenly, the handlers charged into the crowd and the dogs began to feed like sharks, biting several of the youths, affording an Associated Press photographer an image that would burn forever: a white cop in sunglasses holding a fifteen-year-old black boy by the shirt with one hand and giving just enough leash for his dog to sink its teeth into the boy's stomach, the thin, well-dressed boy seeming to be leaning into the dog, his arms limp at his side, calmly staring straight ahead as though to say, "Take me, here I am." There was an irony here, reported Taylor Branch: the boy was Walter Gadsden, of the conservative black Birmingham and Atlanta *World* newspaper family, which had been disdainful of Martin Luther King's entry into the fray; and he would later say, true to his family's black elite status, that the trauma had made him realize that he had been "mixing with a bad crowd," and he had resolved that day to quit such foolishness and prepare himself for college.

It was over by three o'clock, when a police inspector entered the church to call a truce for the day. The advantage had clearly gone to King, not only because the jails were bursting with 250 more arrestees but because now, much more importantly, the world had seen Bull Connor not just blink but lose control altogether. White moderates ranging from the incoming mayor, Albert Boutwell, to Attorney General Robert Kennedy were weakly trying to tweak King for letting children do the dirty work (Burke Marshall, the White House's man on the scene, even said that the kids had contributed to the violence by throwing rocks); King countered by reminding them that they hadn't been nearly as concerned for the children's welfare during all of the years they had endured inferior schools. At the meeting that night inside Sixteenth Street Baptist, where it took an hour just to pass the collection plates that would raise bail money for prisoners now numbering close to a thousand, King was welcomed like a messiah by the ecstatic multitude of parents and movement warriors and common black folk who had never dreamed of a day such as this right here in Birmingham, Alabama. The images of the day's scrimmaging had led off "The Huntley-Brinkley Report" on NBC television that night, he told them, and therefore "we are not alone." He told the parents not to worry about their children who were in jail, calling it a "spiritual experience" for them, and said that the demonstrations would continue through the weekend. "Yesterday was D-day," he said, "and tomorrow will be Double D-day."

Although the battle on the streets would rage back and forth well into the coming week, nothing would ever compare with what had happened on that day of the dogs and hoses. It had been sufficient, for King's purposes, to create a firestorm of outrage around the world that attracted newsmen and show-business personalities like folksinger Joan Baez and black comedian Dick Gregory and many thousands of dollars necessary to fill SCLC's depleted coffers. Nearly six thousand had been arrested during the week of confrontations—so many that at one point the state fairgrounds had to be used as a temporary "jail"—and a total of twenty-five people (only five of them blacks, one being Fred Shuttlesworth) had been injured badly enough to require hospitalization.

On Tuesday, May 7, the pushing and shoving continued to the extent that Connor arrested more than two thousand on that day alone. But by then the real story had shifted behind the scenes, in biracial bargaining sessions at places like the Gaston Motel and over the telephone wires between Birmingham and the White House; and finally, on May 10, King and Shuttlesworth called reporters together to say that Birmingham "has reached an accord with its conscience." There had been a far-ranging agreement on all areas in question, from desegregation of public facilities to the release of those who had been arrested during those chaotic days. The accord was by no means universally applauded by extremists on both sides, but two things were certain: Bull Connor had been broken, once and for all, and Birmingham would never be the same again. "The civil rights movement should thank God for Bull Connor," said President John Kennedy. "He's helped it as much as Abraham Lincoln."

Not surprisingly, with black people dancing in the streets and Klansmen gathering in parks on the edges of town, two dynamite explosions shattered the night air in Birmingham on Saturday, the day after the agreement was announced. One was at the home of the Reverend A. D. King, Martin's brother, whose family escaped without serious injury; the other was at the Gaston Motel across from Kelly Ingram Park, below the room that

King had just vacated in order to return to his home in Atlanta. After that, throughout a relatively placid summer, Birmingham settled into a sort of peace it had never known. At the end of May the Alabama Supreme Court ruled that the city's mayor-council form of government was legal, and within minutes Connor and his crowd were vacating City Hall to make way for Mayor Albert Boutwell and his nine-member council. While Connor went on the hustings as a star speaker on the White Citizens' Council circuit, Boutwell went to work. Jim Crow signs came down in June, and in July the walls of segregation were dismantled: in a two-week period a biracial Committee on Community Affairs was selected, all segregation ordinances were repealed, and downtown lunch counters were desegregated. Martin Luther King, Jr., was a national hero now, thanks to Birmingham, and late in the summer he led some two hundred thousand civil rights demonstrators in the March on Washington and made his ringing "I Have a Dream" speech. Now Kennedy pushed forward the most far-reaching civil rights bill in the history of the nation. "The events in Birmingham and elsewhere," he said, "have so increased the cries for equality that no city or state or legislative body can prudently choose to ignore them."

There remained one final shot to be fired by the white rabble—one so appalling that it made the years of bombings on Dynamite Hill look like firecracker displays. Racial tensions had been thrumming throughout the city in September, when desegregation was due to come to many public schools; and now with Bull Connor gone the diehard racists were listening to Governor George Corley Wallace, who had made his defiant "stand in the schoolhouse door" during the summer at the University of Alabama. On Monday, September 9, five black students integrated three city high schools while Wallace and President Kennedy parried—Wallace had ordered Alabama National Guard troops to surround the schools and keep the blacks out, but then Kennedy federalized the troops and had them withdraw—and during the rest of the week there was much marching and shouting and rock throwing between white students at the schools, who were clearly divided over the issue. On Friday the thirteenth, Wallace flew to Baltimore and declared his intention to run in the 1964 Maryland presidential primary.

That Sunday, September 15, was Youth Day at the Six-teenth Street Baptist Church, the day when the children of the congregation traditionally took over the running of the main service at eleven o'clock, and in the basement four young girls who had left their Bible study classes early to prepare for the service were chattering excitedly about their duties and about the opening of school, which would take place the next day. Three of them were fourteen, the other eleven, and they were dressed in white from head to toe. Mamie Grier, superintendent of the Sunday school, had stopped by to check on the girls and then gone upstairs to sit in on her own Sunday-school class. From *Parting the Waters:* "They were engaged in a lively debate on the lesson topic, 'The Love That Forgives,' when a loud earth-quake shook the entire church and showered the classroom with plaster and debris. Grier's first thought was that it was like a ticker-tape parade. Maxine McNair, a schoolteacher sitting next to her, reflexively went stiff and was the only one to speak. 'Oh, my goodness!' she said." The time was exactly 10:22. Dynamite planted some time during the night had gone off in the basement, causing pandemonium in the church, instantly killing the four girls Grier had seen only moments earlier: McNair's daughter Denise, Addie Mae Collins, Cynthia Wesley, and Carole Robert-son. McNair found out that her daughter was among the dead when she fought through the smoke and the rubble and came upon her father, who was sobbing and holding his granddaughter Denise's white dress shoe. "She's dead, baby," he said. Then, "I'd like to blow the whole town up!"

Once again the city was in disarray. At the exclusive aerie atop Red Mountain known as The Club, where the usual leisurely Sunday brunch was in progress, there was a virtual work stoppage when word of the dynamiting spread to the kitchen help. While black parents swirled about University Hospital, where the four dead girls and twenty injured lay, whites of all persuasions were skittish and unsure of what to do. When Chris McNair, Denise's father, answered a knock at his door that afternoon, he was shocked to see a stunned white couple, their car bearing a Confederate license plate, offering condolences. A pair of white Eagle Scouts, heading home from an aborted segregationist rally at a go-kart track that had been organized by a preacher, aimlessly shot and killed a black teenager who was riding a bicycle. Wallace rushed in three hundred state troopers; and during a rock scuffle between black and white youths a trooper shot a fleeing black kid in the back of the head.

I first heard of the dynamiting when my wife shook me awake in Augusta, where I was sleeping in after covering a football game in Clemson, South Carolina, for the *Chronicle,* and again I found myself on the edge of my chair staring in disbelief at this latest horror in my hometown. Will this shit never end? I thought, feeling shame and remorse wash over me once more, as it had during the showdowns at Kelly Ingram Park in May; wondering if now my father might come around, but afraid to call him and ask. I had no outlet on the sports pages where I could express my feelings, and I wasn't married at that time to the sort of woman who could deal with ideas and issues even as horrible as this.

For the liberal lawyer Chuck Morgan, born and raised in Birmingham, graduated from the University of Alabama, a "pinko" to people like my father, enough was enough, and he certainly had a platform where he could have his say. Morgan had been fighting the good fight for some time now, and had been feeling good about the progress made since King's Project C in May, but now, suddenly, all seemed to have been lost. He had been scheduled to speak at noon Monday to the Young

Men's Business Club, regarded as the most progressive civic club in town despite the fact that it was segregated, and as he went through his notes before the meeting he decided to toss them out and go from the gut. When I read his remarks later, I felt as though he had been addressing my father:

> Four little girls were killed in Birmingham yesterday. A mad, remorseful, worried community asks, "Who did it? Who threw that bomb? Was it a Negro or a white?" . . . But you know the "who" of "Who did it?" is really rather simple. The "who" is every little individual who talks about the "niggers" and spreads the seeds of his hate to his neighbor and his son. The jokester, the crude oaf whose racial jokes rock the party with laughter. The "who" is every governor who ever shouted for lawlessness and became a law violator. . . . Who is really guilty? Each of us. Each citizen who has not consciously attempted to bring about peaceful compliance with the decisions of the Supreme Court; each citizen who has ever said, "They ought to kill that nigger." Every person in this community who has in any way contributed to the popularity of hatred is at least as guilty, or more so, as the demented fool who threw that bomb. What's it like living in Birmingham? No one ever really has [truly "lived" here] and no one will until this city becomes part of the United States. Birmingham is not a dying city. It is dead. . . .

As soon as Morgan had finished, an eager young business-man jumped to his feet and moved that the YMBC go out and find itself a black member, immediately, right now. When the motion failed even to get a second, Morgan knew his days in Birmingham were over. The speech made the New York *Times* the next day, *Life* magazine two weeks later; and in December of that year Morgan wrote a stinging essay in *Look* magazine entitled "I Saw a City Die." It was more or less his public announcement that he, like so many other promising young men before him, was leaving Birmingham.

CHAPTER TWELVE

Other Voices: Junior League and Jail

Mimi Tynes

The Junior League has a white-glove image, but it eventually led me to the awakening I would experience about Birmingham in general and race relations in particular. For the first four years, beginning in 1965, I was involved with the Nearly New Shop, which sold secondhand clothing and other items. In going from salesgirl to treasurer to chairman, I essentially learned many facets of running a small business. We were responsible for all the bookkeeping, paying salaries, generating publicity, manning the sales floor, maintaining a supply of merchandise, as well as understanding all of the Internal Revenue rules and regulations regarding nonprofit organizations. Several years later, I served as treasurer of the League, doing the bookkeeping and managing the investments for three or four hundred thousand dollars. In 1971–72, I was one of three co-chairmen the first time the League held a professional tennis tournament as a fund-raiser. By 1976–77, the year I was president of the League, we put on the first professional tennis tournament held in the brand-new Civic Center Coliseum—the first women's tournament ever to come to Birmingham—with total prize money of $150,000.

More importantly, though, in my active years with the Junior League I was exposed to other worlds and a number of important issues facing our community and our state: foster care, adoption, child abuse, day care, the Department of Human Resources, the juvenile court system, the Department of Youth Services, education, arts, the needs of severely emotionally disturbed children and their families, as well as public and private funding sources for these and other groups or programs. The League provided me with a wealth of opportunities and experiences encompassing all of Birmingham, not just the part over the mountain.

In 1977, I was asked to serve on the board of Big Brothers of Greater Birmingham, which became Big Brothers/Big Sisters about eighteen months later. Two of the staff members and many of the board members were black. I was thirty-seven years old, and this was the first time I was really involved and working around the same table with blacks. Before long, I couldn't believe I sat back in my apartment in Mountain Brook in 1963, teaching school and reading about what was going on downtown, knowing something was wrong, but having no motivation to be involved in changing things for the better.

Still later, in 1983, Leadership Birmingham, patterned after similar programs in other cities such as Atlanta and Nashville, was developed to address what some considered a void in Birmingham's leadership. Because of my involvement in the Junior League and other community organizations, I was fortunate enough to be part of the first class. A major aspect of the program is to have each class represent a really good cross-section of the community: blacks, whites, women, men, corporate leaders, community leaders, liberals, conservatives, and so on. The program year started with a two-day overnight retreat, followed by seven day-long sessions and another retreat at the end. Each of the day-long sessions examined in depth a different topic: local government, education, economic development, the criminal justice system, an open community, health and human services, and quality of life. The agenda included a variety of speakers, site visits, and discussions among ourselves. One experience I remember vividly was visiting the old Birmingham City Jail and feeling what it was like to be in one of those small cells originally designed for one or two people and now having four to six bunks.

During the opening retreat we discussed what had happened in Birmingham in the sixties. The same subject kept coming up in other sessions as well, because our history and race relations were an integral part of each topic covered. Among those in the class were several black women who were to become friends and associates: Odessa Woolfolk and Charlena Bray and Helen Shores Lee. Getting to know them made all that had happened in Birmingham before have new meaning for me. I would think, I can't believe that Odessa couldn't use the Birmingham Public Library, or that Helen or Charlena had to drink from the "colored" water fountain and ride in the back of the bus.

The same kind of thoughts kept coming to me throughout that year. Then came one of the few times when a light bulb turned on in my head. I was listening to Ed LaMonte, who's now a Birmingham-Southern professor but then was the executive assistant to Mayor Arrington, talk to the students at Altamont during a lecture series about Birmingham. He was discussing Birmingham during the sixties, just as he and others had during Leadership Birmingham. It suddenly occurred to me that if I'd had an experience like Leadership Birmingham when I was in high school, maybe my whole outlook and a lot of people's reactions to what happened in the sixties might have been different. There is no way to know what issues and factors today's young people will have to face, but why not have a high school version of Leadership Birmingham?

I mentioned this idea a number of times during the remaining Leadership Birmingham sessions and particularly at the closing retreat. Several others—all women, incidentally—agreed to work on the idea. We expanded the original group and started Youth Leadership Forum of Birmingham. The planning process took about a year: putting together a steering committee; getting information from Louisville, where a similar program had been started the year before; getting support from school superintendents and funding sources. YLF was launched in the fall of 1985. All of my previous volunteer experiences gave me just what was needed in terms of skill and knowledge of the community to serve as YLF's executive director for seven years before retiring last May.

John Porter

When the pastor died at Sixth Avenue Baptist, I was called back to take over in September of '62. I had to give it some thought. For fifty-five years the Goodgames, father and son, had pastored there. I didn't know what it would be like, going back to the church where I'd grown up. One of the first things I did was call my mother and tell her, "Now, Mama, I'm coming, but if you're going to pastor I'm not," because I knew how strong she was. I'd barely gotten there when she came to tell me something that somebody had told her to tell me. I slapped her hands good, not physically, because I knew if I didn't stop her dead in her tracks right then she would keep it up. Thirty years later, she's never interfered again.

I couldn't predict that '63 was going to happen, but the ingredients were all in place. We had Bull Connor. Things were out of control as far as the white power structure was concerned. The tension was there. I remember I used to fly into Birmingham on visits from Detroit, and to walk through the Birmingham airport was a bad experience, because I was scared. I knew I was out of my place. I had been the first in my family to go to college, and now I was the first to fly. It was a very uneasy feeling, though I'd often been where I shouldn't have been even when I was a kid.

But this was it for me. I had left Montgomery before the bus boycott. I wasn't here for the Freedom Riders, or for the sit-ins. And then, in the spring of '63, all hell broke loose. That's when King came to town. It was only then that there was a rallying and a full participation of everybody, and I decided, Well, this is it. I felt as if Providence had delivered me.

Up until that time the former pastor would not allow any of the mass meetings. They didn't really need a larger church until King came, and that's when I invited them to come to Sixth Avenue. I felt it was my time to strike a lick at this thing of separation and segregation. It was never in a mood of anger. The reason I never had much anger is that I had so much joy in childhood. There was fear, but never anger. I had a definite determination to do whatever had to be done. There was no question in my mind that the thing to do was march into that line of policemen when the time came.

The black people here had been down so long, so oppressive was segregation, that they couldn't have done it without King's leadership. Up until then, it had been Shuttlesworth, and he was definitely a one-man show. Fred had a church in North Birmingham, and in the movement he had a rather dictatorial style of leadership. His style wasn't easy for me, but it was effective. He was like a Bear Bryant or a George Patton. All of the plans were in his head, and it was damn the torpedoes, full speed ahead. He'd tell us at a meeting what we were supposed to do tomorrow and we'd go home and see on the six o'clock news that what we were supposed to do tomorrow he'd already gone and done today. When Martin King came to town the whole town rallied, and with everybody involved history was made. Fred is the local hero of the moment and rightly deserves the recognition, but it took King to come and rally the community.

Even so, the SCLC was about the most unorganized organization that ever existed. It was a day-to-day operation with them. I'll never believe anyone anticipated Bull Connor's doing what he did. The movement met every night, at the Gaston Motel or at Sixteenth Street or at my church when they needed a bigger place for meetings, to decide what to do the next day.

Even the Children's Crusade was an unplanned event. The way that came up, James Bevel went to Miles College looking for marchers, but Miles was in the middle of a corporate fund-raising situation and the president locked the school down so the faculty couldn't participate, so in desperation they went by Parker High and waved their hands and the school emptied. It was a day-to-day operation of faith. There was no master plan.

In May of '63 I got arrested twice for marching and a third time for breaking an injunction with King, and each time I went to jail. I'll never forget the first time. Three of us had agreed at the meeting the night before to lead the march the next day. It was almost an unspoken agreement that the thirty or forty who were to be arrested would be allowed to walk ahead, and there might be a thousand in the crowd behind. Really, the safest place to be was up front with the ones who were to be arrested, because the dogs and the hoses were on the rest of the crowd. King was already in jail, writing his "Letter from Birmingham Jail," but he had told us, "Now, when you're arrested, go straight to the paddy wagons. No dragging and lifting is necessary. If you agree to break the law, you agree to pay the price." That sounded safe enough, but you didn't know for sure that it would go like that. In Birmingham in those days, getting arrested didn't guarantee that you'd make it to jail. Sometimes it would turn out that you had "pulled a hidden knife" or "attempted to escape," and they would just shoot you.

The moment came. There was lots of singing in the crowd, very emotional, the paddy wagons were waiting, the dogs and hoses were there, and we were all lined up and ready to go. I heard my mother screaming, and suddenly out of the crowd came my father. He'd always told me, "Now just leave this thing alone, brother." He was afraid for my safety. He had taught me how to "get along" in a racist southern society. "Leave this thing alone." But here he came now, and I didn't know what he was up to. He was pushing people out of the way, moving toward me, and I thought, Oh, my God, not here, Daddy, not now, and he pushed his way through the crowd. And when he got to me, lined up and ready to get arrested, he leaned over and he shook hands with me. It was beautiful, just beautiful. We had both come a long, long way since the Martins' mansion.

During the summer leading up to the bombing at Sixteenth Street Baptist, we had neighborhood watches where each man in the neighborhood would sit for one or two hours at the head of the street, all night, every night, taking turns, all over town. Most of the bombings had been on the north side, Dynamite Hill, where Parker High and Miles College and the upper-class blacks were; but still there was the fear that someone would drive through our neighborhood and do the same thing. So the fear was all over. One or two of the men had guns, but back then there were no guns in the black community because they couldn't afford them. My daddy had an old hunting rifle; he always had just one shell, and every New Year's night he would go out and shoot that shell. I went hunting with him once and he had one shell and he killed a rabbit. Most hunting in Pittsview, where he came from, had been done with sticks and dogs.

I was in the pulpit, ready to go into the eleven o'clock service, when the little girls were killed. We didn't hear it, we just got word. An usher came down to me and said, ''We just got bombed at Sixteenth Street,'' so I made an announcement and we quickly dismissed. The congregation was just milling around. Then we got more details, that the bodies were arriving at the University Center Hospital near us.

We were at Sixth Avenue and Sixteenth Street South then, where Cooper Green Hospital is now, across from the Burger King you see today, and since we were the biggest church around they agreed to have the funeral services here. It takes black folks a long time to put together a funeral, you know, so I guess it was held on about Thursday. At ten o'clock in the morning I went up to the Catholic church to greet the members of the clergy of all denominations, all in their robes and regalia, and we marched the two blocks to our church. It was a broad spectrum of priests, rabbis, black and white, everybody. Somehow, we managed to get most of them inside the door. The funeral was the finest demonstration on the part of the clergy that I've seen in Birmingham, before or since.

Sixteenth Street was the culmination. There were no more bombings after that. It seemed to sober everybody up, even the meanest of the mean. Four little girls in their choir robes—think of it. There were many events following the funeral that kept hope alive, or otherwise us old folks would have been skeptical about any hopes for progress. I remember standing in line until two in the morning, back in the spring, to vote for the change in city government. Soon, Bull was gone. There was always a little sign, a glimmer of hope, a victory here, a loss there, to keep us hoping. There was tremendous hope in the black community, in established neighborhoods like Titusville, where the older folks like my parents wanted so much to recapture what some once thought was just a good relationship with white folk. Everybody was tired of fighting, it seemed, and it had taken something horrible to get us there.

Part Three

EXILE

CHAPTER THIRTEEN

The City
Too Busy to Hate

When I went to work for the Augusta *Chronicle* in 1963, I found myself in an environment that differed from Birmingham only in size. Augusta had none of the mossy charm of its sister city Savannah, 130 miles down the road on the Atlantic coast. It was, rather, a smelly jangle of paper mills, cement and brick plants, lumberyards, and a neon boulevard, endemic to all military towns, catering to every need of the young soldiers stationed at Fort Gordon. The air in the Savannah River area, pungent from the paper mills and the toxic atomic plant across the river in South Carolina, was just as polluted as Birmingham's. The newspapers in Augusta were no less reactionary than those in Birmingham; working-class blacks and whites smoldered and glared at each other down in the sweatshops; a ruling white elite lived above the fray in white-columned mansions on the bluffs; and moral judgments were dictated by deeply conservative southern Protestants. Augusta was just as segregated, inbred, smelly, provincial, and racist as Birmingham. But it was simply too small a stage to attract Martin Luther King and the civil rights movement.

The newspaper was in an antiquated brick building on Broad Street, the main drag, where bands of young GIs swarmed day and night in pursuit of booze and women, and it was there in the corner of the newsroom that I wrote a daily column while my staff of four put out our slim sports section. During the baseball season I covered the Augusta Yankees of the *integrated* Sally

League, getting a much-needed ten dollars a game to be official scorer, and at daybreak on football Saturdays I crammed aboard the newspaper chain's twin-engine plane with the three other sports editors from Augusta and Savannah to be dropped off for college games in Atlanta or Athens in Georgia, or Clemson or Columbia in South Carolina; I'd write my stuff in the press box, then dart to the airport for the flight back home in the dark. Otherwise, Augusta offered slim pickings for a sports columnist: a minor league umpire on his way up or a major leaguer on his way back down; a bluenosed board member of the Augusta National Golf Club on the eve of the Masters; a barbaric high school football coach; the visiting stock car driver Fast Freddie Lorenzen; a barber on Broad Street with a scrapbook of memories from the days when prizefighting was big stuff in those parts.

There was silence from my family in Birmingham after the confrontations in May and the dynamiting in September, along the lines of a news blackout, and I was afraid to ask my old man what he thought about it all. Too busy with my own new life, three hundred miles away, I was staying clear of Birmingham. Besides, now I had found another source of enlightenment: the New York *Herald-Tribune,* which came in the mail at the *Chronicle* and lay unread until I discovered it. I had read the *International Herald-Tribune* while in France, of course, which is where I had first come across the erudite sports columnist Red Smith. Now, after studying Smith's column, I would wander through the rest of the paper. The *Trib* was gallantly fighting for its life in the fierce New York newspaper wars, a battle it would lose in a couple of years, but for a shining moment it was filled with wonderful writing not often found in a daily newspaper: Smith on sports, Art Buchwald when he was still fresh, the bitchy Judith Crist on the movies. More importantly to me, though, a fellow named Jimmy Breslin had just switched over from sports to the writing of a general-interest column that would have a profound impact on my career. In a thousand words or less, Breslin was writing close to literature: sharp vignettes with a beginning and a middle and an end, vivid slices of life from the streets of New York, crisp little journalistic short stories that would become known as New Journalism. (Also experimenting at that time, in the *Trib*'s Sunday magazine, *New York,* was a reporter named Tom Wolfe, who had become "bored" with the standard magazine article format.) The style had its detractors, especially at the straight-laced New York *Times,* which accused Breslin of making up half of his stuff, but I was hypnotized. Breslin owed a large debt to Hemingway, whose economy of style had changed the writing of fiction; and I, in due time, would owe a debt to Breslin. He had opened a window for me and shown me that it was possible to truly *write* in a daily newspaper if given the opportunity.

My chance to try this new style would not come in Augusta, Georgia, but its roots were there. The managing editor of the *Chronicle* was Luther Thigpen, a stern, old-fashioned, just-the-facts breed of smalltown newsman, an unlikely sort to be interested in any newspaper writing that wasn't the straight "inverted pyramid." But Luther turned out to be a well-read man away from the newsroom, and soon I was passing Breslin's columns to him after I had read the *Trib,* and he was encouraging me to try out the style in my sports column. Thus, I would write about a pint-sized outfielder named Ernie Oravetz, a former Washington Senator now playing out his career as a Chattanooga Lookout in the Sally League: "They had lost again the night before, this time in Knoxville, and now, after another seven-hour bus ride to nowhere, he found himself perched on the stool at yet another hamburger joint. If it's Thursday, this must be Augusta. . . ." At some point I wrote the first nonsports story I had ever tried, a profile in the *Chronicle*'s weekend pullout section on a best-selling historical novelist named Edison Marshall, a virtual civic treasure in those parts (to which the great man responded with a postcard saying that "with proper application, you might be able to write for the pulps one day''). Then came the first hard-news story I would write: on the day of John Kennedy's assassination.

It says something about my priorities, because on the afternoon of Friday, November 22, 1963, I was on my kitchen phone with the general manager of the Augusta Yankees. It had just been announced that Augusta had lost its franchise due to poor attendance, that there would be no more professional baseball in Augusta, and I was interviewing the GM for my Sunday column. I felt the column would be among my last in Augusta, that I would be leaving, since there wouldn't be any more baseball to hold my interest. As I was commiserating with him on the phone, he abruptly broke off the conversation: "This is nothing," he shouted. "Turn on your television. We'll talk later." There it was, from Dallas: the death of a President. Soon Luther Thigpen was calling everybody in to put out a special edition of the *Chronicle*. I volunteered to call the only person I knew in Dallas for a report on the mood out there. Aunt Margaret, a sister of my mother known to all as "Mutt," said the people in the neighborhood where she and Uncle Buster, a factory mechanic, had moved after leaving Birmingham were "afraid to leave the house, scared to death about what the niggers are going to do."

For a raise of ten dollars a week and the allure of the Cincinnati Reds' spring training complex, I loaded up my wife and our year-old daughter to move five hundred miles south to Tampa, Florida, where I would become sports editor of a dying little afternoon daily, the Tampa *Times*. Its circulation was down to forty thousand, and it wasn't long for this world, badly outgunned by the bulging Tampa *Tribune* and the excellent St. Petersburg *Times* across the bay; but at least there was baseball. I didn't know it at the time, but the highlights of my seven months in Florida would be riding across the playing fields in a golf cart every day with Fred Hutchinson, the Cincinnati manager, and

later, once the National League season was under way, flying
with a group of Tampa boosters to see a Reds-Braves game in
Cincinnati in Pete Rose's rookie season. The summer was spent
covering the Reds' Class A farm club, often in the company of
two hundred old guys in Bermuda shorts and fishing caps; and
I was glumly preparing to cover the Florida State Seminoles and
the Florida Gators during the football season when, in August,
I had a call from Luther Thigpen. He had just become managing
editor of a new daily paper in Atlanta, and he was inviting me
to come to the big city and write a column for the Atlanta
Times—not a sports column but a "Breslin" column. Goodbye,
palm trees, Class A baseball, jai alai, and saltwater fishing reports. On Labor Day of '64, passing the skeletal infrastructure
of the new major league baseball stadium that would become the
home of the Braves as soon as they could be stolen away from
Milwaukee, I rolled into Atlanta.

The Atlanta *Times* had been started up for all the wrong
reasons. Many of the major stockholders were right-wing nuts,
reactionary John Birchers and White Citizens' Councilers united
in their hatred of Ralph McGill and the *Constitution*. They truly
believed that they could make a difference for their Republican
hero Barry Goldwater in the 1964 presidential race against Lyndon Johnson. Luther Thigpen was apolitical, "just a newsman,"
and he told me to forget about politics and "write your stories
like we talked about in Augusta." In the city of Ralph McGill,
"Hotlanta," the despised old rival of my hometown, Birmingham, I would make a new career. If Breslin had his Mutchie's,
a bar in Queens, I had my Manuel's Tavern, a blue-collar saloon
where I could always find a column when the well went dry: an
Emory University theologian named Dr. Thomas Altizer nursing
a beer and espousing his "God is dead" theory; a sad old lady
on a barstool; Manuel Maloof himself, a second-generation Lebanese who would become chief executive officer of the largest

county in Georgia; an old Jew talking about the Holocaust. I had
no office hours—"Just get the crap in on time"—and I was
learning how to write, making something of a name for myself
in the South's big city. Luther had brought in a feisty little group
of reporters, and we might have been underpaid and under-
staffed and on the wrong side politically, but we were having
fun, sometimes beating the larger *Journal* and *Constitution* on
stories in spite of being badly outnumbered. My father, of course,
was beside himself over this turn of events; to him, as he would
confide to friends at the loading docks in Atlanta, his son had
been called up to the big time like a mercenary, a freedom fighter,
in order to counter "all of that Communist crap" spread by
"Rastus McGill."

There really was an audience for an extremely conservative
newspaper in Atlanta, mainly older people in the suburbs who
resented the strides made toward racial tolerance; and the *Times*
rode that crest until Goldwater was routed by Lyndon Johnson
in November. But so urgent was the paper's founders' mission
to get Goldwater into the White House that they had clamored
into print before they had sufficient backing. And they had mis-
calculated on another point of even greater importance: the white
power establishment in Atlanta, unlike the one in Birmingham,
found right-wing rabble-rousing not only unseemly but, more to
the point, bad for business. "The City Too Busy to Hate" had
already been coined as Atlanta's motto, a direct reference to Birmingham's lack of leadership during the height of racial tensions,
and the major advertisers in town (primarily the monolithic,
home-owned Rich's department store) never came across with
any appreciable support to keep the *Times* afloat. There were
anxious moments in the *Times* newsroom as early as the Christmas shopping season of '64, when the editions were getting thin-
ner by the day; and by the first of the year we were being called
together around the city desk for the same painful scene: haggard
directors, some of them right-wing Republicans who themselves

had been swept out in the wake of Goldwater's defeat, breaking down and crying as they tried to assure us the *Times* would survive.

Across town, at Atlanta Newspapers, Inc., parent company of the *Journal* and *Constitution,* they had to be careful about what they might do to hasten the death of the *Times.* The bosses there knew that the *Times*'s lawyers could accomplish what the ad salesmen had not been able to do if they could nail them with an antitrust suit for "tampering" with editors and reporters. A couple of reporters had already jumped ship when spring arrived, when it was looking like the next payroll might be the last; and I began to hear through third parties that I had admirers at the ANI, "even Mister McGill," and that I would be a fool not to think about doing something. To me, of course, this was like a kid lost in the Dodgers' sprawling farm system hearing that Branch Rickey himself had spoken his name at an organizational meeting. But I still enjoyed being with the underdog, even if the *Times*'s editorial writers were becoming more strident than ever as they got backed into a corner; and I didn't want to run out on my friend and mentor, Luther Thigpen, the man who had brought me that far. The question of whether to make an inquiry was answered on March 7, 1965. At about the same hour that hundreds of civil rights marchers were being beaten at the Pettus Bridge in Selma, Alabama, on the first leg of a protest march to Montgomery, my son, David, was being born in an Atlanta hospital. With another mouth to feed, I began talking to the managing editor at the *Journal* through an intermediary, Joe Cumming, the southeastern bureau chief for *Newsweek* magazine. Early in April, hired by the *Journal* but warned that my column would be posted on the comics pages "if it doesn't work out," I went over to the House of McGill.

The Atlanta *Journal* and *Constitution* were not great newspapers by any stretch of the imagination. They were owned by the Cox Newspapers chain, along with papers in lesser towns like Dayton, Ohio, and Austin, Texas, and even though our weekly paychecks came from Atlanta Newspapers, Inc., the local bosses pretended (for antitrust purposes) that the afternoon *Journal* and the morning *Constitution* were separate entities. True, on the editorial pages the *Journal* took the conservative position and McGill's *Constitution* the liberal; true, there were separate news staffs stationed on different floors. But the papers shared advertising, circulation, and production facilities in order to cut costs and make money, and making money is what they did best. When I arrived in '65, reporters either used their personal automobiles to reach breaking news stories or else had to ask for bus tokens from a secretary in the newsroom. And the *Constitution* had just failed to keep its vigorous, award-winning investigative reporter Jack Nelson, who opened a southeastern bureau for the Los Angeles *Times* right there in the same building. There were several young men on the papers at that time who would make names for themselves later, most notably the humorist Roy Blount, Jr., and the syndicated redneck columnist Lewis Grizzard; but the great majority of them knew that it would be only a matter of time before they had to go elsewhere, primarily into public relations of some sort, in order to pay their rent.

Around the rest of the nation it was presumed that the Atlanta *Constitution* was an excellent newspaper, the conscience of the South; but in fact that reputation lay solely on the presence of Ralph McGill's column. He was listed as "publisher" of the *Constitution,* but he had nothing to do with what went into the news columns. Harold Martin, a *Constitution* editorial writer at that time and a close friend of McGill's, spelled out the situation in his biography, *Ralph McGill, Reporter:*

> It was a grievous embarrassment to McGill that his paper, during the cataclysmic years of the civil rights struggle, chose to play down the news of the great confrontations, leaving the

coverage of such events as Martin Luther King's Birmingham sit-ins and the Selma march to the wire services and the national press. . . . [Chief executive Jack Tarver] was largely guided by the *Constitution*'s lawyers, a cautious lot by nature, [who] were counseling that, in view of the libel suits McGill had already gotten them into, the papers should keep a very low profile when black and white were confronting each other on the streets.

Indeed, the Atlanta papers were among the few dailies of any size in the United States that did not send reporters to Selma, only two hundred miles from Atlanta, for King's march from the Pettus Bridge to the steps of the Alabama capitol in Montgomery; and the word that reached the newsroom was that McGill had been talked out of delivering yet another letter of resignation to Tarver by the editor, Eugene Patterson, just as bullheaded a liberal as McGill.

But it was all right for McGill to say what was on his mind through his front-page column, and he made full use of the opportunity. He had been attending a conference at the Carnegie Foundation in New York when Bull Connor let loose the dogs and water hoses at Kelly Ingram Park in May of 1963, and he uncased his portable typewriter and let fly. He traced the history of Birmingham, making the point that it was not an Old South city but a brawling industrial town. It was, he wrote, "Bull Connor's town, and George Wallace's town, the white man's town all the way; and the Birmingham newspapers and the churches and the politicians and industrialists are content that this is so." Then, when Sixteenth Street Baptist was bombed in September, McGill formally declared that the word "moderate" no longer fit him:

> "Moderate" now means to remain silent, to avoid controversy, to make no commitment, to avoid affirming belief in principle. . . . So now, after the bombing of schools, temples,

churches, homes and motels, comes the dynamiting of a crowded Sunday school where Negro children reading the lesson of the forgiveness of love were killed or maimed. . . . And until the "moderates" and the great body of Christianity make up their minds whether by their silence they give consent to the White Citizens' Councils or the dynamiters, we shall continue to trample out the bitter vintage where the grapes of wrath are stored.

All I could do was sit at my typewriter, on the floor below McGill's office, and, with each edition of the *Constitution,* watch the great man dance. My mandate at the *Journal* was not to ruminate on the South's failings, a task I wasn't yet prepared to tackle, but rather to hit the streets in pursuit of my little daily dramas; and writing was drilled into me once and for all during the five years that I wrote six one-thousand-word columns a week, a million and a half words when it was over. This, for me, was the journalism school they hadn't had at Auburn when I was there, my personal boot camp, where I could learn all of the basics: finding ideas, interviewing, composing the story, and then writing it under daily pressure. Strippers, hookers, athletes, troubadours, politicians, drunks, Klansmen, priests, pilots, plumbers, route salesmen, socialites—all were my people. I was at the Atlanta airport on a snowy dawn to meet one of the first pine boxes coming back from Vietnam; I went on the hustings with Manuel Maloof when he entered local politics ("Take the courage of Churchill and the mind of Einstein and the compassion of Roosevelt, put 'em in a body like mine, and go up against a pretty-boy like Ronnie Reagan on TV, you'll get your brains beat out"); I spent two months of 1966 writing Ernie Pyle–like dispatches from Vietnam; I drove down to Plains, Georgia, the day after a peanut farmer named Jimmy Carter had lost the gubernatorial race to a screwball fried-chicken king named Lester Maddox, one of my old man's heroes, to write a column entitled "The One Who Got Away"; I drove up to the little town of Summerville to hang out with one of the heroes of my youth, Ralph "Country" Brown, who had been a Birmingham Baron when Rickwood Field was my shrine. Although looking over my shoulder was a conservative managing editor, a balding ex-Marine who was there to monitor expense accounts and make sure nothing liberal showed up during his watch, I managed to slip a few columns past him that were favorable toward Martin Luther King and Julian Bond and others of the civil rights movement who were headquartered in Atlanta—a group that also included Chuck Morgan, the former Birmingham lawyer, who now ran the Atlanta office of the American Civil Liberties Union.

It was a prime time to be living in Atlanta. Birmingham wasn't the only city in America to shoot itself in the foot during the sixties; from Boston to Los Angeles, from Miami to San Francisco, cities were in great turmoil throughout an entire decade marked by assassinations, Vietnam, the "hippie" drug culture, and the civil rights movement. But Atlanta, even though it was the headquarters of Dr. King and the place where most civil rights strategy was plotted, managed to escape nearly all of the urban violence of that time. Indeed, the city was on a roll, and from my perspective as a newspaper columnist I had a front-row seat as a mere handful of powerful upper-class white businessmen, with not a little counseling and cheerleading from Ralph McGill and Eugene Patterson, pulled Atlanta through the decade because, as they said over and over again, "what's good for Atlanta is good for business, and vice versa." They had, in fact, laid down the ground rules even before the decade began by saying, "Integration is coming, ready or not, and we're not going to let it destroy Atlanta." Having just witnessed Birmingham's self-destruction, most of it due to reactionary newspapers and shortsighted "leaders," I appreciated Atlanta's "white power structure" much more than did the critics who dismissed them as just a bunch of businessmen looking out for themselves.

The mayor of Atlanta during the sixties was particularly

fascinating to me, especially when compared with the men of his background in Birmingham. He was Ivan Allen, Jr., son of a typewriter salesman from Rome, Georgia, now head of the family's office-supply business in downtown Atlanta. He had been born into privilege, but he had also been taught an old-fashioned civic goodness by his father. Like most of his generation who would become the city's leaders, he lived within the city limits and felt an obligation to put back into the city what he had taken out. In the late fifties, as the incoming president of the Chamber of Commerce, Allen had drawn up a document called the Six-Point Program, a sort of blueprint for Atlanta as it faced the sixties. It specifically covered the need to smoothly integrate public schools, to improve housing for the poor, to build a sports complex that would attract major league teams, and to get started immediately on expressways and a rapid transit system so Atlanta could handle the hordes that were sure to come. (Meanwhile, at the very same time, Birmingham's "leaders" were ignoring the woeful projections in the Metropolitan Audit.) Just as the downtown businesspeople were mulling that over, the sit-ins came to Atlanta—a young Julian Bond and Dr. Martin Luther King, Jr., were among those arrested at Rich's department store—and the Allen-for-mayor movement began after he and a group from the Chamber of Commerce negotiated a settlement that soon would lead to desegregation of all public facilities in Atlanta. Allen went on the attack against his chief opponent, Lester Maddox, the tenth-grade dropout who campaigned on the race issue, and he moved into the mayor's office in January of 1962. On the first day, he ordered that all "White" and "Colored" signs be removed from City Hall.

Allen's record on race relations was all the more remarkable because of his background; like most wealthy white southerners, he had known black people only in their roles as domestics at home and laborers at work. But he became aware that there was a viable black society out there on a night in 1947 when, as head of the Community Chest, he agreed to attend a dinner kicking off the charity's "Negro division" fund drive. A huge black woman kept wildly applauding everything he said during his speech after dinner, thoroughly unnerving him, and when he had finished she charged the podium and wrapped her arms around him. "Lord God, chillun," she shouted, "this is my *baby*. I was his mammy's nurse the night he was brung into this world." Although Allen would write a sizable personal check to the Negro division of the Community Chest later that night, the classic paternalistic response of a privileged white southerner, it set him on his way. During his eight years as mayor, Ivan Allen, Jr., would embody Atlanta's handling of the civil rights movement. While Birmingham was closing down all city parks rather than have them integrated, Allen was fully desegregating all public facilities; while Bull Connor was answering black protesters with police dogs and water hoses, Allen was standing on top of a police car and personally dispersing an angry mob in a poor black neighborhood; while Birmingham was throwing Martin Luther King in jail, Allen was putting together a gala biracial dinner to honor the native son's winning the Nobel Peace Prize; while Birmingham's white elite were refusing to go downtown and mingle with blacks anymore, Allen was going to Washington and becoming the only elected white southern official to testify in favor of the public accommodations section of Lyndon Johnson's Civil Rights Act.

It freed Allen's soul, and it freed his beloved city to become the urban success story of the sixties. Having "solved" the racial situation and thereby turned to other matters, albeit for pragmatic reasons, Atlanta began to boom. There were plenty of blue-collar whites in the metropolitan area (now passing the one-million mark) who were grousing, who spat out "Ivan the Commie," who missed the Atlanta *Times;* but their paychecks were bigger now, and they were further appeased when major league sports came to town. There were city-watchers around the country who were put off by Atlanta's relentless Babbittry ("World's Busiest Airport," "World's Tallest Hotel," "The City Too Busy to Hate," "The Next Great City"), who found the whole idea of a bunch of rich white businessmen working for the common good impossible to swallow; but they couldn't deny the sweet irony that the city that had been burned to the ground during the Civil War exactly a century earlier had found the key to prosperity when it opened its doors to all people. And nobody knew it better than the sulking white elite of Birmingham, a mere three-hour drive away, the city that had been neck and neck with Atlanta in most indices only ten years before.

Never had I dreamed that I would become even a minor celebrity, but that's what happens when your name tops a column on page 2 of a newspaper with a daily circulation of 240,000. You don't even have to be very good—although I must have been doing something right, judging from the offers and feelers coming to me from the New York *Times* and *Newsweek* and other publications outside the South. Big frog, little pond, enjoying every minute of it. Free to roam and write whatever I fancied, I had entree everywhere—City Hall, the state capitol, Atlanta–Fulton County Stadium, strip joints and the symphony, Manuel's Tavern and the Coach and Six restaurant—and if the money wasn't great, the perks were. It was difficult to pay for drinks if I strolled into a bar with one of the recurring characters in my column, a wasted old newspaper guy known as Streetcar (so named because he'd commandeered one on the streets of Knoxville one Halloween night as a kid, leading to the first of many incarcerations), and difficult to say no to the ladies. I had married the first one who had slept with me, this college dropout from Birmingham who had only wanted babies and a white picket fence; and now, predictably, a marriage that had been bad from the outset was falling apart, held together only by two young children and some vague notion that it might all work out somehow. There had been no career planning whatsoever: college, writing, marriage, fatherhood, France, Atlanta—it had all sort of happened. I was just the son of an Alabama truck driver, astonished to be here, enjoying the best of times in the best of southern cities.

Given the hours she was spending on the phone with her mother in Birmingham, it probably was my unhappy wife's fondest dream that one day we would return to the familiar comforts of what she still regarded as home. Thus, her hopes ran high one day in the summer of 1966 when I went downtown to have lunch with a fellow who was flying in from Birmingham to offer me the job as founding editor of a new magazine. He was a courtly gentleman named Emory Cunningham, a graduate of Auburn's school of agriculture, now publisher of the eminently successful magazine *Progressive Farmer*. I must have been a sight when he laid eyes on me at a motel dining room, still wearing a beard and ashen from the amoebic dysentery I had brought home from Vietnam, but he ordered martinis and made his pitch anyway. The Progressive Farmer corporation was starting up a magazine to be called *Southern Living,* he said, and everybody was sure the formula was a winner: think over-the-mountain Birmingham, the good southern life, great color photography, heavy on recipes and home decorating and backyard entertaining. I was shifting in my seat, thinking about the real Birmingham, the one I knew. The magazine was almost guaranteed a circulation of one million right out of the gate, riding *Progressive Farmer*'s subscription list, he said, and he liked the idea of having a good old Auburn boy like me as the first editor. I told him some stories, when he asked, about my old man and McGill and Martin Luther King and Vietnam. He was assuring me that my salary would make it possible for me to move my family back home where I "belonged," but this time to a "nice" place in Homewood or Mountain Brook, when my eyes must have glazed over. We hadn't finished our first round of drinks when he said, in all kindness, "Look, this would be a mistake. You would either quit or get fired after two weeks. Why don't we enjoy our lunch?" When I called my wife to report on the meeting, she cried.

My old man thought I had lost it, too. He might not be the sort of prospective reader *Southern Living* had in mind, but he knew a respectable job when he saw it. "Christ, Pop, I belong at a magazine like that about like you'd belong driving for Greyhound," I told him one beery evening at a steakhouse in Atlanta, where we often had to meet because he so despised my wife. He sputtered and said that was different, and soon was praising my sister's choice of husband. In Jim Lott, he had, indeed, found a surrogate son: a Birmingham boy who had studied engineering at Auburn, returned home to work for a construction company, proposed to my sister on bended knee after showing the old man his financial portfolio, then built a brick house in Mountain Brook that sat on an elevated cul-de-sac, so help me, "so I can get a better bead on 'em when they start coming." In Jim, he had found somebody to talk "nigger" with. So you can see what the prodigal son was up against: "married sorry," had no savings account, rented a duplex, ran around on his wife, "just an educated fool" (he would tell his pals in Atlanta), and, worst of all, worked for Ralph McGill. The fact that I seldom got more than a glimpse of McGill, usually when he ducked into a chauffeured car to avoid the hecklers, didn't calm my father a bit. He was aging fast, as truckers do; but integration had gotten his hackles up like never before. Before the first beer was poured, our meetings, such as they were, sank into shouting matches. "McGill and Martin Luther Coon can have Atlanta if they want it," he would say in the back room of Manuel's, where he knew he could always find me if he waited late enough. "Bull Connor taught 'em a thing or two. Birmingham's doing just fine." Well, I told him, I see where the pollution got so bad they had to shut down some steel mills. "It's that damned Ralph Nader that done it. When there ain't no smoke over Birmingham, there's people

ain't eatin'.'' He was a colorful character or a pain in the ass,
depending on the point of view, and I missed one of his greatest
moments: sharing a bottle in the parking lot after closing with a
black bartender named Howard, on a night when I never showed
up, he wiped the neck of the bottle and took another swig and
then said, ''Howard, tell me the truth, what do you think about
this nigger situation?''

At some point around the first of 1968, when I felt I was
burning out from the grind of the daily column and needed a
change, a writer named Dan Wakefield came to town. He had
been raised in Indianapolis, but now he was identified with New
York and Boston, and he was traveling around the country to
research a book called *Supernation at Peace and War.* A gaggle
of us writers and photographers in Atlanta were in the slothful
habit of gathering on most afternoons at a downtown watering
hole called Emile's French Cafe, in what we fancied was a hin-
terland version of the Algonquin Round Table, where people at
nearby tables strained to hear our irreverent ripostes. One day
the people from *Atlanta* magazine brought Wakefield by to join
in on our tomfoolery. A real author, from the mysterious East!
He was an amiable little fellow, with many stories to tell, and I
wound up escorting him around town during the week that he
spent in our midst. He was reading my column and was surprised
to find something that good in Atlanta, he said, and when I told
him I didn't want to spend the rest of my life hacking out a daily
newspaper column he asked me if I had heard of the Nieman
fellowships at Harvard.

Every year since 1939, when the program was begun in
memory of a Milwaukee newspaper editor named Lucius W. Nieman, a dozen ''promising'' journalists from all corners of the
country had been selected to spend a school year at Harvard.
You got a stipend and were free to do whatever you wanted for
a blessed nine months, whether that meant staying drunk or writ-

ing a novel. Some big names had come out of there: Tom Wicker
of the New York *Times,* John Seigenthaler of the Nashville *Ten-
nessean,* Jack Nelson (the one who had left the *Constitution* for
the Los Angeles *Times*), and on and on. A. B. "Bud" Guthrie,
in fact, had written *The Big Sky* during his Nieman year. Wakefield knew about this because he had become the first freelance
writer to win a Nieman, in 1964, and he felt I would be a perfect
candidate. "The people at Harvard like to think they've taken
a diamond in the rough, so to speak, and had something to do
with polishing it." He said the competition would be formidable,
with maybe five hundred applicants, and then told me what to
do: "Lay on some of that 'ignorant southern boy' shit, and be
damned sure you tell 'em about your old man."

Already in the sixties there had been five Niemans from the
Constitution, due in great part to Ralph McGill's influence; and
when I got an audience with him, he talked first about the tragic
past of my hometown and then said, sure, fill out the application,
he'd be glad to write one of the letters of recommendation. That
is probably all it would have taken, but I followed Wakefield's
advice when I began filling out the forms: "Son of a Birmingham
trucker. . . . Parents married for free on the stage of a movie
house. . . . Auburn was better known as a football factory. . . .
Time to stand back and take a longer view of Birmingham and
the South. . . ." I enclosed a dozen of the better columns I had
written and mailed off the package, figuring that was that, but
in May I was called up for an unnerving interview in the May-
flower Hotel in Washington, and in June I was notified by wire
that I had been selected. As far as anybody could recall, I would
be the first Nieman fellow who had grown up in Birmingham,
Alabama.

Maybe now, I thought, my parents will be impressed. That
seemed odd, that a thirty-two-year-old man would need some
sort of affirmation from his parents; but it had been a rocky road.
After hearing my wife babble over how nice it was going to be

seeing all of those famous places in Boston, I called Birmingham. My mother answered.

I fairly shouted. "Mama, I won that fellowship!"

"Well, that's good, son."

"Guess we'll be moving to Boston soon."

There was a pause. "What school did you say that was, son?"

I sighed. "Harvard, Mama. Harvard."

CHAPTER FOURTEEN

Harvard

There was no doubt in my mind now that my successes were my parents' failures. Not many of my generation were leaving Birmingham except when they were transferred by a large national company, which was the case with my cousin Melvin of Chicago Bridge & Iron, who was jerked around for years to places ranging from Miami to Pittsburgh. It would have pleased my parents mightily if I had stayed right there in the sports department of the Birmingham *News*, covering Bear Bryant and waiting for my turn to become sports editor. But no; here I was, at thirty-two, without a penny in savings, still renting apartments, unhappily married, bags always packed, and in a profession that they would not try to understand. I knew of other writers who had made it in spite of coming from less than intellectual backgrounds—Willie Morris of Yazoo City, Mississippi, then editor of *Harper's* magazine, always came to mind—but they seemed to have become someone's protégé somewhere along the way, if only as a child whose mother read to him. My mentor, if I had one, was the much-reviled "Rastus" McGill. And now I was going to spend a year in that cesspool of Communist thinking, Harvard, which had given the world such dangerous radicals as Roosevelt and the Kennedys and John Kenneth Galbraith and Pat Moynihan and Averell Harriman. Not once in their lives would my parents ever ask me what it was like to spend a year at Harvard—leading me to assume that they were not pleased, they were embarrassed.

My wife and children, the girl five and the boy three now, had gone to Birmingham ahead of me for goodbyes while I wrote my last columns for the *Journal* and loaded up a U-Haul trailer for the journey to Boston. During the spring I had written a proposal for a book about country music, an idea that had come to me after I had written a profile for *Atlanta* magazine on a local boy, Bill Anderson, who was a member of the Grand Ole Opry; and a friend who was regional sales representative for a major publishing house had hand-delivered my book proposal to New York. I had gotten hooked on the music as a kid, riding with my old man, listening to the all-night truckers' radio shows as we rolled through the Blue Ridge, and I figured this was a book I could write. Either the letter had disappeared into a black hole or the idea wasn't any good—I had no agent, knew nothing of the mysterious workings up there, and I was afraid to ask— so I forgot about the book and spent a lot of time celebrating and being celebrated at Manuel's and Emile's, talking with some of the Niemans from Atlanta who had preceded me, and pondered the certainty that I was about to make another unscheduled turn. Just before I left, when he was headed out of town himself, for the 1968 Democratic convention in Chicago, Ralph McGill summoned me to his office to wish me godspeed. "Your life is never going to be quite the same after Harvard, son," he said.

When I drove to Birmingham at the end of August, to pick up my family and head northeast so we could reach Cambridge, Massachusetts, in time to enroll our daughter in the first grade, I found that there was to be a last supper at my parents' house. Since "the niggers" were "taking over" in the old neighborhood in Woodlawn, my old man had sprung for a new brick split-level house in East Lake that was sandwiched between a public golf course and Zion City, the ragged black settlement where our maid of many years, Louvenia, was now buried. This new house had become a very unpleasant place for me. There was nothing there to remind me of my childhood, except for a back bedroom preserved as "Paul, Jr.'s room" to complement another that was known as "Joyce's room." But worst of all there was a tackily furnished, thin-paneled den that had become the place where the old man sat at the upright piano of his youth and, between Hoagy Carmichael tunes, carried on his usual diatribe about "niggers, Jews, and Catholics." The only driving he was doing these days was on a freelance basis, for a couple of old friends in the surplus tire business, and I figured he had too much time on his hands. On top of the piano were framed eight-by-ten photographs of the esteemed Lester Maddox, now governor of Georgia, and George Wallace, who was running for President in direct response to the Civil Rights Act. This good man who once had been my hero, my King of the Road, now was eaten up by racism as though it were a cancer.

It turned out to be the longest night of my life. My sister and her husband were there, and after dinner we retired to the den. The television was turned on; and since all of the networks were carrying the Democratic convention, we had little choice but to watch. On the floor of the convention hall in Chicago there was the usual swarm of delegates and political groupies, but this time there was an even bigger story to be covered outside: thousands of protesters, including hippies and blacks and wounded Vietnam veterans, were squared off against Mayor Richard Daley's battle-ready Chicago police. There was a glimpse of Bull Connor, a delegate this year, passed out drunk in his wheelchair, prompting my old man and my brother-in-law to say what a shame it was that a fine man like that had to be struck with a heart attack. I was surrounded, didn't have a prayer, and when suddenly the Chicago cops rushed the protesters like sharks who had sensed blood, clubbing people to the ground and looking for more, it was very nearly a repeat of what had happened in Birmingham only five years earlier. "It's about time to haul out the firehoses, don't you think, Mr. Hemphill?"

said my sister's husband, sucking up to him. "Reason enough to elect George," said my old man. Shit, I thought, they've worked up a routine—ought to buy a bus and hit the road. All of this was meant for me, obviously: the clucking of tongues, the sucking of teeth, the commentary ("That one ain't bathed in a month" . . . "Lookit that, split his head wide open" . . . "Police oughta get combat pay"). All I could do, like the kids we saw being bludgeoned on the screen, was hunker down and ride it out. Some farewell. Dawn was a long time coming.

In a Volkswagen Beetle with a retractable sun roof for air conditioning, pulling a trailer taller and wider than the car, straining to make four hundred miles a day, we took on the twelve-hundred-mile trek to Cambridge: Dad driving, Mom sleeping, two kids moping in the backseat, Labor Day weekend, hottest temperatures of the year. Onward we chugged, buoyed only by the promise of a new adventure at the end of the road, out of Alabama and over the Blue Ridge, around Washington and New York, onto the Merritt Parkway announcing New England. By noon on Labor Day we had negotiated Boston and crossed the Charles River, where scullers and sailboaters were slicing through the emerald water; and it was while we were darting through the mad traffic on Massachusetts Avenue, my wife straining to spy just one Victorian house like the postcards had promised, that I had to hit the brakes to avoid smashing into a tambourine enthusiast. Harvard Square. The place was crawling with "hippies": barefoot girls, long-haired boys, kite fliers, skateboarders, guitar pickers; the tie-dyed, thong-sandaled, dope-smoking, bourbon-guzzling children of Woodstock and, for all I knew, the future of America. I sat at the wheel, enjoying the show, and wondered how many of them had taken their licks in Chicago. My kids pressed their faces to the rear windows, mouths wide open, saying nothing. My wife, I noticed as the light changed and we edged forward, was crying again.

Having a child to enroll in the first grade, we had arrived ahead of the other Niemans. Good thing, because we needed all of the time we could get to bring order to the apartment we had been assigned: a narrow two-story town house, two bedrooms upstairs and a living room–kitchen area below, on a cobbled alley called Shaler Lane, across a boulevard from Mount Auburn Hospital, where the famous child psychologist and author Dr. Robert Coles was in residence. We could guess from their leavings that the previous occupants had a dog and a motorbike and a baby, because the floors and walls were slung with dog shit, motor oil, and dried chunks of oatmeal and jelly. This wasn't exactly what my wife had in mind when she signed on for a year in the cold Northeast; but she had learned to move into strange abodes, and in due time we had made the place livable. It would be all right, all we needed. Lisa's school was within walking distance, as were all of the places I would need to be during the year, and David had dozens of kids to play with on the alley—Mormons all, mostly the families of M.B.A. candidates, all of them there on subleases that had been passed along from one Mormon to another for twenty years.

Then came the moment I had looked forward to with some trepidation, when I would meet my fellow Niemans. Over Scotch and soda, in a brooding dark-paneled room at the Faculty Club, we came together and it was just as I had feared: hardballers from the East, Harvards and Yalies, a New York *Times*-man here and a *Newsday*man there, a couple of wire-service Moscow hands, not a good old boy in sight. If the old man could see me now! We circled each other, heard from the affable rosy-cheeked curator of the program ("Then, on the other hand, there's nothing entirely unpleasant about spending the year at Cronin's," which was, I would find soon enough, a replica of Manuel's Tavern), refilled our glasses, and began to speak earnestly among ourselves of just how we intended to improve our minds, if not our career situations, during the coming nine months. I was sort of lying back, wondering if the joke had been on me rather than the Nieman selection committee when I told them I was just a misguided ignorant redneck from Alabama. Then I heard a voice: "Well, Bubba, how's the watermelon crop this year?" His name tag said he was Joe Strickland, of the Detroit *News*. He was very handsome and very black, and he seemed to feel as out of place as I. When I looked startled, he winked and said, "Stay cool. I checked my blade at the door."

"I'm a city boy," I told him. "Don't know nothin' 'bout no watermelons."

"I know. Atlanta tags. Saw you moving in."

"Shaler Lane?"

"We're neighbors, Bubba." He leaned over to whisper. "These Harvard cats ain't dumb. Got themselves a token nigger and a token redneck, put us next door to each other so they can keep their eyes on us."

As we were breaking up, a secretary from the Nieman office came up to me, apologizing and handing me a letter. It had arrived ahead of me, and she had forgotten about it. The letter was from a senior editor at the New York publishing house, explaining that somebody had found my proposal for a book on country music while rummaging through the desk of an editor whose head had rolled in a putsch; if I hadn't sold the idea already, could I fly down to talk about a contract? Within a week, before classes had gotten under way at Harvard, I had scrounged air fare, set foot on the streets of New York for the first time in my life, been stroked by one of the hot young editors in publishing, and walked away with a deal: a total advance of $2,500, half up front and the rest upon completion, for a book we would call *The Nashville Sound*. I was giddy, scared, and aware of the irony that I had gone to Harvard, as I had written in my application, "to get away from the South and take a long view of home," but now I would be commuting between Harvard Yard and the stage of the Grand Ole Opry.

This, of course, greatly diminished my anxieties about being thrust into such a heady environment. The most intimidating of our Nieman group was J. Anthony Lukas, who had been editor of the Harvard newspaper, the *Crimson*, while an undergraduate, and had already won a Pulitzer as a reporter for the New York *Times*. There were the two Moscow correspondents, Henry Bradsher of United Press International and Richard Longworth of the Associated Press; Gisela Bolte from the Bonn bureau of *Time* magazine; a columnist for *Newsday* named Mike McGrady (a Yalie, a friend of Jimmy Breslin); a book critic from North Carolina, Jonathan Yardley, son of a private women's school headmaster, schooled at the University of North Carolina, once an intern for James Reston of the New York *Times*; and assorted others with credentials much better than mine—people who actually had questions to ask John Kenneth Galbraith (called "Kenny" by Tony Lukas) when he dropped by for a little evening chat with the Niemans.

Of these, I felt closest to Mike McGrady. We were columnists; we had been affected by Breslin, we had covered Vietnam, and we wanted to write books. He had written a couple of unpublished novels in his youth, when he graduated from Yale and struck out for Europe to "play Hemingway," and he had published a collection of his Vietnam columns in a book entitled *A Dove in Vietnam*, written in response to our hero John Steinbeck, who had gone to Vietnam for *Newsday* and disappointed him with a hawkish series on the war. And now, during our Nieman year, he was having some fun with a spoof of the blowzy best-selling sex novels of Jacqueline Susann: with McGrady coordinating the effort, twenty-four writers and editors at *Newsday* were putting together a terrible novel they would call *Naked Came the Stranger* ("Good writing," he warned his authors in a memo, "will be blue-penciled into oblivion"), a book that would make the New York *Times* best-seller list and lead to a sequel McGrady would write about their prank, entitled *Stranger Than Naked, or, How to Write Dirty Books for Fun and Profit.* He was my kind of guy, and so together we romped through the halls of ivy: drinking beer at Cronin's, making trips in his ancient VW to New York (where he consulted on the progress of *Naked* before we went off to get drunk at the Lion's Head in Greenwich Village with the novelist Frederick Exley, whose fictional memoir, *A Fan's Notes,* had made him a legend among writers), and dutifully attending Scotch-and-soda Nieman soirees for civilized discussions about the United States economy or world peace or the social upheavals going on around us. (Tony Lukas was also working on a book, *Don't Shoot! We Are Your Children,* and would sneak radicals like Jerry Rubin into our midst for clandestine meetings.) It was not the classic way to spend a Nieman year, but Mike McGrady performed a great service for me. Tony Lukas has his thing, he told me, and you have yours; find your power and use it.

And then there was Joe Strickland. When I wasn't hanging out with McGrady, I was with Joe. As a boy he had been put on a bus by his mother in Savannah, Georgia, with his name pinned to his shirt, and dispatched to live with his grandparents in Detroit. He had gone to Wayne State University and then gotten a job as a reporter with the Detroit *News,* where, he said, he was the "house nigger" on a "racist newspaper worse than Birmingham." He was there not to write, he told me, but to "keep the editors posted on what the niggers are up to." He guessed that he had become a Nieman not because of his promise as a newsman but because he had given his editors so much grief for their coverage of the black community following the assassination of Martin Luther King that they had found a neat way to get rid of him. The Nieman Foundation had indeed housed its only southerner and only black four doors from each other;

and we did indeed feel at times as though we were on display. Going along with the gag, we would show up at parties held for the Niemans in huge Victorian mansions on Brattle Street, and soon he would be entertaining his group of eager Brahmin liberals with stories of the ghetto while I was enthralling mine with stories about my old man. Joe had left his wife and children at home in Detroit, freeing him for the pursuit of women and good dope and whatever knowledge he might deem useful. He was handsome and charming and articulate, armed with Hemingway's "shit detector," and once I got past the facade he presented—that of the "jiveass nigger," as he put it—I found someone who had much more reason than I to feel intimidated by the elite WASP culture of the privileged East, epitomized by Harvard. One of the great moments of the year, for me, was when we went together for the very first class on African-American history ever taught at Harvard. The little amphitheater was packed with black militants wearing dashikis as a pasty white history professor began by chalking a map of Africa on the blackboard and explaining that blacks had gone into the interior to flush out tribesmen to be delivered to white traders waiting with their ships. Suddenly Joe, looking like anything but a radical with his close-trimmed hair and nifty tweed jacket, arose and boomed, "Just a goddamn minute. You trying to tell us the brothers were responsible for slavery?" The ashen lecturer sputtered, "Well, it's not that simple, you see, but—"

Joe said, "Let's cut out the bullshit, then, and get on with it." The brothers in the dashikis were dumbfounded.

In the fall, Joe and I went to a Wallace for President rally at the Boston Common, where a bristling line of cops had to stand between the angry students and the cheering Southies; and Mike and I became regulars in the famous creative writing class taught by Theodore Morrison, whose students had included John Updike. All along, I had been gathering my strength for an assault on Nashville, and at the beginning of the "reading period" that is the month of January at Harvard, I flew down there and crammed in the bulk of the research for my book. Bill Anderson, the singer I had written about, allowed me to use his lakeside home and his office on Music Row while he was on the road for the entire month, and I found everybody from Chet Atkins to the stage-door guard at the Opry to be most accessible to a boy from Birmingham who could recite every stanza of "Six Days on the Road." In my absence, Joe was taking my young son under his wing and forcing my wife to go along to the various Nieman seminars and socials as his "date." I returned in February, just as a massive snowstorm struck Boston, and began to write. I had kept quiet about the book, since there was a stipulation saying you weren't to "write professionally" during the Nieman year, but the word got out. How sweet it was when the gentleman from the *Times*, Tony Lukas, sidled up to me one day with what I perceived to be a new respect for the Southerner and said, "So . . . a *book*."

Never again in the years ahead as a freelance writer would I have it this good. The advance from my publisher may have been modest, and the monthly Nieman stipend of eight hundred dollars might have seemed small to the others, but I was relatively flush—which says more about the pay scale at the Atlanta *Journal* than about my watching pennies. Our rent on Shaler Lane was cheap, and I walked through the snow every morning to an office made available to me at Adams House, where another adjunct member was Vernon Jordan, soon to become head of the Urban League. Sharing a suite with a historian named Jack Womack, who was being interviewed almost daily in the wake of the publication of his biography of Zapata, I worked on my book. Once I paused to fly to California, for interviews with Merle Haggard and Glen Campbell; and another time I flew back down to Nashville to fill in some holes in my research. On that trip, in the spring of 1969, word came that Ralph McGill had died. I was so broke that I couldn't afford a plane ticket to Atlanta for the memorial service held for him. But I read about it later: how there had been a bomb threat at the church and how a huge throng of people, ranging from liberals like the ex-Birmingham lawyer Chuck Morgan to old conservative enemies like Senator Herman Talmadge, had come to observe him as he lay in state. They had buried him in his "Harvard tie," a striped crimson-and-black number he had bought when the school awarded him an honorary degree. My wife told me one day when I came home from my writing that our daughter's first-grade teacher, a Radcliffe student from Atlanta, had assumed that we would be leaving; her parents had called to say that I was the heir apparent to McGill at the *Constitution*, that I was being groomed at Harvard. I regarded it as blasphemy, silly gossip, an embarrassing slander on the man's great name. Nobody—ever —would fill his shoes.

But he would have liked the book I was writing, I felt. It was about the music he had known as a young man, growing up as he did in the hardscrabble countryside of Tennessee, and I hoped that I was making more than just a book about fiddles and sequined suits-of-light and all-night rides to the next show; that it was really more of a song about the hopes and fears and even the prejudices of people I had known all my life, starting with my own father. It was already too late for me to catch up on all of the reading I had missed as a young man, to veer off into making broad pronouncements about the state of the world when I barely understood ward politics, and I didn't have the proper constitution for that. I could be a loose cannon, as much as my old man, and that is not attractive in a job that requires patience in addition to a deep well of courage. But in my blind stumblings and ruminations during the year at Harvard, I had learned to my surprise that I wasn't altogether without a story to tell.

.   .   .

On moving day, we had just crammed everything that would fit into the U-Haul and I was forcing the doors closed when I heard Joe Strickland bounding down the alley. He had become a regular at our apartment for dinners of spaghetti or southern fried chicken during the school year—indeed, to my great surprise, had been welcomed by my wife and children without regard to his color—but we hadn't seen much of him during the spring. He had stopped coming to Nieman socials, was seldom seen on campus, had even missed being included in the group photograph. He had told me, the last time I had seen him, that he wouldn't be going back to the Detroit *News* but would become an "ivory hunter" for Harvard, beating the bushes for promising black students in order to increase minority enrollment. I had been leaving notes at his apartment and at the little Nieman office, desperately hoping we could see him again before we left, and here he was.

"Couldn't even spell 'Nieman,' and here I are one," I told him. He had grabbed David in a wrestling hold and was mussing his hair.

"They'll forgive you, bro."

"You got to come see us, Joe."

"I can taste the black-eyed peas already." Letting go of my son, he turned on my wife, busy straightening our little girl's hair, and proceeded to kiss this daughter of over-the-mountain Birmingham firmly on the lips. When she responded with a hug, he jumped back and shouted, "*Yawsuh!* The South's gon' rise again!!!"

CHAPTER FIFTEEN

Home Again

Dynamiting had continued in Birmingham, but now it was of a different nature. As though to accommodate the white flight that had begun almost immediately after the bombing of the Sixteenth Street Baptist Church in 1963, a seven-year project was launched that would create a virtual highway to heaven for those whites who could afford it: the blasting of a broad 210-foot-deep swale through the solid rock barrier that was Red Mountain, just beneath the raised right arm of Vulcan. The Red Mountain Expressway required the deepest highway cut in the Southeast, and it was a development long awaited by the residents of the over-the-mountain communities of Mountain Brook, Homewood, and Vestavia Hills, whose daily escapes from the grim realities of downtown had meant hectic stop-and-go drives up the meandering streets that led them from the troubles in the valley up and over the ridges to the serenity of their leafy havens. Now the trip would take only minutes on a graceful eight-lane freeway, lighted and landscaped, exits clearly marked, with a stark view of the strata of minerals that had created the mountain in the first place. And now the Big Mules were being joined over the mountain by middle- and upper-class whites on the run from a city becoming blacker by the day. When they ran out of room in Homewood, Mountain Brook, and Vestavia Hills, the bulldozers rumbled and belched farther southward through the rich bottomlands and scraped out the new towns of Hoover and Pelham, creating what I would come to call the Five White Kingdoms. The Klan had used dynamite for one purpose, the more discreet whites for another.

In the fifteen years that followed the blast at Sixteenth Street Baptist, Birmingham accomplished a facelift. To be sure, much of it was inspired by a need to do something about the city's image; but whatever the reasons, nobody argued that there was anywhere to go but up. Once Bull Connor and his cronies had been thrown out of City Hall, replaced by a cleaner and more efficient mayor-and-council form of government, the way was cleared for making strides that had been too long delayed, especially regarding the economy. The moderate Albert Boutwell had served well as a transitional mayor post-Connor; and when he was replaced in 1965 by George Seibels, a silver-haired can-do Republican businessman with an edifice complex, the whole face of the city changed: skyscrapers went up; steel mills were closed; the black activist lawyer Arthur Shores became a city councilman; Birmingham was proclaimed an "all-American city" by *Look* magazine (which, in 1963, had published an expanded version of Chuck Morgan's bitter adieu); the Birmingham Barons returned to Rickwood, and minor-league professional football and ice hockey came to town; the UAB Medical Center became a major player; and the Sloss Furnace was turned into a museum (where prematurely retired steelworkers gave guided tours and Shakespeare was performed). Finally, Twentieth Street downtown was landscaped and renamed Birmingham Green. When Bull Connor died in 1973 at the age of seventy-five, there was little outward resemblance between the Birmingham he left and the Birmingham of ten years earlier in the showdown with Martin Luther King at Kelly Ingram Park.

But when I returned from the year at Harvard and resumed making sporadic trips to visit my parents, I could see that the soul of Birmingham had changed very little. Bull might be out of power, but his spirit lingered on. "White flight" was a fact of life in cities all over America, once the desperate battle to retain white supremacy had been fought and lost, and Birmingham was carrying this new kind of segregation to a higher artform. The laws of the Supreme Court and the outrage of a nation might be able to force Birmingham to give up its old ways, but that didn't preclude inventing new ones to escape what it perceived as the flooding of the valley by unwashed hordes of blacks. *The niggers are taking over!* One day the first black kids broke through the mobs of angry parents throwing eggs and shrieking insults outside of dear old Woodlawn High, and the next day, it seemed, the school had gone black majority. The Barons might be back, but the neighborhood around Rickwood had become "undesirable," and whites didn't go there anymore. Now that blacks were able to shop in the downtown stores, Pizitz and Loveman's and Blach's simply closed their doors. Chips on their shoulders, muttering about being singled out, pointing fingers at Cleveland and Detroit and even Atlanta, whites were in full retreat, either to the countryside at both ends of the valley or over the mountain by way of this splendid new escape route, the Red Mountain Expressway. The census figures comparing 1960 with 1990, when the city's population went from forty percent to sixty percent black, would be revealing. In that thirty-year period, the city of Birmingham's population shrank by 75,000 and the Five White Kingdoms grew by 74,200. And here were the populations of the five in the 1990 census (with the number of blacks in parentheses): Homewood 22,922 (1,887); Mountain Brook 19,810 (38); Vestavia Hills 19,749 (223); Hoover 39,788 (1,318); Pelham 9,765 (234). The last annexation referendum had been held in 1964 (Homewood actually voted yes, by seven votes, but it was thrown out upon appeal), and there was not likely to be another. Hunkered down on so many Wisteria Lanes, giving their tax money not to Birmingham but to their Mountain Brooks, using the city only as a daytime office, sending their kids to resegregated schools, dining and playing golf and tennis at private clubs, hid-

ing behind Vulcan's back, they were not really from Birmingham. "Brookies" and "Homies," yes; Birminghamians, no.

McGill's last words to me, that things would never be quite
the same again after Harvard, turned out to be prophetic, of
course. Given how far I had come, I probably changed more
during that year than any of the other Niemans except Joe Strickland. What that interlude had done was open up windows for
me: afforded me my first truly close relationship with a black
person, showed me a larger world and broader possibilities,
taught me that my upbringing was just as valid as Tony Lukas's
if I used it properly. (Once, drinking beer at Cronin's and be-
moaning the fact that I had such a woeful knowledge of literature, I was told by Jonathan Yardley that I might as well go with
what I did have: "Don't try to catch up. You're free to be original. Make your own literature.") Nobody seemed to expect me
to stay very long with the *Journal* when I got back that summer
and resumed my column.

As soon as I had finished touching up the book, I conned
my managing editor into letting me hit the road on a two-month
journey of eight thousand miles around the South, writing what
I found in a series called "Paul Hemphill Rediscovers the
South." In those columns, totaling fifty thousand words, I more
or less said farewell to the newspaper business. Following my
nose, writing on a portable typewriter in fleabag motels, searching for a Western Union office, moving on to the next thing that
caught my fancy, I got an education: integration in small-town
North Carolina; a rodeo in Texas; unemployed coal miners in
West Virginia; old black jazzmen in New Orleans; Judge Roy
Hofheinz giving a personal tour of his Astrodome in Houston;
dropping in on the Hemphill graveyard in Robbins, Tennessee;
visiting the Lorraine Motel in Memphis, where Martin Luther
King had died; hanging out with Cuban refugees on Calle Ocho

in Miami and Cajuns in Louisiana and striking black sanitation workers in Charleston and the sad descendants of the Trail of Tears on the Cherokee reservation in North Carolina. It was the basis for a collection of mine entitled *The Good Old Boys*, and I had no doubt that the year of reflection at Harvard had strengthened my voice.

Still, in September, toward the end of the grand tour, there was an incident that told me I had better get out of newspapering while there was time. I had spent a couple of hours with Fred Shuttlesworth in Birmingham, and by mid-afternoon I was using Benny Marshall's typewriter in the sports department of the Birmingham *News* to bang out a column on my hometown, six years after the dynamiting of the church. Benny was returning that day from receiving a national sportswriting award up east somewhere, wasn't expected in the office that day; but while I was writing Alf Van Hoose came to me and said, "You may have a chance to help out an old friend." Benny had called from the airport, was very drunk, was insisting that he had to come by to do some work; and Van Hoose thought that maybe I could take him over to the Bankhead Hotel for a cup of coffee. Presently, the elevator doors opened and there he was, weaving, a paper cup of black coffee in his hand, a silly grin on his face. "Hemp!" he yelled, moving toward me for an embrace. Then, from across the newsroom, there came the booming voice of the managing editor, Vincent Townsend; he was ordering Benny, who had just been named one of the best sports columnists in the country, to ride down the road to the town of Siluria with a photographer to have his picture made congratulating the winner of the *News*'s weekly promotional pick-the-winner football contest. Benny's face drained ("I don't know, Chief—*Shi-luria?*"), and Van Hoose said he would go to Siluria in Benny's place, but first he would take him home. That was my last look at Benny Marshall, who had championed me and given me my first real job, because

I heard on the car radio as I neared Montgomery two hours later what had happened when Van Hoose had let him out: he had stumbled into his house, gone straight to the bathroom, and put a pistol to his head. I remembered what Hemingway had said about newspapering: "Newspaper work will not harm a young writer and will help him if he gets out of it in time." I was flown up to talk with Bill Moyers, publisher of *Newsday*, about being a columnist there, but I didn't see a future for myself on Long Island. Two months later, I quit the *Journal*.

My old man thought I was out of my mind for giving up a steady job when I had a wife and two kids to support, and it failed to mollify him when I pointed out that (a) he had never approved of my working for "them lyin' Atlanta newspapers" in the first place and (b) like father, like son: he was a freelance trucker, and now I was a freelance writer. *The Nashville Sound* had been blessed from the start—right book, right author, right editor, right time—and when it came out in the spring of '70 I had every reason to think it would always be like this. The book was excerpted in national magazines, sold to a book club, got grand reviews everywhere (daily *and* Sunday in the New York *Times*), landed me on the "Today" show with Hugh Downs, and wound up selling seventy-five thousand copies in hardcover editions alone. I spent the summer co-authoring the memoirs of Ivan Allen, Jr. (*Mayor: Notes on the Sixties*), a book that didn't sell in any large numbers but would become valuable as a reference work for authors and others interested in that decade; signed with the same publisher for a two-book deal (an untitled novel and the collection *The Good Old Boys*); and plunged into writing for the magazines: *Sport*, *Life*, the *Atlantic*, *TV Guide*, you name it. It was the natural progression that most writers go through, I felt, wherein a failed jock finds he can write, begins with sports because it's familiar, goes to a "general" newspaper column, tires of newspapering, works for the magazines, finally writes a nonfiction book on something he knows, and then, like any red-blooded American boy or girl, aspires to write a novel.

Every now and then, but only in a glancing way, I had written about my old man. Then, one day, a writer friend named Marshall Frady, himself the son of a South Carolina preacher who had never quite understood his boy's choice of profession, said I ought to rear back and let it fly; Birmingham and the old man made for a fascinating tale, and it sounded right for the *New York Times Sunday Magazine.* My recollection is that I just sat down one day and began to write: "During the week, when he would be on the road somewhere, the days at home began with the muffled slapping of screen doors and the dull starting of cars. . . ." The piece showed his warts, for sure, but all in all I felt as though I had introduced an authentic folk hero to American life. There was, at the end, a measure of redemption: "Instead of bending or running when the blows came pouring down on his head—his wife harping on security and 'respectability,' his children acting ashamed of him, the unions killing his way of life—he stood and fought and, if forced to retreat, was still standing there, bloody, throwing rocks and cussing, when they found him. . . ."

The writing had taken only a week, and I was exhausted when I finished. It had been a bloodletting, as painful for me as it might turn out to be for him, and I felt I had been to a confessional. On another level, that of a writer and his craft, I knew I had been somewhere I had never gone before. I mailed it off to my agent, who sent it on to the *Times Sunday Magazine,* and quickly I heard that they loved the piece and were buying it under the title "Growing Up in Birmingham." Soon the editors even dispatched to Birmingham one of their more famous photographers, George Tames, for a day of shooting my parents at home and the father and son at a truck stop. My parents must have assumed it would be a wonderful little "write-up" like one might read in *Southern Living* or the Birmingham *News* week-end tabloid, and they never asked. I only knew that it was the best piece of writing I had ever done, and hoped they would see that, despite everything, this was a love story. Life went on; my old man drove other trucks, I wrote other stories, my mother made out other Social Security checks. Then the word came from the *Times Sunday Magazine* (from the same copy editor who once had wept over the phone to me during an editing session, telling me he had never been able to make a separate peace with his own father): it would be in that Sunday's magazine. I called the old man to tell him, and he said he would make some special arrangements to get copies when it came out.

What could I have been expecting of parents whose reading ran from the *Upper Room* to *Reader's Digest*? The old man had arranged with a friend of his at the Birmingham airport to have a stewardess on the first flight of the day from New York to bring ten copies of the *Times* with her. He was there at the gate when the plane arrived, paid her for the papers, and raced back home with them. He and my mother tossed aside everything else (the first New York *Times* she had ever laid her hands on), opened the magazine, and, after looking at the handsome photographs George Tames had shot, began to read. By noon, there was a bonfire going in the backyard. And on Monday, with my sister helping them out, they cruised all of the hotels and newsstands in Birmingham where the Sunday *Times* might be arriving and added them to the bonfire. Paul, Jr., had failed them again.

The pain cut both ways. For days and then weeks I waited to hear something from them, some sort of affirmation, any kind of response—"It sort of upset your mama, son, but I reckon she'll get over it"—but it would never come. I had heard about the bonfire through my wife, who got it from my mother and my sister, and later I would hear thirdhand that my mother had positioned herself among her longtime friends at Lake Highlands

Methodist as "poor Velma," whose son had written "that terrible story" about his parents. When the *Times* began forwarding letters from all over the country in response to the piece, every single one of them favorable, I sent a batch of them to my old man with a note joshing that he had become an American folk hero. He never responded. Finally, I gave up. It was the clearest evidence I would ever have that I had truly become a prodigal son in their eyes. That piece in the *Times,* as it turned out, was the last straw.

A third child was born—Molly—and we moved far, far away from Birmingham, farther than ever before, to an island off the coast of Georgia. St. Simons Island was partly a resort, but mostly a small year-round town connected to the mainland and the smelly lumber-and-pulpmill city of Brunswick by a causeway that ran over the Marshes of Glynn rhapsodized by the poet Sidney Lanier. Soon I was buying a two-story house a block from the Atlantic beach, taking an office across from the lighthouse in the village, and settling down to what I hoped would be an unfettered life of living simply and writing my first novel. Atlanta had been too much of a distraction, with its malls and traffic and bars and interesting ladies, and it was here that I intended to make my marriage and my career as a real live author work. Royalties were still coming in from *Nashville*, so small had been the advance, and I was on contract with *Sport* (writing a monthly column called "Paul Hemphill's America" for the magazine I had devoured as a kid); and when I wasn't traveling for *Sport* and other magazines, I was in a steady groove: bicycling to my office, putting down some words, pedaling home for lunch, back at work in the early afternoon, taking the kids to the beach or a nearby swimming pool at the end of the day, rocking Molly to sleep in the front-porch swing while the moon rose over the ocean. I accepted an invitation to fly to Philadelphia and discuss moving up there to write a daily column for the *Inquirer*, which was becoming one of the best papers in the country, but my heart wasn't in it. Better my little island than Philadelphia.

It worked for a while. My son could walk or ride his bike three or four blocks to the island's elementary school, and a school bus stopped in front of the house to take my older daughter across the causeway to the junior high in Brunswick. Both of the schools were integrated by now, the early seventies, and it pleased me to think that David and Lisa's having known Joe Strickland in Cambridge had made them color-blind to a certain extent. Everybody's favorite author in those parts was Eugenia Price, who lived somewhere back in the palmetto marshes and wrote historical romances tied to the Colonial past of "Georgia's Golden Isles"; so, except for a chummy book signing at a local restaurant for *The Good Old Boys* (the lead piece being the *Times Magazine* article on my old man), I was just another shaggy islander who pruned his oleanders and played slow-pitch softball and bicycled with his son and bought chicken gizzards from the grocery store so his daughter could trap crabs off the pier at dusk. The only real disruption came one day when I was met at the little island airport by my wife and the kids, having been somewhere in the service of *Sport* magazine, with the news that the Boston *Globe* wanted a quote from me about Joe Strickland, since "everybody says you were his best friend of the Niemans that year." Joe had been found dead of three bullets fired through his shower curtain, at his ratty apartment in a seedy black neighborhood of Boston, and the cops didn't have a clue. "It could have been drugs, it could have been a woman," the reporter told me. "Either way, the landlord said people were always coming and going at the apartment. He went up there when he heard the shower running all night." When the Nieman office asked me to deliver a eulogy in behalf of our class, I flew up for the memorial service at a chapel on the campus. Mike

McGrady of *Newsday* and Bob Levey of the Boston *Globe* were there, of our Nieman group, and I'm not sure that the smattering of Harvards in the chapel were particularly amused when I told Joe's story about our being their "token nigger and token redneck . . . next door to each other so they can keep their eyes on us."

Fissures in a marriage become magnified when you live in a small place like an island of only five thousand permanent residents. In Atlanta I had been able to leave the house in the morning and take the interstate and spend all day and half the night in another world, connected to my wife only by the telephone (if she could find me), and at Harvard a walk of less than a mile had transported me to a garret somewhere in the catacombs of academia where there wasn't even a phone. Here, though, we became too close, close to the point of suffocation, and the odds of a divorce became shorter rather than longer. I had wrenched her from a forgiving mother and a forgiving hometown, taken her five hundred miles away from the womb—this squeamish and unfinished young woman who had not been given the self-assurance to ride out even the first quarter of college—and now the fissure was becoming the Grand Canyon. I was writing books, but I was married to a woman who, to my knowledge, had never finished reading one. I was wallpapering and painting the house, but she was so enervated that she wouldn't pick up around the place. While she stuffed herself with food, I stretched the cocktail hour down in the village at the Binnacle Lounge. When the book royalties played out and money got tight, the mere mention of her taking a job created a firestorm of wailing and finger pointing and door slamming and rallying the children to her expanding bosom—followed, naturally, by astronomical long-distance telephone bills for calls to her mother and older sister (herself already bitterly divorced) in Birmingham. I had promised myself that there would be no more philandering, and was sticking with it, and that turned out not to be the problem at all. We had been a mistake from the beginning.

There had not been much contact with my parents since the *Times Magazine* piece, and that had been only part of the reason for our estrangement. The biggest was that they, especially the old man, wouldn't let go of the fact that I had taken a wife who fell far short of the standards being set by my sister. Few women could meet the challenge of Joyce, for whom life had stuck on hold in 1962 when she promised to love, honor, and obey this fellow I now perceived as a smug country-club racist. Joyce could cook, sew, and play the perfect hostess. Joyce was lithe and gracious and acquiescent. Joyce took classes in tennis, dancing, ceramics, and picture framing. I couldn't argue the point that my wife paled in comparison—what woman wouldn't? —but I was still trying to hang on, hoping that by some miracle I could avoid the nightmare of my three children growing up without their father being on the premises, and I wasn't getting much help from anybody. Even my wife, without an ounce of self-confidence, was guilty of helping build the wall between my old man and me that had begun with our wranglings over politics and race by whining that we should stay with *her* parents on our rare visits to Birmingham because, "well, you know how your father is." And I had gone along. We would make an obligatory run by my parents' house to show off their grandchildren, the old man and I swigging from a bottle in the basement where he cached his whiskey, the women upstairs ignoring each other, the kids wondering if this would ever end. They were anxious visits that filled me with guilt and sadness that it had come to this between me and this indomitable old cuss, my father, the King of the Road.

Although he wasn't given to careful strategies, it's possible that the old man planned what happened on Labor Day of '74 as a means of forcing an issue that had festered for too long. They had come to visit us for the long weekend, their first trip to St. Simons Island, and there was trouble from the start. He and I had wandered down to the Binnacle Lounge and were having what was, for us, a civilized drink or two—talking baseball, carrying on with the regulars at the bar, pondering a game of eight ball in the back room—when my wife suddenly appeared at the door, urgently motioning for me. My mother, to hear her tell it, was "criticizing everything I do," and I ought to talk to her. I was caught in the middle again. Through the rest of that day and all of Sunday, the air was tense. Then, getting along toward dusk on Monday, Labor Day itself, while my wife was making potato salad and my mother was entertaining her grandchildren, the old man and I were outside watching the chickens barbecue and getting liquored up.

"Y'all ought to give her a break," I told him.

"She don't deserve any more breaks," he said.

"Jesus, Pop, I'm trying to hang on to this marriage."

"You know damned well you married below your class."

I lost it then, throwing my glass against the side of the house and roaring up out of my chair. "Since when did the Hemphills have any class?"

Suddenly the women were shouting and the children were crying as he and I began storming through the house, hurling wild insults, nearly coming to blows in my son's bedroom. "Take off those glasses and fight like a man," he said, and I slung them to the floor, just as my mother threw herself between us, pleading, "Y'all stop, now, I S'wanee, y'all quit it!" Soon I was ordering them to get packing, to hell with dinner, get out of the house, hit the road.

In the gloaming, while my old man threw their stuff into suitcases and my mother took the stunned children for a walk ("Now we love y'all," I heard her say. "This is just between your daddy and your granddaddy"), I stood alone on a little upstairs porch overlooking the ocean and wondered how we had reached this pass. They drove away, confused and hungry, tail-lights growing dimmer as they headed for the village and then the causeway bridge that would take them . . . where? A diner? A motel? All the way back to Birmingham?

My wife came upstairs, shaken, unable to speak. For an instant I thought I saw the glint of a cold warrior who had just won a bloodless coup. "By God," I told her in a measured voice, "you'd better be right." I spent the night alone on a daybed in my office in the village, drinking from a fifth of whiskey until I passed out.

Messy marriage, messier divorce. I had been fooling around with the idea of a book about George Wallace, had even made some reconnaissance trips to Montgomery, so now at least I had a place to go. Soon after the blowout with my old man, I bor-rowed some pocket money from one of my drinking buddies at the Binnacle, left an anguished note for the kids, threw my type-writer and some clothes and books into a rusty old Chevy station wagon I had bought for two hundred dollars, and ran away from home. I took a dollar-a-day sleeping porch upstairs in a turn-of-the-century Victorian house in downtown Montgomery, a pop-ular address over the years for unmarried newspapermen and visiting writers, and became a husband and father on the lam. Now I could fully empathize with the singer Kris Kristofferson, who had told me of similar digs in Nashville where in anguish he had written one of his better songs, "Help Me Make It Through the Night." That Halloween night I was in a Laun-dromat, watching my clothes spin in a dryer, wondering what costumes my kids were wearing as they roved the island without Daddy. The only other person in the Laundromat was an old black man, who looked me over and said, "Mean you ain't out spookin' tonight?" I said, "I did my spookin' when I ran away from home." Not knowing what to make of this, the old man pursed his lips, shook his head, then snapped open the Montgomery *Advertiser* and said—anything for small talk—"See what th' governor was up to today?"

Although I would get on the state's jet with Wallace and his wife, Cornelia, and accompany them to a Democratic party "mini-convention" in Kansas City, where I spent more time with my friends from Georgia in the Jimmy Carter camp than with Wallace, it didn't take long for his people to check me out and advise him to stonewall me. They found, for one thing, that I was a good friend of Marshall Frady, who had written *the* book on their man—a devastating Faulknerian profile, much more than a political book, entitled *Wallace*—and no amount of telling them about my blue-collar roots and being "just an ol' Auburn boy" and how "my daddy's a trucker in Birmin'ham and he thinks the governor hung the moon" would overcome what their sleuthing had found. I was a consort of the forked-tongued Frady; I'd gone to Harvard with those "pointy-headed liberals that ain't got enough sense to park their bicycles straight"; and I was not only a liberal but a liberal of the worst sort: one who had turned on his own people. There would be no Wallace book from me. There would be hardly anything from me, in fact, until I had looked the devil in the eye.

One timorous return to the island showed me that, yes, it would be easier to live without her than with her. Thus, I began my descent. "The best way to handle the first Christmas away is to hope when you sober up it's over," I had been advised by a friend who had been through it, so that's what I did. My kids weren't even being shown my letters, I would learn, and I was being systematically stripped of them. My wife took them to Birmingham, first to crowd together in her mother's house on the wannabe fringes of Homewood and then to take an apartment nearby. "*We* have decided," she would say, meaning a board consisting of her and her mother and her divorced sister, "that it's not a good time to come see the children." Long days, longer nights, full of whiskey and women and pain and shooting pool until dawn. "But David would miss his little friends if he went to visit you." She took a job at a department store in a mall: "As long as you owe me a penny, buddy boy, you don't see your kids." I moved to Tallahassee, teaching some journalism classes at the all-black Florida A&M University. Next I took a cabin in the north Georgia mountains during the summer of '75, somehow finagling to get the two oldest to be allowed to go with me, but she came to fetch them "just for a visit" for a week in Birmingham, and when I moped into their bedrooms the next morning the only thing left behind was a single sock belonging to my ten-year-old son. Now I had nobody—no wife, no kids, no parents, no sister—who could understand any of this. Before I left the mountains, though, I took the first step out of the pits by writing my parents to apologize for the Labor Day fiasco and to pass the news that I was going to divorce "her" at all costs, which promised to be considerable.

The woman I soon would meet and marry is appalled by this sort of talk, saying it belongs in a bad novel or a country song, but she saved my life. I returned to Tallahassee in the fall, this time to teach evening "adult education" writing classes at FAMU, where they hoped to draw from the throngs of bright people who held dull bureaucratic jobs with the state government. I had heard from one of them just before I left the cabin —Susan Farran Percy, managing editor, news bureau, Florida Department of Commerce—saying that several people in her office were interested in my classes, and asking if they needed my permission to enroll. The more the merrier, I gaily responded, then headed out of the hills to the town where my first wife and I had set up housekeeping fourteen very long years earlier. Taking an eighty-five-dollar-a-month apartment in the dank basement of a house occupied by a divorcee and her adolescent son, I tried to make the place livable, and then, on a balmy night in early September, I drove over to FAMU to meet my students. There were about a dozen of them, the sort of crowd I had seen before in the occasional nighttime writing classes I had taught at junior colleges in Atlanta and Brunswick: women, for the most part, who had married too soon after college and now wanted to resume their dreams of writing. And there, among them, was Susan Percy.

My line is that I was so impressed to meet my first Phi Beta Kappa that I married her. She had been just that, at the University of Georgia; but like too many women of her generation (she was born in 1944, in Atlanta) she had married almost immediately and begun to trail her husband around as he pursued his career. He was a Yalie, an archaeologist, and she had followed him first to New Orleans, where he was associated with Tulane University and she became a reporter on a skimpy biweekly newspaper called the *West Bank Guide*; and now to Tallahassee, where he was with the state of Florida and she directed the mailing of press releases and glossy photographs that made Florida sound like paradise.

My class was a convivial little group, given to meeting as often at someone's house or apartment as at the college, and for a while they became my family. A young woman gave me a cat to keep me company; an older woman kept bringing me food and recipes; and with a young reporter from the Tallahassee *Democrat* I would go to watch a willowy young man named Andre Dawson play baseball for FAMU before launching himself toward the major leagues. More importantly, though, there was Ms. Percy. You don't become smitten by a woman when you are pushing forty, but you have reached a point where you know what you want, and I knew early on that I wanted her in a serious way. This was a handsome, wise, desirable, altogether *good* woman—childless, and trapped, as I had been for too long, in a suffocating marriage. She was separated now. Lingering in the booths at Garcia's Cuban restaurant after the others had gone, we talked about books and politics and Birmingham and the nuns who had practically beaten a classical education into her; and we learned, somewhere between the black-bean soup and the third beer, that we loved each other. I divorced in October of '75, she soon afterwards; and in due time we became a couple.

Just as the school year was playing out in the spring, and I was wondering exactly how I intended to get married and support my kids without some kind of regular income, I reluctantly accepted an offer to write a daily column for the San Francisco *Examiner*. San Francisco represented a fresh start in a new town for both of us. For the last time, Susan found herself taking a "spousal" job, this one with a biweekly paper called the San Francisco *Progress*. The highlight of 1976 was our most unchurchly poolside wedding at the home of Wells Twombly, the *Examiner* sports columnist, who had become my best friend out there. We bought the booze; Wells and his wife, Peggy, rustled up the food; their boys' rock band took care of the music; and two hundred friends came to see a former rabbi marry a lapsed Catholic to an Alabama atheist. I had quit the paper by then, this time in a noble snit with my editor over Jimmy Carter (I championed him, but the boss, a Nieman fellow and former Atlanta *Constitution* editor named Reg Murphy, didn't); but I had put together enough money from magazining to resume work on what we now could call my "long-awaited novel" about minor league baseball. By then I was convinced that San Francisco never had the newspapers it deserved for a simple reason: who the hell wants to work in Baghdad by the Bay? We drank its wine and sang its song until, in the spring, we heard the real world calling. David, who had just turned twelve, flew out to join us, and we loaded up the car for the three-thousand-mile drive back home to where we belonged: Atlanta.

CHAPTER SIXTEEN

Other Voices: Epiphanies

Mimi Tynes

During my seven years with Youth Leadership Forum, 278 students went through the program. We selected about forty each year, from high schools all over the Birmingham area: city, county, independent, parochial, and, later, Shelby County schools. Each class was a real cross-section economically, racially, and geographically. We followed a scaled-down Leadership Birmingham format, with six sessions over a six-month period. The first and last were overnight retreats, and the four in between were all-day meetings dealing with local government, economic development, the arts, and human service issues. Each day we visited two or three sites related to the day's topics, and over a year the students met and interacted with as many as one hundred community leaders.

One of the factors that really made YLF work was the quality of the students who wanted to participate in the program. We had a hundred and fifty applicants the first year and selected thirty-six. The last year I was involved we had about three hundred and selected forty-four. They don't have to be top students, but most of them are. The students had to apply, the school couldn't select them or appoint them; so that meant the door was open for kids the school might not have thought about. Part of the selection process was an interview, so you tended to get articulate, bright, and interesting students. They always had a wonderful time discussing issues among themselves and with these adults. They kept saying over and over again, "I didn't know this was happening in Birmingham." It was not our primary intent to encourage them to come back to Birmingham, but many finished YLF with a very positive view of what Birmingham had to offer. A number of YLF alumni are just beginning to graduate from college, so we're getting ready to find out its impact on them as young adults.

Working with these young people was a joy for any adult who had any connections with the program, and it gave us a very positive outlook on the kind of leadership that could be available to the Birmingham area in the future.

One of the specific YLF activities on the opening retreat was to divide the class into small groups and take each group to spend several hours in a community, a neighborhood, or a suburban city. For several years a group went to Muscoda, a small black community just south of Bessemer. The visit made a tremendous impression, because for many it was the first time they had been to somebody's house in a community like that, and they were quite touched, because they found, regardless of the means available, loving and caring families and residents working hard to make their community better. At Kingston, a housing project, they saw kids playing football, people working in the church, former residents who had come back to provide positive role models for teenagers, and area corporations wanting to be involved in their neighborhood.

We also took a group to Mountain Brook. Before the visit we asked, "What are your preconceived notions about the area you are going to visit?" And then, afterwards, "Did the visit do anything to change your perception?" It's much harder to change a perception that people have about an affluent community, and that's what Mountain Brook is: you do have expensive homes, incredibly beautiful residential areas, a city council set up so everybody is working on a voluntary basis, and a number of residents who have time and expertise to give and are giving both. I got my back up a bit when the kids pretty well bashed Mountain Brook in their skit about the visit. I didn't do it, but I wanted to stand up and say, ''Wait a minute—I'm from Mountain Brook, and you're being prejudiced against me.'' Certainly, some residents want to be insulated over the mountain, but there are so many doing so much for the entire Birmingham area, behind the scenes or openly. Birmingham is their home, and they care deeply—some through their time and talents, others with their dollars, and many with as much of both as possible. They want the whole community of Birmingham to be better.

I never think of my community as being Mountain Brook, never have. It's Birmingham as a whole. That's what Youth Leadership Forum is about. It takes kids out of their own small neighborhood, community, or suburban city and gives them a sense of a broader community, shows them that we're all in this thing together. We hope they'll be interested in being involved. And maybe it won't take 'em until they're almost forty years old, like it did for me, to find the particular niche that is right for them.

John Porter

When I was still a boy, tagging along with my father to help him at the mansion, I got to know of a nephew of the Martins' named John C. Tyson. The Tysons also had a big house in Mountain Brook, not far away from the Martins, and they had a maid named Mammy. I was told by my mother, who worked now and then as an upstairs maid for the Martins and the Tysons, that on the day when John C. turned eighteen they called in Mammy and told her that she and the other help weren't to call him ''John C.'' anymore, that from now on it was ''Mr. Tyson.''

When the Tysons moved to Montgomery, they ''gave''

Mammy to the Martins, and Mammy promptly fired everybody except my daddy so she could take control of the house. She let him stay on because he was mild-mannered, no threat, and he worked outside. The Tysons had left some things in their house in Mountain Brook, so one day in the summer Mammy and my father were sent over there to clean up the place. When my father got home that night, he had toys and clothes and things out of the attic that had been left by John C. It was Christmas in July. In my childhood, all because of Mammy, I played with John Tyson's toys and worn his clothes.

Many years later, around 1978, Governor Wallace said in the paper that if a black man was on the list he would possibly be inclined to appoint him to the state board of pardons and paroles. So I went down to Montgomery with my résumé, went around to see all of the folks in charge of making recommendations. The supreme court justice, the lieutenant governor, they all told me that they appreciated it and they would look at it. Well, pretty soon I found myself sitting before a Judge John Tyson. I wasn't sure whether he was the Mobile John Tyson or the Birmingham John Tyson. He said, "We're meeting tomorrow morning on this, but I'll read your résumé and give you consideration." Then he looked at it and said, "You know, I'm from Birmingham, too." I thought, Oh, Lord, this is Mammy's John C. I said, "Judge, I think we know some of the same people." When I told him I was Robert and Emma's son, and I knew Mammy, he pulled out a file of old pictures and we reminisced for quite a while. Finally, he said, "Tomorrow morning, I want you to be my nominee."

Sure enough, the next day I was on the list. The two black state senators had told me, "You can't get it. George's best friend, the guy who headed up his candidacy for President, is on the list. No way you can get it." Sure enough, George didn't send my name up; he sent up his best friend, this guy named

Ventress. But then some things started happening. To make the story short, the senate got tied up on this for two days until Ventress finally removed his name and the governor sent my name in. John Tyson had put my name up and then lined up fourteen senators behind me. I got the job.

CHAPTER SEVENTEEN

Digging In

In spite of all its annoying boosterish prattle about being a "city too busy to hate" and "the next great international city," Atlanta by the late seventies was as good a place as any for us to settle down. Of my previous addresses, the most promising had been St. Simons Island, with its beaches and good salt air and small-town ambience; but, of course, my injudicious first marriage had made the island something less than paradise. Atlanta was not only Susan's hometown, it also was where she finally might find jobs in editing or writing that were equal to her considerable abilities. This wasn't New York (it was too late for that), but there were certainly better job opportunities for her in Atlanta than there had been in Tallahassee, New Orleans, and San Francisco. Now, at last, she had a husband who was trailing *her* around. It didn't much matter to me anymore where I lived, as long as she was happy and thriving, although there were times when it saddened me to find that I had so divorced myself from Birmingham that I wasn't really *of* any place; I had just made my bed there, whether it was Augusta or St. Simons or San Francisco.

Atlanta, this time around, would become the place where finally I would put down some roots. We started by buying a leaky little bungalow in a funky in-town neighborhood not two miles from the World's Tallest Hotel; and while I worked on books and magazine pieces and even did a stint as a commentator on National Public Radio's "All Things Considered," Susan held a number of editing jobs that eventually led to her becoming managing editor of *Atlanta*, one of the better city magazines in the country by the nineties. Her mother and most of her childhood friends were there, something I envied her for; and I had plenty of friends from my first go-round who had stayed on, among them Anne Rivers of the days on the Auburn *Plainsman*, now married and on her way to becoming the best-selling novelist Anne Rivers Siddons. The neighborhood held an interesting stew of freelance carpenters and artists and social activists and octogenarians; my old haunt Manuel's Tavern was a walk away; and whenever we felt the need for entertainment it was there: big league sports, good restaurants, nightclubs. Both the city and our street were egalitarian places to call home, a far cry from the self-conscious class strata I remembered from Birmingham, and so we hunkered down to make a life together. I found myself gleefully joining in on the Birmingham jokes one heard in Atlanta—like the one about the Delta pilot, upon announcing the approach to the Birmingham airport in a different time zone, advising passengers to set their watches back "about twenty years."

For the first time in my adult life, it seemed, I had done something right in the eyes of my parents when I married Susan Percy. I might still be banging off the walls a bit in the manner of the old man—cowboy boots, beard, whiskey, given to spontaneous judgments ("At least I don't have to hold a mirror to his mouth to see if he's still breathing," Susan would say, alluding to her first husband)—but she obviously had calmed me down, and singlehandedly created a truce between me and my parents on the simple grounds that it was foolish for us to fight like that. Mama saw a smart woman whose education and career were every bit as valid as the path that Joyce had chosen. The old man saw a woman who would simply walk away when he tried to launch a racial tirade, make him feel like white trash. A memorable moment came when he began to blather "Niggers-

JewsandCatholics'' but suddenly caught himself and looked at Susan and mumbled, ''Present company excluded, of course.''

Early in 1979 Susan produced a baby (Martha) and I published my first novel (*Long Gone*). The baby came easier. The novel was placed in the mid-fifties and had to do with a Class D baseball club called the Graceville Oilers, meaning I had gotten something, anyway, out of that distant failed attempt to play professional baseball. But it seemed as though it had taken forever for me to produce what turned out to be a slender little effort, and I knew why: I had spent too long at the teat of journalism, and I didn't recognize a ''point of view'' when I saw one. Although the sales were piddling, the book would get great reviews in places like *Sports Illustrated* and the *New York Times Book Review*, land me on the ''Today'' show again, and eventually become a Home Box Office cable television movie. That was heady stuff, to be sure, and even though I knew I had gotten some breaks vis-à-vis its publication—the flowering of interest in baseball, a serious effort by the publisher, and the gentle treatment often accorded first novelists by critics —I allowed my good fortune to lure me down a treacherous path.

Meanwhile, in Birmingham, the makeover continued apace. The most visible of the heavy-industry operations, Sloss Furnace and Ensley Mill, had shut down for good, and now less than ten percent of Jefferson County's population was even remotely involved in the making of iron and steel. The major employer in town was UAB and the associated medical complex, taking up twenty-five square blocks in Southside where once had been that cluster of ethnic neighborhoods around Ramsay High. All in all Birmingham had become a pretty town now that the air was clear and the unsightly tin-roofed mills had been either dismantled or simply camouflaged by kudzu. There were glistening new skyscrapers downtown; Birmingham Green; an expanded airport; more seats at Legion Field, where the annual "Iron Bowl" game was played between Alabama and Auburn; and now you could actually eat the fish you caught out of East Lake. The slogan created by the chamber of commerce in 1962—"It's Nice to Have You in Birmingham"—might have been premature, but nearly twenty years later there appeared to be some justification for it. Even so, with the black mayor, Richard Arrington, and his black-majority city council calling the shots at City Hall, whites had continued to take flight over the Red Mountain Expressway.

My old man, of course, didn't like the new Birmingham one bit. Truckers age fast from their disjointed lives on the road— eating poorly, sleeping irregularly, having their innards jostled, living with the constant tension of pulling heavy loads through traffic—and he, as a scrambling independent "leased operator," had aged faster than most. By the time he was sixty, in 1971, he had sold his trucks and become semiretired, taking little one-shot jobs thrown his way by a couple of old friends in the surplus tire business. Now he would drive or be flown to an air base, where he would inspect huge lots of discarded aircraft tires, and if he won the bid he would load them onto a rented rig and haul them back to Birmingham or Atlanta, where they would be recapped and sold for use with earth-moving equipment. Often he was paid not in cash but in holidays for him and Mama, so as not to disturb his Social Security standing. Typical was a trip to San Francisco while Susan and I were living there: they flew out and stayed with us for a couple of nights while he inspected a batch of surplus tires in the Bay Area, and when he was done they continued to Seattle, where they boarded a ship for an Alaskan cruise paid for by Sexton Tire Company in Atlanta. In contrast to those glorious bustling days of the regular run to the tire plants in Ohio and Maryland during the forties and fifties, he had been left with too much time on his hands.

Now, with the steel industry virtually dead and a black

mayor ensconced at City Hall, nothing was right in his world. Trips to Birmingham, to pick up my children from my first marriage and run them by for dinner and a visit with their grandparents, became nightmares for me and for the kids. Rather than inquire about their lives, or mine for that matter, he maintained snarling monologues assailing the usual suspects and adding a whole new cast befitting the times: the Supreme Court, "that nigger Arrington," environmentalists (for "seeing that there ain't no more smoke in Birmingham"), the Democratic party. From the stuffy paneled den, where he had been raving and playing the piano over the squawks and drone of the Nashville Network on the television set, he would lurch down the basement steps for a belt of whiskey straight from the bottle he had kept "hidden" from Mama for years, then come roaring back upstairs to pick up where he had left off. Most of his fellow truckers had died before reaching their sixties, leaving him with no friends. Golf? Forget it. Fishing? Too dull. They had bought a trailer on a lake in central Florida, but he found that the only thing to do down there was play Bingo on Wednesday nights. "Sometimes I'll hear an ol' boy grab another gear out on the highway, and it sort of gets to me," he once told me. Without his truck, all he had was his whiskey and his memories. More than once, to Mama's great consternation, he barged into the studios of WBRC-TV, up on Red Mountain next to Vulcan, to sit in at the piano on "The Country Boy Eddie Show" at five o'clock in the morning.

I must say, though, that he went out with style. Regardless of whether he or Mama or my sister knew it, he had a small fan club among my friends in Atlanta. They were writers, for the most part, and they remembered the *New York Times Sunday Magazine* piece, had seen the two-by-three-foot oil painting of him above my rolltop desk (an original, based on a George Tames photograph, used to illustrate a magazine reprint of "Growing Up in Birmingham"), had heard my stories of him:

the heroic run to Portland on the eve of the war; his "three million miles without an accident chargeable to myself"; his devotion to Bull Connor and George Wallace. And so in August of 1981 I announced that there would be a brunch at our house in Atlanta to celebrate his seventieth birthday, and that the man himself would be in attendance. There was much excitement as the day approached—Annie Siddons and her husband, Heyward, would be there, as would my cousin Jim Stewart, an editor for the *Constitution* who had just returned from his own stint as a Nieman fellow at Harvard—but then, three or four days before the event, I couldn't find him. Frantically, I called around, and finally located him at an air base in the Texas Panhandle; he had won a bid on a lot of discarded 250-pound B-52 tires, was rolling them up a ramp into a trailer all by himself, and by nightfall should be ready to haul them back to Sexton Tire in Atlanta. "Tell Mama I'll be there when I get there," he said. He made it on time, shaved and showered and put on some "dress-up clothes," and was standing at the door to greet the celebrants as they arrived for eggs and Bloody Marys. As it turned out, the trip to Texas at the age of seventy was the last hurrah for the King of the Road.

Later in the year, there would be a final shining moment in my parents' lives. On November 19, my sister and I hosted a golden wedding anniversary party at her house on the hill in Mountain Brook. Invitations had gone out to family and friends, and I had interested a *Post-Herald* columnist in writing about their free wedding on the stage of the Ritz Theater during the Depression. The house was cheerful and toasty, filled with my aunts and uncles and cousins from all over, plus survivors from the old neighborhood in Woodlawn and a woman who had baby-sat me in the thirties and even my old childhood chum Wallace Graddick. Mama sent shivers of envy through the other women when she wore the dress she had been married in and advised one and all that it had fit perfectly; she hadn't let it out an inch.

With a crowd of three thousand gathered for the showdown at
Kelly Ingram Park in downtown Birmingham on Friday, May 3,
1963, black youths were sent cartwheeling by special water cannons
capable of tearing bark from a tree at one hundred yards.

- -

Frustrated when demonstrators refused to disperse, Birmingham Police Commissioner Bull Connor ordered eight "K-9 units"—policemen with German shepherds—to threaten the crowd.

The world watched in horror, via television, as the police dogs were unleashed on black protesters, some of whom were first-graders.

Students clung to curbs, bushes, utility poles, or whatever was available, under blasts from the water hoses. Two young girls had their clothes stripped away, and others were sent dancing like puppets on a string.

Although only five demonstrators required hospitalization after the day of dogs and hoses, the world was outraged. President John F. Kennedy said the civil rights movement "should thank God for Bull Connor. He's helped it as much as Abraham Lincoln."

Paul Hemphill in Vietnam, June 1966, as a columnist for the *Atlanta Journal.*

BELOW: Paul Hemphill (in striped jacket) during press conference with Robert F. Kennedy at the Atlanta airport, during Kennedy's campaign for the Democratic presidential nomination in 1968.

Class of 1969 Nieman Fellows at Harvard. Far left, second row, is Mike
McGrady, then of *Newsday*. Far right, front row, is J. Anthony (Tony) Lukas,
a *New York Times* reporter at the time. Next to him (cigarette in hand) is
Jonathan Yardley, now book critic for *The Washington Post*. Paul Hemphill is
in the second row, above shoulders of Yardley and Gisela Bolte of *Time*.
Noticeably absent on the day of the photo is Joe Strickland of *The Detroit
News*, Hemphill's friend and the only black Nieman Fellow that year.

LEFT: Paul
Hemphill with a
hopeful young
country singer—
John Wesley
Ryles—in a
Nashville record-
ing studio,
January 1969,
while author was
researching his
first book, *The
Nashville Sound*.

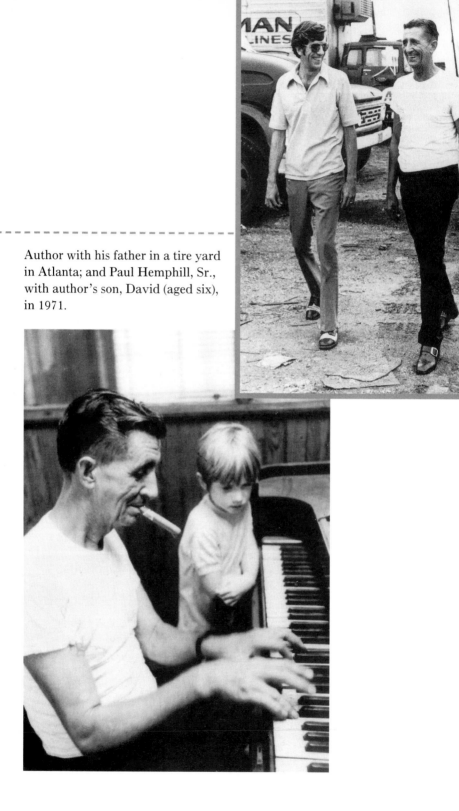

Author with his father in a tire yard in Atlanta; and Paul Hemphill, Sr., with author's son, David (aged six), in 1971.

Author and his father ca. 1986 in den of parents' last home in Birmingham. Father had had his stroke by then. Cap reads *Poole Truck Line*, for which father had hauled stuff.

RIGHT: Paul Hemphill and his wife, Susan Percy, on the beach near Charleston, South Carolina, 1988.

Children of Paul Hemphill, Christmas 1987. Left to right: Lisa, Martha, Molly, David.

Birmingham Mayor Richard Arrington during dedication of Kelly Ingram Park, September 1992.

BELOW: The Civil Rights District in downtown Birmingham, dedicated thirty years after the violence of the early sixties. Foreground is Kelly Ingram Park. Upper left (domed) is the Civil Rights Institute. Upper right (twin cupolas) is Sixteenth Street Baptist Church.

The old man wore a ghastly double-knit suit, and except for the visits we made to his four-door Chrysler, where he had a bottle stashed in the trunk, he was on his best behavior. Almost all of the conversations that I overheard as I floated through the rooms dealt with how tough times had been during the Depression and how sweet they had been in the twenty years thereafter. It was clear that those had been the times of their lives. No one spoke of the sixties.

My life began to unravel shortly after the anniversary party. There are scores of theories about what "causes" alcoholism, ranging from sloth to a bug in the genes; but whatever the reasons, I found at the beginning of the eighties that I couldn't leave alcohol alone. Almost every writer I knew drank, some of them much more prodigiously than I, and I had regarded it as an occupational hazard, something that went with the territory—until I reached my early forties and discovered that I was having vodka and orange juice for breakfast. I had deluded myself into thinking that I was doing okay—a novelist now, a network radio commentator, a loving husband and father—but evidence was beginning to build that whiskey was no longer my friend. I picked up a couple of drunk-driving tickets (once on a camping expedition with my son), screwed up several magazine assignments, sank to writing a fifty-dollar-a-week column for a ragged little underground paper in Atlanta, began bouncing checks, and more than once found Susan crying herself to sleep. There's a joke about the drunk whose doctor asks him if he's ever thought about joining Alcoholics Anonymous and the guy says, "Aw, hell, it ain't *that* bad." I didn't think it was that bad, either, so around '82 I began the first of several attempts at stopping cold-turkey. My old man had been one of my best drinking buddies, even if it often had led to trouble, and he was shocked to hear I had quit: "Hell, I could quit any damn time I had a reason to, but I ain't been shown no good reason yet."

It worked for a couple of years—sort of. In 1981 I had put together another collection of magazine and newspaper pieces for my fifth book, *Too Old to Cry*, but the well seemed to go dry as I concentrated on living in a strange, new, sober body. By the first of 1984, figuring I had won the fight, I tackled two books back-to-back: a novel called *The Sixkiller Chronicles*, its protagonist being an old country singer who was my old man in disguise, and an account of a hike of the Appalachian Trail with my son. On a morning in March of that year, exhausted from pounding out the novel in fifty-seven days flat, I dropped off the manuscript at the post office and Susan drove David and me to the southern terminus of the Appalachian Trail in the north Georgia mountains. I would entitle the book *Me and the Boy*, because I intended it to be a great deal more than just a narrative of a walk in the woods. This was going to be, all at once, a celebration of life, a farewell to alcohol, a coming-together with my son, and, I hoped, the chance to make some kind of separate peace with my old man and with Birmingham itself. The best place to try doing all of this, it seemed to me, was somewhere far from the normal distractions: in the deep woods.

There was a lot of sorting-out for both of us to do as we strapped on our packs and stepped out on the 2,100-mile trail that rides the spine of the Appalachians from Georgia to Maine. As the only son, David obviously had suffered more from the divorce than the two girls. He had just turned nineteen and had failed miserably in his first quarter at the University of the South in Sewanee, Tennessee, in spite of a stunning score on his Scholastic Aptitude Test, and it seemed a propitious time for him to be taking a sabbatical. The same, of course, could be said for me. In times of emotional stress, some people turn to religion, others to psychiatry, but this seemed to be the best therapy for us: father and son, side by side for six solid months in the forest, working things out. There would be many times when unspoken animosities would finally erupt (*"Didn't you even love Mom?"*

"Watch it, son—whiskey's in the Hemphill blood"), and often it felt like an ongoing confessional and general bloodletting. But that's what it was supposed to be, and on that level the project was a success. My knees weren't up to the task, eventually forcing us to abort the trek at Harpers Ferry, West Virginia, after nearly one thousand miles. But, as my friend Joe Cumming of *Newsweek* used to say, we had "seen the elephant and heard the owl" on those one hundred days and nights away from civilization as most people know it. At last, I had embraced my son; and also, perhaps just as importantly, I had made a unilateral decision about how I should regard my father. There was the Good Daddy and there was the Bad Daddy, and I was determined not to allow the sins of the latter to outweigh the good. And as the years went by, there would be evidence that David had made the same decision regarding me, *his* father.

We had a few more steps to go. I began swimming in whiskey again after our return from the trail, and I finally turned myself in at AA when Susan kicked me out of the house on Thanksgiving weekend of '84. While I was trying to assemble *Me and the Boy* during the daytime and attending AA meetings at night, David was discovering booze and marijuana at Sewanee and, consequently, was being shown the door. In the spring of '85, my own recovery somewhat tenuous, I raced to Birmingham after David's half-assed attempt at suicide (the boy knew his metaphor and symbolism, all right, trying to asphyxiate himself with our Peak I camp stove in a car that fortunately was anything but airtight) and hustled him to his first AA meeting on Birmingham's Southside. By the time the book came out in the spring of '86, we both had managed to stabilize somewhat: I took *Me and the Boy* on the road and he enrolled at UAB, at one glorious point scoring perfect 4.0 grade averages in philosophy in successive quarters. Lisa had graduated from the University of Alabama, become a born-again Christian (surprise, surprise, Daddy!), and taken a job at the publishing house attached to

Southern Living in Birmingham; Molly was turning out to be slim and beautiful and bright, a student at Homewood High; Martha was in the first grade, fortunate now to be growing up in a stable household where ideas and books were discussed over the dinner table.

The old man did not go gentle into that good night. For forty years, three million miles of gallivanting across the countryside without a map because he knew it so well, he had been defined by his truck. "Your daddy's the most honest man and about the best truck driver I've ever known," said Toby Sexton, the tire man in Atlanta, his last true believer. He had no hobbies, no buddies, only his wife and his truck and his piano. Trucking was all he knew, and there were times, toward the end, when I would privately muse that my old man had been a lot better at what he did for a living than I was. He certainly had his warts, the racism being the worst of them all; but as his life wound down I began trying to comfort myself with an old country saying that Ralph McGill had used as the title for a collection of his columns: "The fleas come with the dog." Maybe it was put better by Mama once after he had set my kids to crying with a tirade about their mother on one of their rare visits, when I asked her how she was putting up with him in his declining years: "I've thought about leaving him, son, but he's a good man and I love him." It was clear that she was suggesting I do the same.

He went down with a stroke in the spring of 1985, as he roared toward his seventy-fourth birthday, and they literally strapped him to his bed at the hospital to keep him from tearing out the needles and tubes jabbed into his wiry body so he could go out for a drink ("Hell, I've gotta get out of here," he kept yelling in his delirium; "I got to make Anniston in the morning"). When he returned home, bent over and so shaky he could barely feed himself, the only way he could calm down was by drinking and playing the piano. Soon after that, my mother was diagnosed as having Alzheimer's, the same disease that had snuffed out Mama Nelson and had already made a vegetable of my aunt Ethel Lacey, prompting my sister to arrange for our parents to move into a room at a hushed Methodist nursing home in Birmingham.

This was the pits for the old man, now a cowboy who had been sent to the barn. "Sometimes Mama don't even know who I am, son," he would say, tears welling up. He kept the good Christians at Fair Haven on their toes—pounding Hank Williams medleys on the white baby grand in the main lobby, swigging in broad daylight from the bottle he kept in the trunk of the Chrysler parked out front, shouting about the "nigger" attendants, startling the dying old widows in wheelchairs by jogging through the halls—and they seemed relieved when he began spending most daylight hours at the house in East Lake, which he had refused to sell, so he would have a refuge where he could "do any damned thing I please." Finally, when his shenanigans became too much, the directors at the nursing home said either he would straighten up or both he and "poor Mrs. Hemphill" would be kicked out. The only solution, it seemed, was to send him to an alcohol rehabilitation place in Hattiesburg, Mississippi.

It was called Pine Grove Alcoholic Recovery Center, and they may still be telling stories about him. When he checked in and they told him he was the oldest and the healthiest of the sixteen there, he told the doctor, "Don't feel bad, Doc, we all make mistakes"; and when it came his turn to speak at his first formal AA meeting, he stood and puffed up and said, "My name is Paul Hemphill, Sr., and I'm not guilty of a damned thing but living." He had, in fact, so convinced the other "inmates" of his not being alcoholic, of having been "put in prison by my own daughter" when he really ought to be at the bedside of his dying wife, that the directors there feared a revolt and pondered asking him to leave.

He solved the problem for them. A doctor called me one day

and said he was standing at the main desk, bags packed, wanting "the money y'all stole from me when I checked into this joint" so he could catch the next bus to Birmingham. He snatched the phone away and told me he was leaving, if it meant walking all the way home. He handed the phone back to the rattled young doctor, who said the next bus didn't leave until ten o'clock that night, and I extracted a promise from him: "Personally put him on the bus, because if you let him hang around at the station long enough he'll call the wrong guy 'nigger' and I'll never see my father alive again." He rolled into the Birmingham bus station at dawn the next day, took a cab to the house in East Lake, and caught up on the whiskey he had missed.

He spent the last two months of his life dividing his time between 403 North Eighty-ninth Street and Fair Haven: making an effort to stay sober and look his best for a visit with Mama, who by then had almost lost her mind to Alzheimer's and was in a special health care unit, then returning to the house to booze alone, wander the rooms, inspect his treasures in the basement, undoubtedly to cry. He was in a panic by now, as frightened of death as anyone I'd ever known, and when he called me in Atlanta on three consecutive nights (something he had never done) I drove over that weekend for a visit.

I got to the house at noon and had to wait a half-hour until he rolled up, freshly shaved and well dressed, having been to Fair Haven for a visit with Mama. Since he was too embarrassed to eat in public places now because of his shakes, we went through the drive-in window at Andrews Barbecue in East Lake. Back at the house, we sat in the den and shoveled in our plates of barbecue and beans and cole slaw.

"I'm just an old man, waitin' to die," he said, tears coming again, wiping barbecue sauce from his lips with the sleeve of his shirt.

"Hell, Daddy," I lied, "the King of the Road will never die."

"Might as well." He waited for another jet to rumble over the roof, flaps down for landing, rattling the windows. "Ain't much demand for me anymore."

"There's Mama. You could do it for Mama."

"She don't even know who I am, son. I'll walk into that cell they keep her in and she'll look at me and say, 'Have you seen my husband? Paul? He was here a while ago.' I tell you, boy, it seems like the Ritz Theater just happened yesterday. . . ." He was blubbering now.

A writer never sleeps. Unknown to my father, although I suspect he knew I wasn't going to let our lives go unreported, I had already begun to scribble the opening pages of a novel I would call *King of the Road.* The prologue, already written, was a flashback to a father and his young son settling into a battered truck in the middle of the night, the first leg of a great adventure. "Truckin's good enough for me," the man says, "and I notice there ain't nobody starvin'." This time I planned to bring him in on the book, once I really got it going, by spending time with him and plumbing his memory. That would be good for both of us, especially the old man at twilight.

One night about two weeks after that visit with him, I was in my office at home, shutting down for bedtime, when the phone rang. Joyce's voice broke the minute I answered. "Paul," she said, "Daddy's dead." He had snatched Mama out of Fair Haven the day before and brought her home for her seventy-sixth birthday, both so addled that they didn't celebrate it at all, and at some point during the afternoon as she slept he was hit by a massive heart attack and fell to the floor in the dining room. Mama could only remember later that she wandered into that part of the house, looking for him, and she saw him on the floor, his head bloody from the fall, saying, "Get help . . . get help." He was dead when the paramedics arrived.

As I took the news, I felt his presence. Staring back at me

was the oil portrait, with those tortured blue eyes and the floppy ears and the lined bronze face that looked like an eroded river-bank. He had done a lot of living, my father; and as I returned his stare, a jerky black-and-white newsreel flashed through my mind: him playing the piano, rolling his cigar in his mouth, throwing a ringer in horseshoes and kicking his heels; the two of us at ball games, at the Opry, pulling the Blue Ridge at night. There were no images of our bad times, only the good.

Dazed, turning off the lights for the evening, I shuffled to the bedroom. Susan was propped up with a book, and I went over to sit on the edge of the bed. My throat was dry, and I wasn't sure of where I was.

"What's wrong, hon?" she said.

"My daddy died."

"Oh, Paul." She took me in her arms, and I began to jerk and cry for the first time in my memory. "I'm so sorry," she said.

"He could be a sonofabitch," I said. "But by God, he was *my* sonofabitch."

In Birmingham, after taking care of business and holding a "viewing" at the funeral home, I chose to spend the night before the burial at the house in East Lake. The piano was still adorned with the framed photographs of George Wallace and Lester Maddox, and the television seemed permanently set for the Nashville Network, but now there was a dark red blood spot in the carpet where he had fallen after striking his head on the dining room table. The house was ghostly quiet, swirling with memories, and I stayed up well past midnight: wandering the hallway, where every inch of wall space was covered with family photographs; rummaging through boxes of snapshots dating to the late thirties, when I was riding my tricycle; finding cigar boxes that held receipts for gasoline he had bought during the fifties. I had been aimlessly watching Channel 6, WBRC, when I fell asleep in my clothes on the sofa, and I bolted awake just before daybreak when I heard my old man's name being called. It was Country Boy Eddie himself: "We've lost a dear friend, folks," he was telling those in the television audience who might remember the audacious old trucker who used to drop in and play the piano at daybreak. "Paul Hemphill died yesterday. . . ."

It was, as they say, "a nice funeral." Joyce and I decided against a religious service, understanding the blasphemy in that, and cut straight to the burial at Forest Hill Cemetery. The pallbearers included Toby Sexton, the tire man from Atlanta who was his last good friend, and when the hapless preacher lied about having heard Daddy playing "Amazing Grace" one day on the baby grand piano at Fair Haven, Toby and I had to contain ourselves. Mama sat between Joyce and me under the tent, and nobody can be sure whether she knew that her love was gone. The cemetery was on a knoll overlooking the confluence of Interstates 20 and 59, and the one thing everyone did remember from that day was that the preacher kept being interrupted by the roar of eighteen-wheelers down below, grabbing gears, whining, belching smoke, making time, headed west, leaving Birmingham.

Part Four

RETURNING

CHAPTER EIGHTEEN

Siblings

And so, early in 1992, soon after my fifty-sixth birthday, I leased an apartment on Birmingham's Southside where, from the landing outside my door, there was a splendid view of Vulcan's statue on the crest of Red Mountain. With Daddy dead and Mama dying, with my first three children having survived the divorce and begun to thrive to varying extents, with the mere passage of years, I figured that maybe now the coast was finally clear enough for me to take a longer look at the city of my birth. Having an apartment would give me a small measure of permanence—more, at any rate, than I might have gotten from checking into a different motel every time I drove the three hours from Atlanta—and from there I would poke around town at my leisure throughout the spring and summer. I would put in a phone, haul our old television set from home, buy a spare word processor, even outfit the place with kitchen and bathroom stuff. I would decorate the walls with a map of the city and the well-traveled oil portrait of my old man. I would become a citizen of Birmingham for a while: shopping at Bud's Grocery across the street, cooking and working and sleeping in the apartment, getting my news from local radio and television and the *News* and the *Post-Herald*, going out to see the Barons play, feeding the pigeons at Linn Park.

At mid-morning on St. Patrick's Day I was crossing the Alabama line on Interstate 20, to officially take residency, when my mother died, a month short of her eightieth birthday. Unlike my

father's death, which had come like a thunderbolt, Mama's passing was regarded as "a blessing" by those who came by Roebuck
Chapel the next night. She had lingered with Alzheimer's for the
last four years of her life, unaware that her sister Ethel was
strapped to a bed in the same wing of Fair Haven with the same
disease, and there were dry eyes all around when her casket was
put into the ground beside my father's at Forest Hill Cemetery.
There were two notable differences between her burial ceremony
and my father's: this time the preacher knew whom he was eu-
logizing, and the gaggle of rough-handed workingmen at grave-
side had been replaced by church ladies. My sister and I sat alone
together beneath the tent with the knowledge that only now, with
both parents gone and with grown children of our own, had our
childhoods finally ended.

There are those who say, not entirely in jest, that surely my
sister and I were separated at birth. How could such a sweet,
efficient, forgiving soul as Joyce be even remotely related to Paul,
an emotional, caterwauling misanthrope who changed addresses
as often as he changed socks? Once in the early eighties, I casually asked in the postscript of a rare letter to her, "Joyce, are
you happy?" I suppose I wanted to know whether her life was
going as badly as mine was at the time: swimming in booze,
career stalled, kids being withheld, ex-wife raising hell, second
wife crying into her mirror to see the lines I had put on her face,
at another impasse with the old man. I had almost forgotten my
question when Joyce came right back with what she said was
"the hardest letter I've ever had to write." Yes, she wrote in the
perfect Palmer-method cursive she had learned at Minnie Holman, she was happy and fulfilled: "I have the church, and I have
Jim. . . ." With that, it occurred to me, she had said it all.

It was clear in our childhood years that she was her mother's
daughter and I was my father's son. Children of our generation
and social class were reared like that. *We will raise a family / A*

boy for you, a girl for me. . . . The boys played ball and got dirty and learned the manly arts of painting the house and mowing the lawn and fixing things when they broke, all of these considered to be preparations for their becoming the man of their house. The girls, on the other hand, were set on a course toward marriage almost from the day they were born: how to cook and sew, how to be graceful, how to catch and keep a man who would be a "good provider." And during those glorious years of growing up on Fifth Court South in Woodlawn, we both made our parents proud: Paul, Jr., with his baseball and Mary Joyce with her dancing were exactly what Paul and Velma had in mind. We stayed on course as we reached our twenties: I was pursuing an acceptable career as a sportswriter right there in Birmingham; Joyce, coming along behind me at Auburn, was pursuing a degree and a husband. But then Paul went on, "married below [his] class," and began picking up funny ideas in Atlanta and at Harvard. They could deal with her, but not with me. Almost in a blink, I became the wayward son and she became the good daughter.

Time froze for Joyce on Mother's Day of 1962 when she married Jim at Woodlawn Methodist Church, promising to love, honor, and obey. The life they built was out of "Father Knows Best." After living for a couple of years in an apartment, saving their money, they built the three-bedroom brick house in Mountain Brook where they would stay forever. While he brought in a paycheck, doling out an allowance to her, she became the dutiful housewife: cooking, sewing, washing, cleaning, paying the bills, raising two boys and a girl, her only outside interests being her college sorority alumnae group and her church and hobbies like tap dancing and ceramics. She was totally subservient to her husband, himself a throwback to a past time, a rigid man who took the kids down to the basement to dish out corporal punishment. My first wife and I were in the backseat of their Cadillac once, ready to go somewhere with them, when Joyce got in and angrily slammed the shotgun-side door, obviously at the end of a snit. Jim got out from behind the steering wheel, slowly walked around the front of the car, gently opened the door, then said to her in a level voice, "Don't ever slam *my* car door again." She said nothing.

Now, thirty years after the wedding, Joyce had become Mama with money. She had the life that our mother had only dreamed of: an enormous burgundy four-door Cadillac, membership at the Birmingham Country Club, a cool brick house on a cul-de-sac over the mountain, long days filled with tennis and church work and her pastimes and lunch at the club. Her kids had attended Mountain Brook schools and left the nest: Jimmy, the oldest, had gone to Birmingham-Southern and now was a doctor married to a doctor (a Catholic, at that) in Cincinnati; Alan had graduated in business from Auburn, taken a job at a Birmingham bank, then married a Montgomery girl who was a dead ringer for his mother, right down to the lazy drawl that makes "Jim" come out "Jee-yum"; and Debbie, who had caused Joyce much consternation by dropping out of sorority rush at Auburn and then by moving out of the house in rebellion against her father's stern rules, was working in a restaurant and attending UAB. Queenly, gracious, serene, Joyce had become the keeper of the flame in the family—the hostess, over the years, for holiday gatherings that brought together all of those cousins who could remember the Sunday-afternoon feasts at Mama and Daddy Nelson's Victorian house in Woodlawn during the forties and fifties. Like Mama, who had worn her wedding dress at her golden wedding anniversary, Joyce at age fifty-two had a waistline that hadn't expanded an inch. Like most of her friends, career "homemakers" who lived over the mountain, she made an assumption that women who worked did so because they had to; indeed, her letters to my wife were addressed not to "Susan Percy" but to "Mrs. Paul Hemphill." Like Mama, she said "I S'wanee" to register surprise, and her favorite word was "nice," even to describe someone I might consider an absolute rascal, because she didn't want any trouble. When *King of the Road* was published, I got a call from one of Joyce's best friends, a sorority sister now living in Atlanta: "I don't have much to say about that Neanderthal she married, but let me tell you about your sister. Joyce is . . . Joyce is . . . *good!*"

There is a body of jokes about the wealthiest of the women who inhabit the brooding old mansions of Homewood, Mountain Brook, and Vestavia Hills—"Homies" and "Brookies" and "Vesties," I would hear them called—along the line of the Jewish American Princess jokes one hears in, say, Cleveland: "What's she making for dinner?—Reservations." They are the wives of the men still referred to, with equal parts of disgust and envy, as the Big Mules. While their husbands manage endless reservoirs of old money, most of it taken from the days when coal and iron ruled the city, they are solely responsible for lavishing it on themselves and their families: on gargantuan automobiles, on clothes from Paris, on art and furnishings from Italy, on second homes in the Rockies and on Maui, on vacations to any point in the world. Their husbands have first names like Talmadge and Simpkins and Roebuck, the last names of wealthy ancestors, shortened to the more cordial "Tal" and "Sim" and "Roe"; their daughters are debutantes who go off to college at any of the Seven Sisters before returning to marry inside their circle; and their sons come back home to take over the family business, even if it is to manage the trust fund, after a hiatus in the Ivy League. They are supremely wealthy together, up there in their mansions on the hill, venturing no farther than to their country club when they deign to go out, shopping not at the malls but in Atlanta or New York; and the only "common" people they know are their servants and the men who come to fix things. When they give money, it is to further their own causes, from the Republican party to beautification fund-raisers, for they are not known for their charity or their sensitivity toward the common good. A book dealer I would get to know told me of making a delivery of antique books to one of them and catching her on the phone to a friend, "in an absolute fury" that Hillary Clinton might become the country's first lady: "The bitch even filed income taxes under her own name," he quoted her.

It relieves me to report that my sister, however comfortable and insulated her life seemed to be, had not become one of those—although she did seem to speak of them with some awe, much as I might of a novelist who has reached unattainable heights of brilliance and renown. True, she belonged to the Birmingham Country Club and Canterbury United Methodist Church (four thousand white over-the-mountain members strong), lived in what is technically Mountain Brook, traveled in familiar circles far from the grit of the real Birmingham, and knew virtually nothing about politics and race and government except what her husband had told her. Jim's fixed salary as a construction engineer and her modest upbringing precluded her soaring into the ranks of those gaudy superstars who do lunch. She and Jim would go to Colorado that summer of '92, but only because a friend had a place in Aspen. They would often spend weekends forty miles up the road at Logan Martin Lake, but at the cottage of another friend. On those excursions the "girls" went shopping while the men played golf, she told me; and for jollity over dinner, after the lads had tired of needling each other about their day on the links, they would play a game called "MOQ"—"most over quota"—to see which wife had spent the most of her husband's money that day.

A couple of weeks after Mama's burial, I drove by Joyce's house in my dusty Chevy Blazer to pick her up for a leisurely ride around town to all of the places of our youth—research for me, an outing for her, a sort of rite of passage for the two of us. It was a brisk spring day, the first Saturday in April, with azaleas

and jonquils and dogwood beginning to color the leafy neighborhoods over the mountain. Although Joyce didn't live in one
of the stately dark Tudor mansions that characterize the more
spectacular crannies of Mountain Brook, houses where old black
men were already outside picking up the winter's debris from
the carpeted lawns and pruning privet hedges, this house less
than a mile from their country club was certainly more substantial than any I had ever owned: solid, settled, lived-in, several
cuts above Woodlawn and East Lake.

She came to the door wearing a shiny royal-blue jogging
outfit and running shoes, makeup on, hair coiffed, fifty-two years
old but still a knockout. As usual, she said, Jim and their son
Alan were playing golf at the country club. She had just gotten
back a batch of prints that had been made from some old family
snapshots and thought I would like to see them before we left
for our drive. This had been an obsession of hers since our father's death, when she had spent months separating trash from
memorabilia in the house in East Lake before putting it on the
market, and she was assembling a remarkable photographic history: the cabin where Daddy had been born in Tennessee; our
mother as a "flapper" when they were dating in the late twenties; both of us as the years washed by; Mama and Daddy Nelson's house; faded glimpses of birthday parties and vacations and
picnics. The new ones included a shot made in the late 1800s of
one Cicero Alexander Caldwell, Mama Nelson's father, proudly
posing beside his printing press on the sidewalks of downtown
Birmingham, where he cranked out business cards on the spot.
She was putting together a family tree, and thought that later in
the day I might help her shop for a simple computer she could
use in organizing the material.

We spent nearly an hour rummaging through family things,
shoulder to shoulder in the darkened den of the house, the
brother who had left and the sister who had stayed, catching up.
The snapshots kept coming, spilling from shoeboxes and peeking

from yellowed envelopes. Here she was, tap-dancing to "Stairway to the Stars" at age twelve, on a three-step pedestal Daddy had built and gilded with sequins. Here I was, a fifteen-year-old at Ozark Baseball Camp, my buddy Wallace Graddick grinning and draping an arm over my shoulder. Louvenia, posing in the backyard in her apron and Aunt Jemima bandanna. Our parents on a cruise ship, tanned and beaming, seated at the captain's table. Joyce with a doll, me on a "skatemobile," Mama dressed for church, Daddy posing beside one of his trucks. The good gay times.

As she was putting the stuff away she said, "How's it going so far?"

"Slow," I said. "I did have lunch with Alf Van Hoose the other day."

"He was at Mama's funeral. That was nice."

"Alf's a good man. Retired now, you know."

"You could be sports editor of the *News* now."

"I don't want to think about it."

"Anybody else?"

One of the snapshots had been made at Panama City Beach, Florida, in the late forties, with Hemphills and Laceys and friends named Lawler sitting at the edge of the surf. At either end were young Paul Hemphill and Stanley Lawler, who later would take over the family foundry with his brother. "Stan Lawler gave me his card at Mama's funeral," I said, "so I may go by and see what a foundry looks like."

"You know Wallace Graddick is living here again. He's got a new wife."

"Yeah, we're going to try to take in a Barons game at the new ballpark."

"Just like old times."

"I'd like to think so."

She brightened and walked over to a bookcase that held more framed family photographs than books, although I certainly noticed that all eight of mine were there, and when she had pushed aside a stack of *Southern Living* and *Birmingham* magazines, some coffee-table books about the city, and the tabloid *Over the Mountain Journal,* she came back with a copy of a Woodlawn High annual from the fifties. "Well, let's see," she said, riffling the pages of the *Woodlog.* "You know about Lelias Kirby's death. Terry Oden retired from the Secret Service, and now he's in charge of security for AmSouth bank. Johnny Sudderth's a lawyer in Woodlawn, Horton Smith's a doctor in Huntsville, Ralph Loveless is a lawyer in Mobile. But most of them stayed in Birmingham—Dan and Reeves Sims, Mack and Deacon Jones, Bunky Wolaver. Peggy Gafford—she was a cheerleader, remember?—she's very active here in Republican politics." Joyce was a walking Rolodex; give her an address, she could give you the zip code.

I was boggled. "I tell you, this is hard to do. Everybody's got a life, and here I come barging in after all these years. I never had that many good friends in the first place."

"Oh, Terry asks about you all the time."

"I hardly knew Terry, Joyce. He kicked my butt all over the gym one day in Bloody Blaine's PE class."

She shrugged. Boys' stuff. "Well, you just let me know if you need any phone numbers. I can probably find it for you."

"I'm sure you can, Sis."

"That's nice."

"What?"

" 'Sis.' That's what Daddy always called me."

"Well."

In the weeks prior to this I had already done a great deal of driving around the city, regaining my bearings. I had spent a while touring Sloss Furnace, following the arrows in the company of a vacationing couple from Pittsburgh, of all places, to see how the plant had worked. I had parked at Rickwood, used for high school games now, its parking lot a staging area for city school buses, and sat for a while in the rotting grandstand where once I had dreamed. I had to ask directions to Stockham, the neat little ballpark where industrial-league games used to be played, and saw that it had been turned into a storage area for the adjoining mill. Most of the major downtown stores had been boarded up, their owners having moved to suburban malls; and the Ritz Theater, where our parents were married, was long gone. My son was living in a ramshackle bungalow behind a house in Ensley, and on his twenty-seventh birthday he gave me a tour of what had been one of the city's most vibrant steel villages but now looked like Dresden after the bombs: kudzu entwining the soaring brick chimneys of the devastated Ensley Mill; a forbidding housing project known as "the Rockpile," so fraught with drugs and weapons and the black "underclass" that cops simply left it to its own fate; almost all of the businesses nailed shut with plywood covered in graffiti. Much of the west side of town where steel had reigned was like that now, in fact: abandoned, desolate, left to the poorest of the poor by whites and blacks alike who had fled to the suburbs.

This would be different, though—a return by a brother and sister to where their lives had begun. Joyce and I headed straight for East Lake, keeping up a running commentary as we cruised the streets. There was the little shotgun house where she was born in the back bedroom in 1940, right against the sidewalk on Fifth Avenue North, still in decent shape, across from where the Laceys had lived ("I can still see Dr. Lovelady walking out of the house, giving me the high sign"); our next house, also inhabited and in good repair, where our father had converted his dump truck (of the kids who lived next door, she said, George Quiggle had become a preacher and his sister, Carolyn, "lives up north somewhere"); Curry School, where I had gone before transferring to Minnie Holman, still in operation overlooking the airport ("Every time I see the movie *Summer of '42*," I said, "I think of a teacher named Miss Doran. She wore bobby sox, had a boyfriend off in the war, and I was in love with her''); Zion City, the hardscrabble black colony where Louvenia had lived, changed not a whit (although now, by a band of black teenagers hanging out on a corner, we were met with sullen stares and the sharp shout "Honkies!''); our parents' last house, above the public golf course at 403 North Eighty-ninth Street, neater than ever and enclosed by a bright new chain-link fence; Mama's favored church, Lake Highlands Methodist; East Lake Park, down in the bottoms on First Avenue, fully integrated and teeming with joggers and picnickers on this bright spring day ("The old pavilion where we used to have family picnics is still there," she said).

And finally we drove to Woodlawn, where our true growing-up years had taken place. We didn't have to mention the irony in the fact that not a hundred yards away from where Mama and Daddy Nelson's house sat before it was razed, just a whiff away from all of those incredible Sunday dinners after church, there now squatted a McDonald's. The last time I had been to Woodlawn it seemed headed the way of Ensley and West End —stores battened, prostitutes soliciting from windows, movie house and bowling alley gone, little sense that once it had thrived as a municipality unto itself. But now trees were planted along bricked sidewalks, awnings adorned doorways, a drugstore and a hardware and other small businesses had reopened, there were a couple of antique stores, and the turn-of-the-century City Hall had been restored. At the heart of Woodlawn, though, there was still the solemn brick presence of Woodlawn Methodist Church: scene of some "troubles" during the civil rights years, some of them centering on our preacher, Brother John Rutland, and a parishioner named Eugene "Bull" Connor—Brother Rutland being someone else I hoped to find, provided he was still alive.

Soon we were jouncing over the double tracks of the Southern Railway system, where Johnny Sudderth's father, Jake, had been killed, and suddenly coming upon the corner of Fifth Court and Sixtieth Street South that was the very center of our child-hood lives. The house where we had grown up showed all of the signs of renters' neglect: spotty yard; scraggly bushes; flaking paint (now a hideous chocolate); Daddy's backyard barbecue and flagstone patio sprouting weeds; roofing stained and buckled; rusty tricycles and tools and buckets lying where they last had been used. Up and down the block it was much the same story. We had known the neighborhood at its peak in the afterglow of the Second World War, when everyone was a proud first-time homeowner and had a good job and was building a family; but when their children began leaving home and they began moving away—selling to the first buyer, black or white, individual or realtor, they didn't care anymore—this was the result. Several of the houses were empty now, "No Trespassing" and "For Sale" signs staked in their overgrown yards; and on the cracked sidewalk in front of one there was a pickup truck jacked up on concrete building blocks. No one was outside cutting the grass or washing the car or trimming the hedges, even on a splendid day such as this, and no matter how hard I tried, I could not summon up the joyous cries that once floated over these rooftops when all the world was young. Joyce and I were silent, some-where between stunned and saddened, as I wheeled away.

We had cruised through the hills of Crestwood, the subdi-vision where Mama had pined to live, following the route we had hiked to Minnie Holman (now the headquarters for some-thing called Girls, Inc.), and presently I was pulling over to the curb and cutting the engine. For a few minutes we sat there and took in the sweeping view of the city—a view I never noticed as a kid, perhaps because Birmingham in the forties was always clouded in smoke. Now we could see in the foreground Sloss Furnace, then the cluster of skyscrapers that had remade down-town, and finally, on the green ridge far off to the south, the brooding statue of Vulcan.

Two days earlier we had met in one of the tall office buildings overlooking Linn Park to have our parents' wills probated, and on this day Joyce had brought along a yellow legal pad and some documents so she could show me "what Mama and Daddy left." Having money left to me was something I had never thought about; trust funds and inheritances were matters for Big Mules to ponder, not Woodlawn boys. During my visit with the old man at the alcoholic place in Mississippi he had told me, casually, "I never knew this ol' trucker would be leaving this kind of money." I had no idea what he was talking about, and it would have been unseemly to ask. There were the proceeds from the house, I figured; but Mama's health care and his last travails probably had eaten it up.

"It might be a quarter of a million dollars," she said.

I was flabbergasted. "Great Godamighty, Joyce."

"Daddy left it all over the place."

"Are you sure?"

"It could be more," she said. "They had savings bonds from the war, stocks, all kinds of investments. Daddy had about thirty thousand dollars in two different checking accounts, afraid the government was going to steal it from him. It's a wonder he didn't keep some in the mattresses. I'm still calling around, trying to find it all."

My first thoughts were that there would be no more sweat about these last two college educations, and it looked like none of mine would be dying alone in a trailer camp. But then it all came back to me: their saving money in a jar even during the Depression; paying cash for the house in Woodlawn; waiting until one minute after ten o'clock at night to make long-distance phone calls (and then speaking for only three minutes); clipping grocery coupons; making a pot roast last into the "hash" stage; she making clothes and he doing the house repairs. They had lived their lives as though the Depression would last forever. Only the day before, in my readings at the archives, I had discovered what was referred to as "an old Birmingham adage": "Hard times come here first and stay longest." Who would know that better than a couple who got married for free on the stage of a movie house? That was their real legacy. They had taken on life and beaten it.

CHAPTER NINETEEN

Woodlawn Redux

When we lived in Woodlawn, the day officially began at the first gray wash of daylight, the screen door slamming across the street at the Robinsons' house loudly enough to awaken the neighborhood. For us it was a dependable alarm clock, but for Reuben Robinson it was the first step on another grim eleven-mile odyssey across town to the TCI steel mill in Ensley. He could be seen trudging away from the house across the street from ours every weekday at dawn, black metal lunch pail in hand, greeting the milkman, walking nearly a mile to catch a trolley that would drop him within four blocks of the vast Ensley Mill. In marked contrast to my father's clamorous arrivals in his dusty rig every Friday afternoon, Reuben would return to the neighborhood about four o'clock every afternoon: slouched and shuffling along, lunch pail empty now, to be welcomed only by his aproned wife, Belva, with news of plumbing disasters and childish pranks and plans for supper. Reuben made that trip for thirty-nine years, his entire adult working life; and when he took early retirement in 1975 at the age of fifty-nine, frustrated with the workers sent around by the unions, most of them untrained black men he couldn't understand, he was nearly deaf from the din of the mill.

There were other men in the neighborhood whose lives revolved around machines and industry—a train engineer, a Greyhound bus mechanic, my old man, even one who wore a coat and tie and worked in the downtown offices of TCI—but Reuben was the only genuine steelworker. He had gotten a job at the

Ensley Mill in late 1936, earning thirty-three cents an hour in the brass foundry, and it took twenty-two years for him to become foreman of his shop. By the time he decided to chuck it in, he was making eighteen hundred dollars a month in an iron foundry that produced ingots for TCI's rail mill. He retired on about one thousand dollars a month, without a mention of any disability payments for his loss of hearing on the job, and the Ensley Mill closed for good in 1982. That mill, as it turned out, was the one my son and I had viewed one day from the Twentieth Street bridge in Ensley, the one that looked like Dresden after the bombings, with little yellow bulldozers still scavenging about the rubble for usable scrap metal, nothing left but rusty abandoned railroad sidings and fields of kudzu and black brick chimneys rising nearly one hundred feet into the sky as stark memorials to the past.

Belva and Reuben Robinson had been the first to come to Fifth Court and the last to go, living for forty-seven years in that little three-bedroom frame house near the bottom of the hill. The house had been priced at $1,500 when they put down $100 and began making payments of $15 a month in '39, and fetched $31,000 when they sold it to a black couple in '86. They had raised two children there, Mickey and June, about five years behind my sister and me in ages; endured strikes that seemed to come to TCI every summer, times when Reuben would begin hiring himself out as a handyman, once painting four houses during a six-week strike; remembered when a man next door had committed suicide in '41, and when another man across the street had shot his son-in-law dead sometime in the fifties; saw the arrival of the first automobiles in the late thirties and the first television sets in the late forties. Reuben had built a two-car garage out back, not for two cars but for a place to build short-wave radios and television sets, using what he had learned through a correspondence course out of California. They had been the pioneers on the block; and now, with the death of my mother, they were the only original set of parents still alive.

Since I would be driving through Woodlawn to get to the Robinsons' house in Center Point, anyway, I phoned Johnny Sudderth and we agreed to have lunch. Although he was a year older and had married young, Johnny was one of the childhood gang at Fifth Court and Sixtieth Street: only child of a private nurse and a laundry and dry-cleaning deliveryman, a middling pitcher and quarterback at Woodlawn High, taller and skinnier than even I had been. When my cousin Melvin once told me that Johnny was "quite an activist" and I asked what that meant, he said, "He's still living in Woodlawn, isn't he?" I hadn't seen him since the early fifties, when we finished high school and went our separate ways. I knew only that he had divorced, spent some time in California, returned to set up a law practice in the heart of Woodlawn, and had represented my father in a dispute over some retirement property in the Florida swamps.

Reentering a childhood chum's life after nearly forty years was weird, almost an out-of-body experience. Johnny had thickened in the middle, sprouted silver hair, and taken to sporting lawyerly suspenders and somber suits, his overall appearance being that of a small-town dandy. His offices were in the Somerset Building, actually a house that had been the medical offices of the beloved Dr. Somerset—his partner was John Somerset, the doctor's son, and Johnny had even bought the staid old Somerset house in Crestwood—and after some backslapping and sizing each other up, he was giving me a tour: introducing me to his second wife, Tara (who taught tax law at Birmingham-Southern and spent her off-days keeping the Somerset & Sudderth books), and his partner, John; and showing me the lead-lined room where Dr. Somerset had taken X rays and another where he had performed minor surgery in a simpler time. The place was furnished with antiques, a passion of Johnny and Tara's, and out back there were their his-and-hers Mercedes convertibles. We took the red one and rode up the street to John's Restaurant, a meat-and-three diner I had known as Mills', where he was greeted as though he were the mayor of Woodlawn.

Maybe this was the way to go, I thought. Johnny had graduated from Samford University, worked as an accountant at Hayes Aircraft for eighteen years, and after his divorce had wound up in California as a controller in the aerospace industry. He spent eight years in Orange County. "I'd go flying into some town with the big boss, find something wrong with the books, fire the local manager, and fly on to the next one. I hated the place, the people, everything about Orange County. They don't even have Sunday in California." It took him eleven intermittent years of night school to study law and pass the bar, and in the early eighties he moved back home to open his practice.

He felt a sense of place in the old neighborhood, and I envied him for that. He had gone off to see the world, found it lacking, and now was back home among people he had known all his life, doing what he could to improve the place where he grew up. "We thought about moving over the mountain to Vestavia or Mountain Brook," he said. "You know—get one of those big old mansions, join The Club, put on the dog, all of that. But hell, Paul, it's not that big a town. If we want to go out and eat at the Highlands Bar and Grill in Five Points, I just call and say, 'Jay, this is Johnny, how about a good table?' and we're there in fifteen minutes. This is home—Dr. Somerset's house, his old offices, everything." He regaled me with stories about running the drug dealers and prostitutes out of Woodlawn, pointed out the new businesses that had come to First Avenue, and ran me by the refurbished City Hall, where an exhibition of Woodlawn's history was being mounted (it had begun as a pioneer outpost called Wood's Station). "You shouldn't have stayed gone so long," he told me as we said goodbye. Then, as an afterthought, "Your daddy and I had a lot of fun messing with those rascals in Florida. He was a hell of a guy."

Belva and Reuben Robinson lived in a yellow brick house on a one-acre lot about ten miles beyond Woodlawn in Center Point, which had been called "the country" when I was a kid but had become a tangle of strip shopping centers and white middle-class subdivisions, and they seemed comfortable in their retirement. The house was carpeted, stuffed with Early American furniture, paneled walls hung with framed pictures of their grandchildren, with a full basement where Reuben made golf clubs and still tinkered with television and radio sets, and a deck overlooking a fenced backyard that had become a playground for squirrels and birds. Their son, Mickey, now fifty-one, was a fireman. June, forty-seven, lived right up the street, played competitive tennis, and three days a week helped out at her husband's BP Oil station twenty miles away, over the mountain, in Vestavia Hills.

"You remember Dot Sudderth, don't you, Paul?" Belva, an attractive woman with sharp features and dancing eyes, had just brought tall glasses of iced tea to me and Reuben, who sat in a recliner in the den, his ears stuffed with hearing aids, watching the birds flit about in the backyard.

"Johnny's first wife," I said. "Saw her at Mama's funeral."

"You sure? I didn't see her."

"Actually, it was at Roebuck Chapel the night before. She'd given somebody a ride for another service, and didn't know about Mama until she saw me."

"She admitted she was Johnny's ex-wife?"

" 'Admitted'?"

"Lord, Lord." This was going to be good; Belva Robinson was a delicious gossip. "One day when June was working at the station over there, this woman in a fancy car filled it up and came in to pay with a credit card. June just knew it was Dot, because she used to baby-sit for her and Johnny all the time. So she started naming the kids and asking how they were doing, but you know what? Dot said, 'You must be mistaken, I'm not Dot Sudderth, I'm Dot so-and-so, I'm married to the mayor of Vestavia.' June kept insisting she was, and Dot kept insisting she wasn't, so June just let it go. The credit card said Dot something, not Dot Sudderth, and she paid up and went out to her car. When she got there, though, she thought about it and came back in and whispered to June, 'You're right. I used to be Dot Sudderth. I just don't talk about it around here.' And she left.''

Reuben had stirred in his recliner when he heard Johnny's name. "Mickey's ex-wife asked Johnny to represent her when she tried to get more alimony and support. Johnny said he couldn't do that, since we used to be neighbors and all, said it was too close to home. But then you know what he done? He turned the case over to his wife, or a partner, some other one of them damned lawyers, and they got Mickey good. I didn't appreciate that one bit. Called Johnny on the phone and chewed him out. Never talked to him since.''

It wouldn't be the last time I would come across these intertwining lives. For instance, my friend Stan Lawler was vaguely connected to Mimi Tynes, because his father had gotten into the metals business back in the twenties by going to work at the Hardie-Tynes foundry established by Mimi's father-in-law. When my children were removed to Birmingham after the divorce, I wrote many a check for dental work done by a fellow who had played trombone alongside me in the Woodlawn High band. Both my oldest daughter and her mother had served as house-sitters for the publisher of the Birmingham *News,* the paper I now blamed for contributing to the city's problems over the years. And now my son was living just a brisk walk from the site of the mill in Ensley where Reuben Robinson had spent his life at labor. In an inbred medium-sized city such as Birmingham, where there had been little infusion of outside blood, it seemed that everybody was connected in one way or another.

Belva was off on a breathless tear. "Now, of the old ones, Mr. Graddick's still alive, but he's been living with his new wife over near Crestwood ever since Myra got run over by a train. . . . Gay's gotten real fat, you know, since Pete died. . . . Barbara actually hit Karl's mama, it got so bad, and not long after that his mama died, but I don't think that had anything to do with it. . . . David Hudson, that was his name, his mama kept him in curls until he was thirteen. . . . Our number was 595-1991, and I still want to write that down. . . . There's only two or three whites living on the block now, including y'all's place. . . . There was one man, I forget his name right now, an engineer, and when he was coming home from a run he'd toot his whistle over on the Southern tracks to alert his wife. . . . Phyllis Wade, now, she was a pretty one, think they moved to New York and then to Boston, somewhere up there. . . . Your daddy'd get home and start playing that piano, and it was like a neighborhood concert because there wasn't any air conditioning and everybody kept their doors and windows open. . . ."

Reuben sat patiently, figuring the neighborhood was hers, now and then correcting a name or inserting a date or adding bits and pieces ("That was the summer that me and Mr. Beckett both was on strike, and I painted his house while he did brick work on our front steps"), mostly grinning and rocking and enjoying the show. He knew his time would come. When Belva had exhausted her store of tales from the old neighborhood, he launched into a rambling monologue about a life spent at hard labor in the near-prehistoric world of dust and heat and relentless noise that marked the steel mills before their demise.

It was in 1936, the year I was born and Vulcan was put on Red Mountain, that Reuben got a job at the Ensley Mill with the help of his stepfather, a man he still referred to simply as "Mr. Tutt," a timekeeper there. "This was the Depression, and they wasn't hiring nobody," he began. "Mr. Tutt knew one of these fellas in the foundry, and they was good friends, ran a baseball pool together, got along just fine, so he told this fella, says, 'Any time you can use a boy, I got one that needs a job.' So the fella says, 'How tall is he?' and when Mr. Tutt says, 'He's six feet tall,' the fella says, 'I can use him—I need somebody tall that can finish the ingot molds down here.' It was like painting, except it was putting a coating on 'em to keep the metal from burning into the sand. So he had me come out to the employment center, but then they tell me, 'We ain't got a thing, but if you hang around maybe something might show up.' Looking back now, I can see they was testing me, that there was lots of men out of work back then and they could pick and choose. All the time, I knew they'd asked for me, but they was makin' sure that I wanted a job. Anyway, I waited 'em out while they all went off to dinner, and when they saw I was still there after dinner they sent me to what they called a dispensary to be examined, and I finally got wrote up. That was on a Friday, and they told me to come in to work on Monday.''

He reported to ''Forty,'' a building that housed the labor pool, blacks and whites desperate for any kind of work, the flunkies and gofers. ''My stepdaddy tells this fella that I'm up there at Forty and he calls up there and asks for me. So I go down there and he carries me into the foundry and there's fellas there making these molds and he says, 'I want you to watch these fellas today. I don't want you touching anything—just watch 'em, watch what they do, and tomorrow I expect you to do just what they're doing.' Well, that was going to be my training, so I commenced to watch everything, take it all in, but then before the day was half over the foreman came down and I could tell he was miffed about something. Says, 'You go down to the other end of this building and on the right-hand corner there's a fella by the name of Scharber. Henry Scharber. They want you down there.' That's where the brass foundry was at, and that was a lot nicer place than where I'd been. My stepdaddy had been looking out for me some more, I guess, because this Scharber had talked the superintendent into letting him have me to train as an apprentice in the brass shop. That's where I stayed, right there in the brass shop, until it got shut down in nineteen and fifty-eight. I went from labor to supervisor in that shop, wound up running the place, but it took me twenty-two years.''

He was still amazed at the scope of the operations on Birmingham's western side during steel's heyday. ''I was lucky—I worked from seven in the morning till three in the afternoon most of my life, but Ensley was an around-the-clock mill. The rail mill had three shifts, since you couldn't shut down the blast furnaces, but the brass foundry ran five days a week. The Ensley Mill kept growing so big, they just built a viaduct right over it, the Twentieth Street bridge, just like they done at Sloss on First Avenue downtown. The accounting office at Ensley, where Mr. Tutt worked, had a hundred and fifty people in it just to keep up with our time and pay before automation come in. We had six blast furnaces, five or six open hearths, even had a lime plant that ground this lime up, and it covered Ensley so the whole town was white from lime powder. We made molds for the Fairfield plant, too, that was owned by TCI, and I'd sit there with my dinner and see engines loaded with coal coming from Pratt City in open boxcars, headed for the coke plant over there, and they'd be so heavy they'd stall and they'd have to call for another engine. Seemed like they were making everything out there: pig ingots, some of the best rails in the country, tin cans, nails, slag to mix with cement to make concrete for highways, these big 'screwdowns' that was used to nail the plant to the ground, these big flat rolls of sheet like your daddy used to haul that they'd use to make automobiles and refrigerators and no telling what all, and during the war we made hundred-and-fifty-millimeter shells. They even had a fertilizer plant.''

What went wrong? Why did the mills die? Reuben Robinson thought he knew why: the unions, civil rights legislation, antipollution regulations. "Personally, I never would've joined the union if I hadn't had to. I remembered how they had a commissary when I started. It was the Depression, but they allowed my stepdaddy to charge groceries, and I thought that was real nice, I appreciated it. The union movement started right after that, around '37 or '38, and maybe the foreman wouldn't exactly threaten you not to join, but he'd sure remind you that there were a lot of men out there that wanted work real bad.

"Well, years later they just priced my brass foundry out of business. The union kept getting raises and benefits, and it got to where a man who had fifteen years' service was eligible for thirteen weeks' paid vacation every five years. So when you get a dozen men in a shop and all of 'em get thirteen weeks' vacation, you can see what it's costing the company. I had to fight the union, the men, and the company. I'd spend two hours on the phone just calling men to come in, and those that I got on the phone came in and got double overtime. The ones that hadn't come in, they'd just lay off, wouldn't come to work, but it had gotten so you couldn't fire 'em. I reckon that worked in my favor at the end, because when they closed the brass foundry they just transferred me to the iron foundry and even give me a raise."

The last strike came in the sixties, he said, "and that's when the company lost control. They were just trying to manage their business, trying to make some money, but Washington said there were people out of work and there wasn't any steel getting made, said, 'Pay 'em what they want, and raise the price of steel to pay for it.' That did it."

And if it wasn't the unions, it was government in general. "The politicians made the city move the city limits to take in the Ensley plant so they could get more taxes. Then OSHA [Occupational Safety and Health Administration] came along and said the nail factory in Fairfield was making a terrible racket, and the company said it wasn't practical to build a new plant, so they just closed it down.''

Although Belva had told me on the phone that Reuben had taken early retirement because ''the niggers wouldn't work,'' he was careful not to use that word, and to downplay integration of the work force as a reason for his giving up his life's work; but the resentment was still there. ''They were always there, as laborers at first, and some claimed to have an education,'' he said. ''But Lyndon Johnson changed the laws of the land. Now you had to change the fountains, the restrooms, the separate bathhouses for blacks and whites. There'd always been a line of promotion—look how long it took me to go from laborer to foreman—but now you kept hearing 'discrimination, discrimination.' You had to move 'em right along, whether they were ready or not, and I tell you, sometimes it got dangerous. There'd be this man who was untrained, working with a crane and a twenty-ton ladle full of metal more'n two thousand degrees hot, and it got right nerve-racking. They got better in time, once they got the hang of it, but it wasn't much fun watching 'em learn.''

Reuben wanted to show me his basement. Like all the men of the old neighborhood, including my father, he was a do-it-yourselfer, having learned self-sufficiency during the Depression. (I remembered calling to ask him to serve as a pallbearer for my father, when Reuben was seventy-two, and Belva had to call him down off the roof of the house, where he was blowing leaves from the gutters.) When we got to the basement, I wasn't surprised to find that it looked like a hardware store: lathes, saws, paint cans, buckets of nails and screws, old homemade radios and television sets, automobile parts, gas cans, quarts of oil. What did surprise me was a collection of golf clubs he had fashioned, and a portable net like the ones used by placekickers warming up on the sidelines during football games.

"Golf?" I said. "An old steelworker?"

"Used to caddy when I was a teenager. I'd walk eight miles from Ruffner to Roebuck Golf Course. Made fifty cents an hour."

"Yeah, but playing is different. A gentleman of leisure."

"Aw," he said, "when I was about forty-five, I wasn't doing anything for exercise, just working, so I started going over to Sam Byrd's driving range. Pretty soon I was playing every weekend. Even got the wife to playing, and we joined Cumberland Country Club."

He sauntered over to the net. Nearby were a cluster of drivers and a pail of golf balls. This was where he practiced his driving, he said, only now he used plastic balls instead of the real thing. He grinned when he told me why. "We'd barely moved into the house when I got this idea for the net," he said, "and one day I was just driving away, putting balls into it, having a good time, but I didn't notice that every time I drove a ball into the net it slid a little closer to the sink over there. Well, pretty soon I wound up and let one fly and it came right back at me, like a shot, banged off that sink and hit me right between the eyes. For a while there, I was stone deaf. What TCI started, my golf game almost finished."

CHAPTER TWENTY

Vulcan's Last Stand

A Cleveland, Ala., man died yesterday when he was trapped inside a furnace used to heat metals at the Pinson Valley Heat Treating Co. at 6169 Sunrise Drive.

Ollie M. Anderson, 35, was last seen working inside the furnace around 7:30 a.m. just before it was turned on, company President Don Hendry said.

Hendry said it was unknown how the accident occurred, but said apparently the hood to the furnace closed, locking Anderson inside.

—Birmingham *Post-Herald*, June 1992

The news that Jane Fonda and Bo Jackson had stopped by the medical complex for repairs naturally got more play in the Birmingham newspapers. But these unspeakable little horrors like the death of Ollie Anderson occurred often enough to remind those who may have forgotten that the city once known as "the Pittsburgh of the South" was still a place where men labored to make metal from minerals wrested from the earth. About once a month I would see these items buried on the inside pages— "James R. Hicks, 39, was killed when he was trapped in an air-operated molding machine about 3:56 a.m."—and it was enough to sober the drumbeaters who were promoting the "new" Birmingham as another modern American city, like Atlanta, where things were "processed" rather than made; boasting that paper clips had replaced I beams. In a morbid way, these death notices were reminders that Birmingham was still a city of muscle and sweat and danger.

There were enough ghostly signs of the past, like the detritus of Reuben Robinson's Ensley Mill and the museum at Sloss Furnace, to convince the casual visitor that Birmingham was no longer a major steel town. The days when the majority of blue-collar jobs in Jones Valley were in the great booming mills on the west side of town were long gone now; but there were signs —in addition to these deaths in the remaining plants—that metallurgy would always be with Birmingham. The one remaining steel mill of any size was in Fairfield, on the city's western end; but there was a handful of efficient "mini-mill" operations, using not ingots of iron but scrap metal as their raw material, plus scores of little specialized foundries operating in open tin-roofed sheds from one end of the valley to the other. Clearly, making metal was still in Birmingham's blood.

Among the people attending the services for Mama was Stanley Lawler. Our parents had been close for years, Helen being a member of my mother's church and Delmas being the owner of a small foundry for whom my father occasionally hauled stuff. On at least one occasion during the forties, as evidenced by the snapshot Joyce had shown me, our families had vacationed together at the Florida beaches. Since the death of Delmas, Stanley and his brother, Lacy, had carried on Lawler Foundry, begun by their father in 1933, a modest operation that cast small ornamental pieces from iron and aluminum molds. When I told Stanley (now bearded, now fifty-five, now "Stan") that I would be hanging out in Birmingham for a while, and probably would be looking into the steel business, he offered to show me "what's left of the steel industry," with a warning that his place, though typical of the many small foundries in town, "isn't even a cousin" to those great booming mills that once had dominated the city's skyline and formed its very soul.

A few weeks after Mama's funeral, Stan and I sat in a little room that was part of the business offices and shipping dock of Lawler Foundry in Woodlawn. Not two blocks away was the steel Quonset building where, during my newsboy days, I had pedaled my bike to pick up my copies of the Birmingham *News,* without a clue as to what was going on in all of those rickety tin sheds across the tracks. "Our being in this business probably started seventy years ago," Stan was saying. "Dad was young, a traveling man, handy with his hands, and he spent several years in the merchant marines, going from machine work to oiler to assistant mechanic on ships. He got out and settled in Birmingham in the twenties to work in the machine shop at Hardie-Tynes, and pretty soon he and his brother, Lister, started a machine shop of their own. They'd go over to Thomas Foundry in East Birmingham and pick up castings and do work overnight that Thomas couldn't handle, like boring holes, threading, maybe some milling. Evidently, Dad thought the future was the foundry business, so he enticed some friends at Stockham to come and start one of their own. They didn't borrow any money to start up, because in '33 there wasn't any money to borrow."

He pointed to a framed copy of Lawler Foundry's first product line, primarily cast-iron bean pots and kettles and skillets. "It was pretty basic work. They did sand molding then, as now, but there was no automation, no overhead machines, no division of duties. A man would start with a pile of sand in the morning, making moldings, and when he'd gone through his pile of sand it was time to have a lunch break, and after lunch he would turn into an iron pourer. I can't believe what some of the things they made are getting at flea markets these days. In 1936 a thirty-three-gallon cast-iron sugar kettle brought six cents a pound—that's ten dollars and eighty cents—but today people are paying two hundred dollars for something to plant petunias in. Their intrinsic value is as antiques. But still, the most popular piece of cast-iron cookware made in America today is the eight-inch skillet, although if it was bought in the last ten years it probably came from China or Taiwan.''

Stan was born in 1937, and his memory of the foundry during the war years is hazy (''The place was just too small then to turn out war matériel, except maybe hand grenades, so they went back to machining''); but by the time he was a student at Woodlawn High, in the early fifties, he was hooked. ''Every afternoon I had a choice, Boy Scouts or play sports or work, and it seemed like I always chose work. I'd take the bus from school, walk to the foundry, work until quitting time, then ride home with Dad to East Lake. They were still producing a lot of cookware then, but also there were these water-meter lids like you see in your yard. The castings came to us in fifty-five-gallon drums, and we'd get 'em out of one drum and grind 'em off and drop 'em off in another drum. There was this one fellow, F. E. Hallmark, and he loved Payday candy bars. As soon as I'd finished grinding all of the castings and filled up a drum, he would hand me a Payday candy bar, like a reward for doing my job, but right before I could reach it he'd drop it and it would wind up in the bottom of the drum, and I'd have to grab like hell to get that Payday. I think about him every time I see a Payday bar. And there was Dwight Ayers, 'Jelly' Ayers. Those two fellows were more important in getting me and Lacy into the foundry business and keeping us there than anyone else besides my dad. Jelly was from the old school, and he insisted that everything be done right, didn't allow any slack for himself or anyone else, never raised his voice to do it. I remember how he came to work in a shirt and tie, changed clothes, and during the day he got as black as the sand, but when he left that evening he was as clean as when he had come in. He was a neat guy. He just died, about five years ago.''

In '62, after doing a turn in the Army and spending four aimless years at the University of Alabama, Stan decided that Lawler Foundry was where he belonged. Lacy was already there, having finished his Army tour, and the brothers "felt a little dedicated to carrying on the family business. I'd never really gotten it out of my blood, and it just seemed like the natural thing to do, to dig my furrow where I'd already gotten a head start." The growth of the business in the thirty years since has been steady. In '62 they were pouring five tons of molten metal a day, listing only three dozen items in a four-page catalogue, and grossing a quarter of a million dollars in sales. Today they pour twenty-eight tons of metal every day, list nearly fifteen hundred items in a 150-page catalogue, and gross eight million dollars. Their customers are "the modern-day blacksmiths, small iron fabricators, small rolling shops," who fashion custom household railings and burglar bars and even flower-pot holders. "All we do is supply these people with the component parts to go into furniture and railings and the like. They do the designing, the fabricating, the finishing and the installation. So we're strictly the parts suppliers."

We took the short drive over to the foundry itself, across railroad tracks and Birmingham's primary east-west artery, First Avenue North, past corner groceries and used-car lots and sad little bungalows with flaking paint and pots of geraniums lining the porches, and suddenly entered a clamorous area of warehouses and loading docks and tin-roofed foundries. Lawler Foundry employed about one hundred people in the office and at the foundry, he said, and the men who labored in the foundry were about ninety percent black. "I suspect it's always been like that. They're mostly laborers, making between five-fifty and eight-fifty an hour, and they don't last ten years. It's hard, sweaty, repetitive work, and a foundry is the coldest place in town during the winter and the hottest in the summer. We've never been unionized, never had to, because we pay ten percent more than minimum wage and a little family foundry like this with a relatively small income doesn't much interest the union. Probably only half of our people have a definite job to do all day, anyway, with the rest of 'em having two or three jobs, so we'd have a hell of a time working through the strictness of union work rules. We talk up 'be a partner.' They make pretty decent money, given their education level, for as long as they can take the work.''

To someone who works in the comfort of an office, a foundry is a vision of hell. The first workers had come in at 4:30 that morning to begin the process of firing up the mixture of iron ingots from Brazil and limestone from around town; and by 6:30, when dawn was sending shafts of daylight through slits in the corrugated tin roof, the huge ladles held molten metal (aluminum melts at twelve hundred degrees, cast iron at twenty-eight hundred) ready to be poured. Now, in a huge shed open to the elements, about eighty men in hard hats and safety glasses and rubber boots and fire-resistant gloves, their ears stuffed with cotton, bandannas tied around their foreheads to keep the sweat from their eyes, slaved in a nightmarish din of clanking and hissing and groaning that would continue for twelve hours without interruption. The muscled molders, yanking cords to release loads of sand in a whoosh through funnels suspended perilously near their heads, furiously pulled levers and worked foot pedals to compact the wet black grit into molds that would receive the hissing orange liquid as they moved down the line on conveyor belts. *Jerk-whoosh-pull-plop-clang.* They would finish one mold, kick aside the pile of sand growing at their feet, and begin again. *Jerk-whoosh-pull-plop-clang.* There were no computers here, no robotic arms at work, no soft fluorescent lights, no Muzak, no signs saying ''Have a Nice Day.'' There was only the muscle and sweat of men at work, swarthy men, human beings who had drawn this lot in life. Now and then one of them would break away from his station, where he had furiously worked the ropes and levers and pedals for fifty minutes, and would burst out into the daylight for a cigarette or a breath of outside air, his ten-minute break, before donning his gloves and glasses and hard hat and plunging back into the inferno.

"My God," I said when we got back to the office, "how can they stand it?"

He shrugged. "They take what life hands them."

He tried to give a broader perspective on where Lawler Foundry, with its turn-of-the-century Rube Goldberg machinery, fits in an age of automation and worldwide competition. "I think [government] is going to rue the day when they made it hard for the Lawler-type businesses to be here anymore. We've exported all of those jobs, for whatever reasons, and we find ourselves on the short end of the stick. Our biggest competition now is Taiwan, where they don't have to play by the same social rules. By the time we pay close to an eight-dollar-an-hour timeclock wage plus benefits, that's about thirteen cents a minute; and if you're selling a thirty-five-cent product like a gatepost finial, the most profit you can hope for is maybe a nickel. These aren't products where you sell a million a year on a super-fast production line, so this is where they beat us. But what's interesting is, Taiwan's trying to be a developing nation, pushing up their costs because of an awareness of health and pollution and wages. And now their business is floating across the sea to China, where they don't have *any* regulations. The same thing's happening to them that happened to us."

He fumbled through the stack of papers on his desk until he found what he was looking for. "We can't afford lobbyists," he said. "We belong to things like the National Association of Manufacturers, the Chamber of Commerce, Alabama Cast Metals. We all have kind of a conservative approach to slowing down some of the changes in the business, the modernization and all, but we can't make a ripple. I get this Kiplinger newsletter every week. This one's February twenty-eighth, 1992." He opened it and looked for a passage. " 'We have wondered for several years, seeing what all of these regulations were doing to our industry, where the people were going to go to get work.' Well, you can talk about all the cross-training and retraining you want to, but our people aren't trained to start with. Most of my people, the only training they have is on the job. We're not going to teach 'em to be computer experts. It's an industry that's not going to be here unless everybody wakes up and realizes that not everybody can operate a computer. Twenty years ago they said, 'This is going to be the computer age. We're going to teach everybody to use computers and have a stockpile of workers who can do that. Everybody's going to be educated for this.' Well, my stockpile of people can't do this work. They can do the same work they were doing fifty years ago, but the industries that had those jobs fifty years ago aren't here anymore."

As it neared the sixtieth anniversary of its founding, Stan wouldn't say how much longer Lawler Foundry might stay in business, but his eyes lit up when we began talking about the efficient new steel mini-mills ("lean and mean" kept coming up to describe them) that had sprung up in Birmingham in place of the dead old giants. I had read about Birmingham Steel, a hot number on the stock exchange these days, which was actually *exporting* twenty percent of its steel to Japan, South Korea, Mexico, and Taiwan. "And there's SMI, right across the street," Stan said. "It's the old Connors Steel, and it's the biggest success story I've seen in my life. Connors Steel was an old-line small steel company that was going down the tubes. Ten years ago these people bought it out and converted the operation into a modern-day mini-mill. Boy, I tell you. Twenty trucks a day must roll out of there."

"You been inside?" I asked him.

"No. I don't even know what SMI stands for."

"I guess I ought to check 'em out."

"Tell you what." He was already reaching for the phone

book. "Let me make the call. If they have plant tours, maybe you and I could go together. Little family-foundry man like me, I get a hard-on just thinking about a place like that."

Stan Lawler had every right to be envious of his big brother across the street. SMI stands for Structural Metals, Inc., whose parent is a trading company out of Dallas that deals in scrap metal, recyclables, foreign trade and investments. Whereas Lawler Foundry employed one hundred people, poured twenty-eight tons a day, turned out cookware and railings and fenceposts, SMI was quite another animal. With four hundred employees, SMI was pouring nearly one thousand tons a day, producing big items like rails and rolled flats and structural beams for buildings and bridges, and generating nearly $7 million a year in freight costs alone. It was no wonder, then, that Stan showed up for a tour of the SMI plant, on a steamy afternoon in July that promised the usual "afternoon-and-evening thundershowers," as skittish as a Little Leaguer on his first trip to Yankee Stadium.

We were met by a steelworker's steelworker, a husky, red-faced man in his fifties named Dale Bass, technically SMI's superintendent of shipping but, as it would turn out, much more than that. Bass was a steel man to the bone, having spent his entire adult life at it in New Orleans and in Birmingham, through good times and bad, meaning more specifically from the rise and self-destruction of old Connors Steel to its reincarnation in 1983 as SMI. He normally roams the grounds like a football coach exhorting his troops, still seemingly awed by the very idea that such a simple waste as scrap metal can be melted and poured and shaped and rolled until it reappears as massive beams of steel capable of holding up bridges and skyscrapers. There was a special spring in his step on this day, because word had just come down that the stockholders had agreed to spend $27 million for further modernization and expansion. Thus, in

January of '94, only eighteen months hence, SMI's annual production would nearly double without the addition of a single man to the payroll.

Although SMI is small when compared with the giant mills of Birmingham's past, it is a sight to behold in its own right. The grounds cover an entire city block, right there on the dingy warehouse fringes of Woodlawn, and everything comes in large sizes: the two-story, tin-roofed plant itself; forty-five-ton ladles holding molten steel; giant cranes with magnets for hands to deftly pluck the scrap from fifty-foot-tall pyramid-shaped heaps and feed it into roaring furnaces; open boxcars on railroad sidings; huge bags of limestone and carbon and more exotic mixes; and, at the end of the production line, neat gleaming stacks of finished flats and beams and rails ready to be loaded onto eighteen-wheeled rigs lined up at the loading docks.

Everything being on a grander scale here than at Lawler, the sensations were doubled as we fell in behind Dale Bass and entered the jaws of the plant. The hissing, the breath-sucking heat, the choking dust, the monstrous ladles brimming with bubbling liquid metal, brought a tingling sense of danger as we swept along the sooty earthen floor and then mounted iron-railed steps and trod precarious catwalks to take in the view. There is indeed something downright sexual about being in the belly of a steel mill throbbing at full production. On this afternoon, in the center ring, as it were, a menacing machine was producing lengths of rail, each pelvic thrust of the groaning black monster producing another foot of red-hot steel hardening and straining to reach its full length of fifty feet, and when that happened the rail was shoved aside to cool and the machine shuddered before the thrusting began anew.

We had watched all of this from the vantage point of a glassed-in booth suspended above the production line, from which a worker at a computer screen could see the entire process. Dale Bass had to shout over the din: "Our worst nightmare is a lightning storm." There had been these booths throughout the plant, little private aeries strung out along the catwalks above the floor, each of them manned by one or two workers intently focused on a color computer screen listing vital signs in much the same way that surgeons might monitor a patient on the operating table. Everything they needed to know was there on the screen, from the temperature of the steel to the speed of the emerging rail as it inched along. As if he were playing with a new toy, Bass tapped the screen with his finger, the mere touch of human warmth serving as a "mouse," passing along a change of orders to the machine, and then he quickly rescinded the order by tapping the screen again. He grinned and shouted, "The modern steelworker!" Down on the floor and out in the yard there were, to be sure, men with hay rakes walking around scooping up bits of scrap metal and tossing them into bins, and others ripping open sacks of limestone to be used in the next day's melt. But nowhere were there men in leather aprons shoveling coke, yanking levers, working foot pedals, lugging fifty-pound ingots of pig iron to the maws of furnaces, or dancing across simmering beds of piglets on thick wooden shoes while breaking them loose with mallets, as the case had been at Sloss Furnace. This was the new order, the world that hadn't come in time for Reuben Robinson.

To trace the history of this plant is to tell the roller-coaster story of steel making in Birmingham, except that in this case there is a happy ending. Connors Steel had begun at the turn of the century on the banks of the pristine little Cahaba River near Helena, some twenty miles south of downtown, where a dam powered its first crude rolling mill. The operation was moved to Woodlawn before 1920, when steel making was still in its rudimentary stages, and by the thirties, during a time of major construction, Connors had become one of the nation's major suppliers of reinforced structural steel. During the Second World War, employing large numbers of women on the production line, it was turned into a bomb factory (my father being one of the truckers who hauled war matériel from Connors to the ports in Mobile and New Orleans). But the company's true heyday would come in the three decades following the war, when the economy was strong and there was an insatiable demand for reinforced steel to underpin the interstates and the skyscrapers sprouting all across the American landscape to accommodate the "baby boom." By the mid-seventies, Connors Steel employed nearly one thousand workers, and the plant operated twenty-four hours a day, seven days a week, the furnaces never stopping. So great was the demand, their customers were limited to quotas.

Dale Bass had arrived in 1969, after ten years of breaking into steel work at Connors's New Orleans plant, and by 1972 he had been promoted to superintendent. This was heady stuff for someone born poor in rural Blount County, son of an electrical contractor, who would attend a total of sixteen schools all over the Deep South following his parents' divorce before playing some junior-college football in Mississippi and then finding himself in the steel business. Business may have appeared to be booming, but he saw trouble coming. Connors's owners in Pittsburgh paid little attention as the unions began to see how far they could push and the equipment began to wear out. Foreign steel became more than competitive, leading to layoffs and cutbacks in production. Cries for cleaner air were being heard more and more now, stinging a city where it had always been said, "You can't trust any air you can't see." And then there was the legacy of race in Birmingham.

"I was the first superintendent at Connors Steel to promote a black person," Bass was saying later, in his makeshift office. "I didn't just promote one, I promoted three, and of course you know what I was called then. But I was full of piss and vinegar—I didn't care. The South had a problem with the racial situation, and all of the steel mills down here had two lines of progression: you had the white line, and you had the black line.

A company would have nine hundred people, six hundred of 'em blacks making two dollars an hour to pick up stuff and three hundred whites running the jobs and making five dollars an hour. The civil rights movement broke this up, and the government stepped in and said, 'We've got to correct this thing.' Through stupidity we had hired gang labor, but now they had time and grade, which the unions recognized, and that entitled them to jobs that the whites had always had. So now there was one line of progression, based on seniority. Okay? Now what you've got is people with a second-grade education who can't run a machine, can't be taught, and yet that's their rightful place. It was all management's fault. They just never thought the day would come, hadn't had enough foresight to see what was happening. Now they had to have six people to do a job that normally would've taken three, because you had three who didn't know what the hell they were doing and three to make the job go.''

I had heard that before, from my old man and from Reuben Robinson, but then Dale Bass surprised me. ''Look,'' he said, ''they could have done what's natural to do in everyday living. They could have recognized black people as human beings and tried to train them coming in, or tried to hire some who had enough education so they could have done something with 'em, rather than just going out and hiring somebody to pick up a piece of steel and put it in a stack. That's the way it's supposed to be. That's what they should have done.''

He told me the story of a young black man named Tommy Fincher. ''Tommy was a great worker, sort of a union leader looked up to by the others, had these gold stars in his teeth, and one day I called him in and told him I was going to promote him to foreman. At first, he didn't know whether he wanted that or not, but he finally agreed and asked if he could have the next day off to take care of some business. I said sure, and when he came back I saw why. Somebody'd finally appreciated his work, given him his due, and now that he was going to be a boss at Connors Steel he had gone and had a dentist take the gold stars off his teeth. He was a great foreman for me.''

The first shoe dropped, he said, when the workers at Connors went on strike in 1979. ''The union, not the company, had become their home. The owners had always given the union whatever it wanted, whatever Big Steel gave at other places, and it had become very hard for them to make the workers feel they were a part of the company. In '79, they went on strike for no reason, really—maybe just to see what it was like. That lasted two weeks before the company gave in to the union again, and then we started going through some very tough times. Business got very bad. We had a lot of specialists come in and find cost-cutting measures, got the union to agree to some concessions in wages, said we'd pay 'em back when we got back to profitability. But things kept getting worse and worse, and then contract time came up again in '83 and the union started making demands that the owners simply were not going to give 'em. The owners just threw up their hands and closed the plant down, rather than bend. That was in December of '83. That's when we started SMI.''

What emerged was a new kind of steel mill, nonunion, no fat, ''lean and mean,'' incentive-driven, about evenly mixed racially, operating on a team concept. ''Right off the bat, we started with training classes right here on the premises. We said, 'We're interested in making money but we're also interested in the employee who makes the money for us.' We said, 'We're going to give you a job and we want you to appreciate that job, and in turn we'll show that we appreciate you.' This office is never closed. Anyone who wants to see me, they can see me. If they've got a problem and it's confidential, I'll keep it confidential. We have no time clocks here, no layoffs, and we rarely terminate anyone. Understand, we don't tolerate absentees or a lot of tardies, but we make a lot of personal contributions to our people, and we give 'em funeral leave with pay and seven or eight paid holidays. The whole thing has changed in the way management is addressing the work force today—that's where the big difference is.''

A man with eight years' experience earns upwards of thirty-five thousand dollars a year these days at SMI, said Bass, and he has his job forever if it's in his blood. ''There was a fear that the new technology would keep cutting into the work force, but we don't let that happen. We don't fire anybody just because his job has been eliminated. When I put in radio remote cranes, I took the crane operator and put him on the floor. Same thing when we went into magnet handling, which eliminated your hookup people. When we put in a new mill, making one job out of several, we didn't fire anybody. Put in a new caster, same thing. Nobody was laid off. We don't do that. Time has a way of taking its toll. Some people we hire just aren't cut out for the steel business. These computers and radio remotes and other stuff have changed things a lot, you bet, but when you get down to it, it's still men making steel. It takes a special breed. Always did, always will.''

CHAPTER TWENTY-ONE

Red and Yellow, Black and White

On the very first Sunday morning after we had gotten our meager furnishings inside the house in Woodlawn, Mama saw to it that Joyce and I, ages three and seven, were properly scrubbed and dressed, grimly told Daddy to check on the pot roast if he didn't have anything better to do (his alibi this time being that the truck needed some work if he was going to leave out that night for Mobile), and, still able only to dream of having an automobile, marched off with us in our Sunday finery, across the railroad tracks and along cracked sidewalks past rows of sooty shotgun houses, to our new church a mile away in the very heart of Woodlawn. This was late in 1943, with the Second World War still raging, a time of great piety and patriotism in America, when Birmingham boasted of having more children enrolled in Sunday schools than any city of like size not merely in the United States but in the whole *world*. Attending Sunday school and church was a ritual followed by all ''good'' people. And so it would be there, at Woodlawn Methodist Church, a fierce dark brick fortress of God right on First Avenue, that I began a fitful dance with organized religion.

In spite of my father's protestations, church was okay by me—a sanctioned diversion, sort of neat. The ladies who ran the Sunday school classes and Vacation Bible school seemed full of goodness, incapable of ill will, as they taught us the books of the Bible and read verses and led us in song—''Red and yellow, black and white / They are precious in His sight / Jesus loves the little children of the world"—trying to ensure that we remained good little boys and girls. Woodlawn Methodist demanded little more than respectful attention, offering in return a haven where a kid could feel, well, *adorable* in his new pair of "Sunday shoes" or his first coat and tie. Later, when we came of age, at Methodist Youth Fellowship meetings in the gymnasium on Wednesday nights, it became a good place to meet "nice" girls over the Ping-Pong tables and at the punchbowl.

That mild interest in the church was turned up a significant notch in 1950, just as I was preparing to enter high school, when a new preacher arrived: the Reverend John Rutland, a ruddy little fellow only thirty-six years old, who looked like a jaunty parish priest when compared with the stoical Methuselahs we kids had associated with the pastor's chair. Unlike most of the deacons, stern and ponderous old guys who kept their distance, he was as plain and straightforward as Harry Truman—a feisty tornado of a man who had been raised in the distant backwoods of north Alabama and had pastored churches in a series of rough milltowns before finally being called to the big city.

He became known as "Brother Rutland" almost overnight, absolutely adored by the kids of the congregation. It seemed that he was always moving in our midst, tousling hair and cracking jokes and needling us about our puppy loves (even winking at our group of fidgety teenagers, clustered in the balcony, while an assistant pastor droned from the pulpit), and soon there was a cluster of pastors-in-training known as the Preacher Boys. I never went that far, but I can report that I strode down the aisle one Sunday night to be baptized into the church by Brother Rutland himself, and that for the decade of the fifties I was, technically, a Christian.

But those dour elders of the church knew things that we didn't. To wit: Brother John Rutland was an unbending liberal on the matter of race. As the decade wore on and Birmingham became more and more shackled by its racial stance, trouble was boiling between Brother Rutland and the older people of the church—one of whom happened to be Bull Connor, now in place as Birmingham's police commissioner, who lived in Crestwood and was a regular in one of the adult men's Sunday school classes. I knew nothing of the tension that was going on inside the church, although I had continued to attend Sunday services when home on weekends from Auburn and later when I came back home to write sports at the *News.* I was many miles away, in fact, working for FSU in Tallahassee during the football season of 1962, when the bombshell hit: Brother Rutland had been summarily fired for deigning to give the annual "needy family" Christmas offering to the nearest and neediest he could find—a *black* family living in the alley behind the church—and had been exiled to the boondocks for the rest of his career. *Red and yellow, black and white / They are precious in his sight. . . .* I never set foot in a church again.

His banishment had been complete, I would hear—he had pastored small churches in mid-sized towns across the state before retiring in 1982 at the age of sixty-eight—and nobody seemed to know whether he was still alive, including Joyce, whose wedding he had performed at Woodlawn Methodist on Mother's Day of '62 while I was in France with the Air Force. Dead or alive, though, he was regarded as something of a legend by the small minority of liberals who had stood up in the bad times. Taylor Branch had reported in *Parting the Waters* that John Rutland had rushed down to City Hall on the morning of Mother's Day '61, with the Freedom Riders on their way, to plead with his parishioner Bull Connor not to let the Klan have their way. When I mentioned this to David Vann, the ex-mayor, who had been cited as Branch's authority, he said, "That ain't the half of it. He wasn't afraid of Bull or anybody. One time John told me he'd said from the pulpit out there that if Jesus were to walk in the door they wouldn't let him in because they had their minds made up it was *their* church, not his."

One afternoon in June, wondering if John Rutland had indeed died in the anonymity the board of deacons had wished him nearly thirty years earlier, I came across a listing in the Birmingham phone book: RUTLAND John E Rev. The address was in Vestavia Hills, the very last place I would expect him to be found. Figuring it was a son who could fill me in, I dialed the number. I told the woman who answered, "I'm looking for the Brother John Rutland who was my preacher at Woodlawn Methodist in the fifties."

"This is Mary, his wife," she said. "He might be going to a political meeting tonight, but I can have him call you. Who is this?"

"Paul Hemphill. I was just—"

"Why, Paul"—with barely a pause—"you still voting Democrat?"

"Yes'm. I'm a 'yellow dog' all the way."

"Good. We need all the help we can get."

The events of 1962 at Woodlawn Methodist had hurt John deeply, she said, but at seventy-eight he was still fighting. They lived in the parsonage next door to the all-white Vestavia Hills United Methodist Church, where as a member of the staff he conducted daily prayer meetings and made visitations and preached on Sunday nights. They had been married for sixty years. Their son and daughter lived in Huntsville, where he was a pastor and she, married to a lawyer, was an "activist hothead" in a conservative upscale church.

By one o'clock the next afternoon, Brother Rutland and I sat across from each other at a desk in a stark office at the church, behind a door that said, simply, JOHN RUTLAND. The temperature outside had already reached ninety degrees, but he wouldn't shed a bulky speckled-wool sports coat or loosen the garish flowery tie that was held in place by a heavy tie clasp that resembled an Iron Cross more than a crucifix. ''Ruddy'' and ''rumpled'' still described him: about five-eight, wispy blond hair turning white, deep lines in his bronzed face, oversized bifocals that kept slipping down a battered nose. I had already begun to draw parallels between his lonely fight at Woodlawn Methodist and the plight of the Hollywood Ten against Senator Joseph McCarthy during that same period in history, and I wanted the rest of the story from him. In the course of the next hour, shuffling his worn and dusty black wing tips on the floor and slapping a yellow No. 2 pencil on the desk for emphasis, he gave it to me.

He had grown up in Haleyville, one of those raw sawmill towns with a sign at the city limits saying, ''Nigger Don't Let the Sun Set on Your Head,'' and his mother had set him straight early on. His father, a country preacher, had died when John was still a boy, ''putting me on the wrong side of the tracks since I didn't have a daddy,'' and his three best friends were the only black, the only Jewish, and the only Catholic boy in town. ''My mother was an extreme fundamentalist who believed that God had personally dotted every *i* and crossed every *t* in the Bible, the most beautiful Christian I ever saw. If it said they are 'precious in His sight,' it meant *all* of 'em. So she kindly taught me that as I came along.''

He was in trouble from the very beginning, when he was posted near the mining-and-lumbering town of Jasper, fifty miles northwest of Birmingham. ''I was absolutely flabbergasted when I began to see what the church thought about black people.'' It was 1940, and when he invited a black preacher and his gospel quartet to entertain at a church banquet, he was jumped by the wife of the only doctor for miles around. ''She was in her seventies, a spitfire if I ever saw one, and I tell you she let me have it. 'Now I've got some keys to the church and those niggers are not coming into my church,' she said. Well, I was young and foolish and easy to try to show my authority, so I said, 'Miz Stephenson, we're new and we need all the friends we can get, but I've invited Dr. Steele and his quartet to come and there's not any way I can uninvite them. They can sit with Mary and me so none of the black will rub off on you.' Boy, she turned white as a sheet. And I said, 'I've been appointed by the mission and I'm in charge of this church, and while I'm here I'll make these kinds of decisions. So please don't try to lock that door, because I'd hate to have you arrested.' Well, the Lord was with me, Paul. She became the very best friend I ever had in that community. She went all over town telling 'em, 'That little preacher's got guts.' "

After Jasper there were stops in Gadsden and Tuscaloosa (where he recalls baptizing a twelve-year-old named Bobby Shelton, later Grand Dragon of the Alabama Ku Klux Klan), and then Woodlawn, "where I really got into it." The members of Woodlawn Methodist were "good, loving, kind, Bible-loving, *family* people except for this one thing [racism], and it wasn't long before they learned who I was. More than one time I saw Bull get up and say, 'I'm not gonna listen to any more of that kind of preaching,' and walk out."

As the fifties wore on, the two great phobias gripping the South were communism and integration. From the pulpit and in the church bulletin and even down at City Hall, Rutland pounded away on the side of what he felt was right—revealing the Methodist Laymen's Union as nothing but a front for the racist White Citizens' Council, saying that there would never be a truly Christian church as long as there was discrimination, once even appearing before the city commission to ask that black policemen be hired to patrol black neighborhoods—and by the late fifties he was the eye of a storm.

"We got all kinds of threats. My little lady changed from a beautiful young woman to an old woman in nine months' time.

Thank God she regained her beauty, but it absolutely almost killed her. She just couldn't answer the phone. They'd start off with, 'We're gonna rape you, you slut,' or something like that. They broke out a window one time, burned a cross in the yard, and there were always threats of bombing the parsonage in Crestwood. Mary and I got to staying out late at night, when the children were asleep, sitting on the steps and singing 'How Firm a Foundation' as loud as we could. We found out that one of the cars that kept circling the block was an unmarked car sent there by Bob Lindberg, a neighbor and a good man who was police commissioner that time when Bull was out of office, and I tell you, that didn't give me a bit of confidence. Those were the days, buddy—those were the days.''

A story that my sweet aunt Ethel Lacey never dared tell anybody in the family was about the day a parishioner burst into the pastor's study brandishing a shotgun. "He said, 'I'm going to kill the first nigger that sets his foot on the grounds at Wood-lawn High,' '' Brother Rutland recalled. '' 'You've been preaching this integration business ever since you've been here, and you've got people worked up, and it's all your fault.' I said, 'Well, I'd be glad to take credit for that, but they've had some laws passed in Congress that have something to do with it.' Miz Lacey was our church secretary, and she was behind him and she managed to back out of the study and call Bob Lindberg. The guy finally said, 'I think I'll just shoot your head off right here.' I wasn't scared one bit. I said, 'I don't think you want to do that. You wouldn't want to die in the electric chair, would you?' In about five minutes the police came in and got the guy's gun and said they would take him down and book him, and I said, 'Please don't do that. Just keep his gun and let him go. He's all right, he's a good man, he's just upset right now.' So I talked 'em out of it.''

The sequel to the story: "When I came to Vestavia Hills, one of the first calls I got was from the son of this man, who now lived in Brookwood. He was very sick, and the son wanted me to see him. So I stayed with him, and when he died I held his funeral. That's happened many times, with people who were so ugly with me out there. The first Sunday we were here, the one who had been chairman of the board when they got me came across the parking lot and grabbed me and twirled me around and said, 'John Rutland, if I had half as much guts as you had, I would've come to see you a long time ago to tell you that you were right and I was wrong.' " And in the summer of '92 he continued to drop by the nursing home where Aunt Ethel was curled up in the fetal position, all but dead of Alzheimer's, to pray for her soul.

Bull Connor was always a presence. "One Sunday morning before church I saw Bull and two other men standing on the steps with their arms folded across their chests, like they were guarding the place, and I said, 'Mr. Connor'—I never called him 'Mr. Connor' before or since—'what are you doing?' And he said, 'I'm not going to let any niggers in my church.' I said, 'Mr. Connor, you're mistaken. This isn't your church, it belongs to the North Alabama Conference of the Methodist Church, and I'm in charge of it, appointed by the bishop, and I'm superintendent of this building. You are trespassing, my friend. Now I'm going around here to my study, and if I come back here in ten minutes and you're still here I'm going to call the sheriff and have you arrested.' When I turned the corner I heard him say, 'Come on, boys—that SOB'll do what he says.' I don't know what I would have done if he had called my bluff."

Then came Mother's Day of 1961, the day of the Freedom Riders. "Bull and I had talked about it the week before, and I had pleaded with him not to let happen what was about to happen. That morning I called him at City Hall, where I knew he would be, and when he asked me if I knew when the buses were due I told him if I knew I sure wouldn't tell *him*. I tried my best to talk him out of it, but he was down there ready to go. He wouldn't listen to any reasoning. That was a sad, sad day for Birmingham. The odd thing about it was, the Klan hated the whites who were helping the blacks more than the blacks themselves. It got for a while where I thought my name wasn't John but Nigger Lover or Communist.''

There were times when he nearly broke under pressure, "thought I was a damned fool for doing what I was doing. Nobody else was doing it, and I'm talking about the church in general: Baptist, Methodist, or any of 'em. There I was, doing what our church says do, what the New Testament says do, and everybody was mad at me. So one day I went home and told Mary, 'I'm through, I'm quitting, I'm just not going to take this anymore.' '' He remembered a friend from the days in Gadsden, Ben Carr, an executive with an oil company, so he called him to say he needed a job. Carr came to Birmingham the next day and made a "fantastic offer" of a job in personnel. "Mary was trying to tell me to go slow. She said, 'You've got some work to do. We don't run from something like this.' But I was pretty well sold on going with it until Ben called me that same night. He said, 'I can't do this. God won't let me do this. You're the hope for the Methodist Church right now, and if I help you get out then I'll never forgive myself. I'll come down there and fight for you. If you need any money, I'll give it to you. But you've got to stay where you are.' Well, I stayed.''

Woodlawn Methodist, in 1962, became less of a haven for the pious on Sunday mornings and more of a battleground pitting John Rutland and his coterie of backers against Bull Connor and the rank and file and even the regional bishop. Students at nearby Woodlawn High, some of them kids from my old neighborhood, would storm the streets, headed for the church, waving posters saying "Kill the Black Bastards." Now and then rocks would fly in the night, shattering windows. Brother Rutland would preach entire sermons not about God but about the White

Citizens' Council and its counterpart the Methodist Laymen's Union, reprinting the highlights in the church bulletin, bringing a summons from the bishop. I had married and left Birmingham by then, but I would hear that my mother now was driving back to her old church in East Lake rather than have her Sunday morning reveries jostled. His choosing to give the annual Christmas offering to a black family was simply the last straw, Rutland's final obstinacy. He was given six weeks' notice before the bishop exiled him to Decatur, cutting his salary in half, replacing him with one of those weary old men who had quietly stood aside while the battle raged.

Rutland seemed bemused when I told him that my belief in religion of all kinds died all of those years ago, because of what they did to him. "You could think sometimes, 'Well, foot, you just wasted your life.' Except—now I'm gonna preach at you for a minute, Paul—except there's something vital in the church even when it's covered up with all this mess. Deep down, there's something there. And what is there is when you go to see some person who is really up against it, emotionally, socially, financially, and look in the face of that person and say to them honestly, and believe with all your heart, 'God has not forsaken you.' It's the message of the church. We've botched it so bad that it's hard for it to get out sometimes, but the message is there, and that's why I stay with the church."

True believers never quit. A staff job at a wealthy, all-white, over-the-mountain church isn't much of a platform for a warrior like John Rutland, but it's the only one he's got. "I'm the one person in this church that everybody knows would be happy to have it half black and half white. I have a black preacher come and preach to us some Sunday nights, and Joe [Elmore, the pastor] is happy for me to do this. He's always been on the right side; he's just not the outspoken person I am. He'll say things in the pulpit like he did last Sunday, that we've got to have people of all kinds, but nobody thinks about his going out and actually getting anybody.''

Rutland raked a weathered hand through his thinning hair. ''It's been a long battle, and I don't know if we ever will win it. Some of us had to work like the devil to get black people into our Methodist Conference, and now I don't know whether it's good or bad. When I go to the conference I see all of the black members standing back, not mingling with the whites. The blacks and whites don't become what you might call good buddies.''

He remains best when on the ramparts, out in the field, mixing with the people. We had left his office and were standing in the shimmering asphalt parking lot when I saw the fire return to his eyes. ''Mary and I have been going regularly to a black section of town, meeting in different houses where there's usually about twenty kids and eight or ten mothers,'' he said. ''They're poor people, project people. Anyway, last week a woman came in drunk and disruptive, made the meeting a shambles, and I turned and said to Mary, 'This isn't doing any good. It's no use. I don't think I'll come anymore.' Well, a little black boy, couldn't have been more than ten years old, must have overheard me, because he said, 'Preacher, if you're not gonna come anymore, then who's gonna be my daddy?' So I guess we won't be giving up those gatherings after all.''

CHAPTER TWENTY-TWO

You Can't Go Home Again

A remarkable number of people from my childhood had simply never left in the first place. And it seemed that most of those who had moved to other parts of the country in pursuit of a vocation had carefully planned all along for the day when they could finally go back "home" to settle down. Of those who had stayed, there was Bunky Wolaver: an amiable fellow I used to double-date with, now about to retire from the same hardware store where he had worked while a student at Woodlawn High. On the other hand there was my cousin Melvin, an engineer who had retired from Chicago Bridge & Iron after some thirty years of being transferred around, now settled into an old house over the mountain and selling exercise equipment to stay busy.

Most likely, I determined, this reluctance to explore other worlds was due to the fact that few people I grew up with had chosen a "career" in the purest definition of the word. They had, rather, prepared themselves for "jobs," for a way of earning a decent living, most of them in some branch of engineering. The Birmingham we grew up in was a city founded on muscle and sweat, not matters of the mind. I found hardly any old acquaintance or relative who wanted to sit down and talk about social issues (other than the fact that blacks now ran City Hall), who spoke with any passion about his work. Except for the handful who had become preachers, they saved their passions for Alabama or Auburn football, for their children and cars and homes and toys, for their social clubs and children, for their golf games.

Whatever was going on in Iraq or Europe or Los Angeles—or downtown Birmingham, for that matter—was of no concern to them as long as it didn't show up on their monthly bills.

There was no denying that Birmingham had become a pleasant place for conservative middle- to upper-class whites who wanted an unfettered life. It was much cheaper to live there, for sure; the money I was paying for an ordinary brick fifties ranch-style house seven miles from downtown Atlanta would fetch a palace in over-the-mountain Birmingham. There were no traffic jams in Birmingham, except on the Red Mountain Expressway at rush hour; Birmingham Green and the new skyscrapers now gave the city a handsome face; golf courses and city parks were everywhere; the air was clean now that steel was no longer the dominant industry; and if there was any unpleasantness going on, the media generally kept it quiet. True, the city had no major league sports and its symphony orchestra lived on the brink of bankruptcy and its airport was a white elephant and there was only one gourmet restaurant; but, hey, there was always Atlanta, only three hours away. Birminghamians had long forgotten their antagonisms about their onetime sister city. If they wanted excitement, they drove to "Hotlanta," sampled its pleasures, and got out before dark on Sunday.

That's exactly what Reeves Sims and his wife intended to do on the first weekend of June. It was difficult for me to call him anything but "Zor," for the dashing movie character Zorro, his nickname when we had met on the sandlots as teenagers. He had been an odd-looking young fellow, with a pocked face and an aquiline beak, but he was a loyal and true friend, liked by all. We had gone through high school and college together—loving baseball, rooming with each other for a couple of years, riding to Auburn and back in his spiffy '54 Chevy—but I hadn't seen him since we returned from France with the Alabama Air

Guard in 1962. I remembered how his life had changed when he met a spunky little churchgoing redhead named Charlene; first went the beer, then the cigarettes, and soon she had him in church.

On the day after Memorial Day I found him at Vulcan Rivet and Bolt, a place similar to Lawler Foundry, one of a series of small tin-roofed sweatshops strung out on a gritty industrial boulevard in Tarrant City. He had retired a year before as an engineer and personnel officer for Alabama Power Company, but boredom "and Charlene's plans for me around the house" had brought him back to work as a foreman at this little foundry that once employed 250 laborers but now was down to 39. He was doing all right: his elder daughter had married and moved to North Carolina; the other had "tried college but it didn't take," and still lived at home while she managed an apartment complex; and with his retirement pay from Alabama Power and the Air Guard, plus his salary at Vulcan, money was no problem.

"I can't tell you how hard it is to call you Reeves," I said when we settled into a booth at a noisy meat-and-three diner in Tarrant City.

He grinned. "Charlene never much cared for 'Zor.' "

"And you've bulked up."

"Nautilus machines at Alabama Power." Like his father before him, at Stockham, Reeves had been in charge of his company's recreation program. His upper body straining at a burgundy Alabama Power T-shirt, he was no longer the scrawny Zorro I had known.

As we tore into steaming plates heaped with what must be Birmingham's favorite lunch next to barbecue—huge truck-stop gobs of country-fried steak, mashed potatoes, pinto beans, beets, corn muffins, washed down with sweet iced tea—we tried to find a common ground. Most of our friends had been jocks, including his brother, Dan, who was on a football scholarship at Auburn until he was hurt in his freshman year. Dan, in fact, had shown up at my mother's funeral: graying, but still at playing weight, idly working at a well-drilling outfit owned by a legendary sandlot pitcher named Deacon Jones. "Dan, Jr., spent three years in the Braves' farm system, but didn't make it," Reeves said. "Hindman [Wall, another friend and ex–Auburn football player] is athletic director at Tampa University now. Herb Pearce [a pitcher of note at Auburn] got an ugly divorce from Liz, then had a heart attack that almost killed him—still sells real estate in Tampa. You remember what a couple Jerry Elliott [Ensley High and Auburn football] and Mertie Roberts seemed to be? The marriage just died, dried up."

When I asked him about Birmingham and the sixties, he merely shrugged. "I've tried to do what Daddy did at Stockham," he said. "Everybody loved him out there because he treated them like individuals, human beings. He didn't make the laws about segregation, but he wasn't a hater, either. They *had* to have segregated teams at Stockham. He just made sure they got equal treatment." Reeves Sims, Sr., in fact, was the man who hired the great local star of the Negro American League, Piper Davis, Willie Mays's first manager when he was with the Black Barons, to manage Stockham's powerhouse black baseball team when the Negro Leagues went under. Zor slugged down some iced tea and called for the check. "I don't have any animosity towards anybody. I didn't write the rules any more than Daddy did."

Back at the foundry, having taken less than an hour for lunch, he seemed eager to get back to work. He and Charlene had always talked about how they might move away from Birmingham once the children were grown, but now there was his mother: widowed for ten years, "kinda lost without Daddy," still in the old home place in East Lake. For now, he said, they would have to be content with driving to Atlanta that weekend to take in the family amusement parks, Six Flags over Georgia and Stone

Mountain. After a quick goodbye, he dashed through a sudden rain shower and disappeared into the dark bowels of Vulcan Rivet and Bolt.

Our lunch had been cordial, and Charlene had said over the phone that "we'd like to see you while you're here," but there was no further contact. Fair enough, I figured. It worked both ways. My efforts to rekindle friendships had been as uninspired as theirs over the years, in spite of Atlanta and Birmingham being only 150 miles apart; and, as I had told Joyce, it really wasn't easy just to roll into town after thirty years and pick up where we had left off. There was something else, too: a misperception, based on the simple fact that I had left Birmingham to become a writer, that Hemphill had "gotten too big for his britches." I remembered running into Bunky Wolaver during the wake for my father at Roebuck Chapel, where his father-in-law happened also to be lying in state, and his presuming that I was a "big writer now, living in New York," and my trying to convince him that not all writers live in New York and that "success" is relative: "Bunky, you sell more lug nuts in a year than I do books."

A disconcerting number of people I had known either didn't return my phone calls or were on vacation or else we simply couldn't work out an agreeable time to meet. I'd had visions of warm reunions—being invited to the house for spaghetti or hamburgers on the patio, long summer nights of teasing and catching up—but that wasn't happening. Even those reunions I did manage to arrange, like the lunches with Johnny Sudderth and Reeves Sims, turned out to be stiff and forced, as though we were trying to revive a flame that had died long ago. Maybe it was true, for a number of complex reasons, that you can't go home again. "Bubba," I would say with all jocularity over the phone, "it's a name from your tawdry past . . . Paul Hemphill." More often than not, this would be met with some degree of shock, a distant fumbling, then a vague promise that we would "have to get together." (For one thing, he hadn't been called "Bubba" for thirty years.) All I could do, in that clammy temporary apartment at the foot of Vulcan, was keep riffling through the phone book.

Thus, it was with much relief that I made contact with one of the ten who had been in my graduating class at Minnie Holman in 1950. Earl Freedle had lived up the hill from us in Woodlawn when we moved there in 1943. He was the son of an upholsterer, and even then, as a second-grader with jug ears and a round face and wavy hair, he resembled the popular character actor William Bendix in a television show that would come along later, "The Life of Riley." Earl became a regular part of our neighborhood gang as we played corkball and raced skatemobiles and teased the girls and instigated rock fights with the black kids in "Niggertown." I knew he had worked as an artist at Oxmoor House, the book-publishing arm of Southern Progress, the *Southern Living* magazine people, where my oldest daughter had worked for a while, but we hadn't seen each other since our graduation from Auburn in the late fifties.

Over the phone one night, he seemed as jovial and wry as I had remembered. He had married and had two children after college, divorced and remarried, picking up a couple of stepchildren in the process, and now lived in Vestavia Hills. He had been out of work for months, since an upheaval at Oxmoor House, so he had a lot of time on his hands these days. We agreed to meet for lunch the next day and catch up, but he said he ought to warn me that he had "a bad case of CRS."

"What the hell's CRS?" I asked.

"Can't Remember Shit."

When he stepped out of his car in front of a hole-in-the-wall neighborhood sandwich shop in Homewood, next door to a Laundromat, I fully expected him to roll his eyes and say, like William Bendix, "What a revoltin' development *this* is," so little had he changed over the years. Instead, he said, "How 'bout a hug," and after we had embraced and slapped backs we went inside for homemade hamburgers and milk shakes served right out of chrome shakers. The little diner was jammed with kids, whose mothers kept running through the light springtime drizzle to check on their laundry next door.

His house on Fifty-ninth Street had been catty-corner from that of Betty Jean Rase, Miss Birmingham of 1944, and he remembered well the day that year when Mickey Rooney tooled into town in a Chrysler "woodie" convertible to take her as his bride. Earl and I ticked off the names from Minnie Holman days: Harris Cooper, Thomas Dodd, Ed Case, Ronnie Nelson, Jacqueline Brechin, Jimmy Gillespie. . . . "I've seen Jackie a time or two," he said, "and I heard that Sara Frances Woodrow is in Florida. Beyond that, I don't know. There's my CRS again."

He had never left Birmingham; just came back home after four years at Auburn, took a job, and burrowed in for life. "I haven't been a success in business, Paul," he said, telling of a small printing firm he once established, turning out brochures and flyers, a business that did well until computers came along and made it possible for the smallest outfits to do their own printing jobs. In his divorce he had gotten a two-story brick Tudor mansion on Key Circle, the same street on the crest of Red Mountain where John Porter's father had served as a yardman; but when his stepdaughter "couldn't cope with busing" to a mostly black school in the seventies, he had moved farther out to Vestavia Hills. He seemed to have become a man of no great joys and no great sorrows.

Somewhere in there, he snapped. Maybe it was when I began to talk about what I was finding on this sojourn in my old hometown: the breadth of Bull Connor's police state, the stark statistics I had discovered only the day before about white flight, my year at Harvard. I had misread him, thought I was talking to a soul mate. At any rate, we had moved to a park bench outside of the Laundromat, beneath a green striped awning protecting us from the drizzle, when suddenly he took off.

"Those riots in L.A.?" he said. "The beating of Rodney King didn't have anything to do with it."

"Oh?" I said.

"*They* did it."

"Who?"

"The Kennedys."

"Christ, Earl—two of 'em are dead and the other one's a lush. What do you mean, 'the Kennedys'?"

"You know what I mean. The conspiracy. Harriman, the Council on Foreign Relations, Communists, all of this one-world crap. It was all planned and orchestrated. Rodney King just happened to come along."

"Where do you get all of this?"

"I read."

"Read what?"

"The *News.* All of Pat Robertson's books. Couple of financial newsletters out of Texas and California."

There was no stopping him. He wasn't talking to a childhood chum anymore but to a cursed "pinko" who had run off to Harvard and Atlanta, somebody who ought to be set straight. I hadn't heard this sort of diatribe since my old man. I thought at first that he might be pulling my leg, simply wanting to watch my knee jerk, just being the same old wry Earl Freedle, the devil's advocate. If he voted at all this year, he said, it would be for Pat Buchanan. Communism hadn't died at all, he said; the fall of the Berlin Wall was just a sham, smoke and mirrors. I didn't have to ask what he thought about Birmingham's black mayor. "It's these people who won't work," he said, launching into a litany of "Afro-Americans, Native Americans, Mexican-Americans, everything but just plain Americans." For an instant, I thought fondly of my brother-in-law. *Pat Buchanan?*

What a day. I had awakened in a foul mood, the Braves

having lost in the ninth inning the night before, and then discovered that my cut-rate coffeemaker had gone on the blink. Now this. It was embarrassing to find that someone I knew had taken such a turn. The only way I could explain it was to fall back on my theory that staying too long in Birmingham would stunt your growth. I remembered Brother John Rutland's story of going inside Woodlawn Methodist and "crying like a baby" after a band of boys he had known since they were infants had gotten on the loose, chanting "Kill a nigger," back in the early sixties. Earl told me how to get to the nearest K Mart to buy a new coffeemaker, and we shook hands and agreed that it had been too long.

During those days of white bread and baseball, my very best friend was Wallace Graddick. We had been living on Fifth Court South for nearly six years when a moving van backed up to the house next door in 1949 and deposited a playmate, a pal, someone with whom I would negotiate adolescence. Having a sister had been okay, but it wasn't like having a brother. I was thirteen at the time, already a bit of a loner living in a fantasy world, dreading Saturdays, when I would be dragged along as Mama hauled Joyce off to various venues for her dancing practice and recitals. With Daddy on the road throughout the week, I felt like an orphan adrift in a world of women who stayed at home. I was a mopey little boy whose father was gone all the time, left with male companions who were but distant icons: the Barons at Rickwood, Harry James on records, the Cardinals' Harry Caray on KMOX, Hank Williams on the Opry, Hopalong Cassidy at the Woodlawn Theater.

That changed the minute Wallace moved in next door. He was a year younger, a spunky, round-headed little fellow with a burr haircut and a twangy drawl, and we were in similar predicaments. His father was a clerk at Alabama Power, a quiet man who bobbed along in the wake of his energetic wife, Myra, and their delectable teenaged daughter. Rosemary was a dimpled high school cheerleader, the center of attention in the Graddick household, the object of palpable lust from the crew-cut suitors who seemed to come and go in shifts. It didn't take long before Wallace and I became the brothers that our parents hadn't given us.

The next five years, until we graduated from high school and went quite separate ways, would constitute the closest friendship with another male that I would ever have. Wallace and I seemed to be at the center of street life, living side by side as we did at the bottom of the hill, the neighborhood's recreation directors. We were behind most of the action—skatemobile races, corkball games, Halloween pranks, "war" games—together, thick or thin. On our balloon-tired bicycles we trekked all the way to Vulcan and back, got lost in Tarrant City and had to phone home for directions, went fishing at abandoned mining pits. Later, double-dating girls in East Lake, we endured two miles of walking and twenty miles of riding on city buses for the privilege of groping in the balcony of the Alabama Theater.

But what really held us together was baseball. We were obsessed by it. Our attempt to carve a ballpark out of a cornfield was merely the final evidence of our devotion. We lost track of how many times we made the long journey across town to Rickwood, gaining free admittance by returning foul balls caught outside during batting practice, lustily cheering our Barons against the hated Atlanta Crackers, begging dead batting-practice baseballs from the players afterwards, sometimes sharing the bus back to town with a Chattanooga Lookout who couldn't afford a cab. Summer days found us packing sack lunches and pedaling to Stockham, where we would spend hours in the stultifying heat taking two-man batting practice and fielding ground balls with the collection of scarred "Baron balls" we had learned to relace with waxed kite string. Together we memorized the Official Rules of Baseball; learned to compute earned-run averages and slugging percentages; hunched over a portable radio beneath the streetlights listening to Gabby Bell's fanciful re-creations of Barons road games; practiced sliding in a pit I had scraped out beside our house.

Our sojourn at the Ozark Baseball Camp in 1952 turned out to be our last great adventure together. Soon Rosemary married and the Graddicks moved across the Seaboard tracks, to the fringes of Crestwood. From time to time Wallace and I would double-date or go to a Barons game, but we were moving into the last years of high school. I would make my futile baseball attempt and then enroll at Auburn. Wallace would become a star shortstop for the Eastside's fearsome American Legion team, rejecting a contract offer from the New York Yankees in favor of enrolling at Birmingham-Southern College. Now and then I would hear reports, the most somber being that his mother had been killed by a train within view of their house. But over the years there would be only random meetings, usually at gatherings such as the one celebrating my parents' golden wedding anniversary, when Wallace and I hardly knew where to begin catching up.

Finally, forty years after that glorious summer of Ty Cobb's visit to the baseball camp in Missouri, I tracked him down. Unknown to me, Wallace had been a computer supervisor for a bank in Atlanta for the past four years; but now, remarried with two stepchildren, he was back in Birmingham, where he was working for a bank during the day and attending night school in order to "get back in touch with actual computer work." In fact, he said, the house he had owned for years, bought before the suburban sprawl had begun, wasn't too far from the new home of the Barons, Hoover Metropolitan Stadium, so why didn't we take in a game for old times' sake? "The Met isn't Rickwood," he said, "but it's baseball."

He didn't have to tell me about the demise of the church of

my youth, and its replacement. Rickwood had gone the way of most of the grand old ballparks in America. The neighborhood had become "undesirable," a code word for "gone black," and by the mid-sixties white fans simply quit going. Whereas the Barons of 1948 drew 445,926 paying customers, the teams of the late sixties and the seventies did well to draw 50,000 despite being stocked with such future Oakland Athletics stars as Reggie Jackson and Rollie Fingers. There was a resurgence of baseball interest in the early eighties, enough to embolden a new group of owners to abandon Rickwood after the '87 season and move the Barons to a "modern" $14 million park nearly twenty miles from City Hall. Soon the franchise, which had cost a mere $150,000 in 1981, was worth $3.6 million, and there was an irony: the new owners were the Suntory Corporation, the liquor people from Japan, the country that had played a large part in making Birmingham a former steel town.

In the summer of 1991, having heard that the Barons were drawing nearly five thousand people per game to this wonderful new "facility," enough to have the new owners applying for a step up in classification to Triple A, I wanted to see it firsthand. On the drive over, I remembered Rickwood: its odd dimensions; the hand-operated scoreboard; the determined urchins (I among them) outrunning old men for foul balls beneath the rickety bleachers; the steam engines chugging along just beyond the outfield fences; electrifying catches by Jimmy Piersall and orbital home-run shots by Walt Dropo; fans passing the hat for change and bills in appreciation of such daring deeds; umpire baiting from the roof by an ebullient Irish general manager named Eddie Glennon. But most of all I remembered the fans, men of a Birmingham that was mostly gone now, callused workingmen reeking of Lava soap and Mennen's after-shave, out for a beer and something to cheer about, braying through the turnstiles for a night on the town before going back to the grind.

As soon as I left the interstate and drove through the pillared entrance to an office park and followed the landscaped Stadium Trace Parkway, I braced myself. The Met was built for a generation of white suburbanites who wanted comfort and order, not quirks and surprises. This ballpark was like those new exurban neighborhoods where they lived, miles from the sweat and clamor of Tarrant City and Ensley. Someone had gathered all of the ingredients—concrete, bright colors, symmetrical dimensions, picnic areas, batting cages for Little Leaguers, ten thousand seats without a single column to obstruct the view, even fluorescent lighting in the dugouts—and produced an Instant Ballpark in much the same way developers were creating bland suburban tracts that could be anywhere in America. Worst of all, they had managed to hide it from the hoi polloi of both races. White yuppies were everywhere, wearing their White Sox caps and Reeboks, beepers snapped to their designer khakis, their Jeep Cherokees cooling in the parking lots. On that night, in a crowd of about five thousand, I saw two black people: one a strapping young fellow on crutches, probably a Baron on the disabled list; the other an old-timer who could have been a survivor of the "nigger bleachers" at Rickwood, Stepin Fetchit, wearing a white straw hat and tap-dancing in the aisles between innings, showing his audience of little white kids everything their parents had told them about black folks.

Now, less than a year after that discombobulating inspection of the Met, I found myself passing through the turnstiles again, this time in the company of someone I hoped would tell me I was right about all of this—that I wasn't just an old fart living in the past, that Rickwood had been viable and good. It was a brisk Friday night, and the Barons would be playing the Greenville Braves, some of whom I had been tracking through the Atlanta minor league system on outings to Macon and Durham. An unusually large number of kids had shown up for the proceedings, eager to see the "World Famous Chicken" go through his clown routine during the game, and after Wallace and I had purchased some snacks and a scorecard we weaved through the gangs of preteens and sought out seats in a peaceful area behind third base. Barely three thousand were in attendance.

I had already been told by my old YMCA coach, Bill Legg, who now ran the Alabama Sports Hall of Fame in downtown Birmingham, that the only physical difference he could see between me and my old man, now that I was turning gaunt and gray, was that "the cigar's missing." Wallace's resemblance to his father was even more remarkable, I thought, as we settled in and began measuring each other. Wallace had the same humble demeanor as his father, the quiet and pensive Wallace Ward Graddick, Sr., like a man who would take the news of the end of the world under advisement. He had come out at about five-nine, a little thick in the gut, the sort who easily disappears into a crowd. He was wearing a frayed green windbreaker, wrinkled cotton trousers, a faded plaid sportshirt, soft-soled shoes, the same pair of clear-rimmed glasses his father had always worn, and a forty-year-old Hamilton watch he gets cleaned once a year. I had the idea that he cut his own hair.

He began to fill me in on a life that seemed to have meandered without much design after Woodlawn High, where he was voted "Friendliest Senior" of his class. He had spent four years flying with the Navy, tried night law school, then wound up in the trust department of a bank in Birmingham "to save my marriage." That wife first moved out on him with their daughter in 1972, and he spent the next decade enduring his bank job in hopes the marriage would survive, only to see it finally break down in '83. Since then he had gotten into computer work for banks. The daughter from his first marriage had gone to Florida State, and now, at twenty-four, was with the Christian touring group Up With People. He had recently remarried, a woman named Barbara, who had brought two kids to the union.

"Paul, we were *consumed* by baseball, weren't we?" He

was keeping score in his program so he could "stay involved" in the game, something not many people do these days. He brought up the demise of "pepper," a traditional baseball calisthenic wherein a batter lazily taps thrown balls back to a line of fielders stationed ten or fifteen feet in front of him. "These kids today, they don't even know what pepper is. Can you believe that? Of course, around the ballparks these days they have these 'No Pepper' signs, afraid a fan'll get hurt and sue, so I don't guess anybody plays pepper anymore. On top of that, I don't think my stepson's team even practices. They just show up a couple of times a week, play games, and forget it. The other day I came across my old spinner game, where you spin a dial and move players around like chess pieces, except they're on a cardboard diamond. You probably remember my spinner game." He paused to watch as the World Famous Chicken, in the first-base coaching box, waggled an enlarged *Playboy* centerfold at the Greenville pitcher. "Well, my stepson wouldn't have anything to do with the spinner. He wanted to go play Nintendo. Can you imagine these kids riding bikes to Stockham and taking two-man batting practice all day in the sun?"

Obsessions had been a pattern in his life, he said. "When I got out of the Navy I was single, about twenty-seven, didn't need a job at the time, so I took an apartment near the Charley Boswell golf course and for a year I played thirty-six holes of golf, alone, every single day. Then I met Vicki and married her six weeks later, so I had another obsession, and I never played golf again. I tend to get fired up about things and plunge in without thinking. Another time I'd decided I wanted to be a lawyer. I filled out the paperwork, got accepted at Emory, paid my money, drove to Atlanta, turned off the engine, and just sat there looking at the law school building for a while, decided that wasn't what I really wanted to do, cranked it up and drove back to Birmingham. I never even got out of the car."

I said, "Well, you did have the patience to hold on to a bad marriage for—what, eleven years? I can't imagine being separated for that long."

"Protestant ethic. I just didn't believe in divorce."

"But turning down the Yankees, Wallace. I would've killed for a chance like that."

"Aw, I wouldn't have made it. Two hundred dollars a month, playing in Joplin, Missouri?"

"Yeah, but all of those years of working toward a chance like that."

"We had fun, didn't we? That was the thing."

Afterwards we stood in the parking lot as the banks of lights were turned off, one by one, and soon even the Greenville Braves' bus had peeled away. The Barons had won on a two-hit shutout shared by two pitchers. Beneath the eerie blue lights of the lot, nearly empty now, we shivered against the chilly wind and talked about things other than baseball.

Out of nowhere, Wallace said, " 'Getting and spending, we lay waste our powers.' "

"Come again?"

"Wordsworth, I think." He pointed to a faded blue Ford van, his chariot. "Bought it new in '81. More than two hundred thousand miles, after all of that running back and forth to Atlanta. Anyway, I remember that quote from an English professor my freshman year at Southern. It's true, you know."

And then, when we started talking about Rodney King and the riots in Los Angeles and the presidential campaigns and where he had been when Birmingham blew up in '63 (Maine, playing out his time in the Navy), my heart fairly soared. I was still sour from the lunch with Earl Freedle, and was getting an overdose of Birmingham's smug white Christian Republicanism. But now here was my very best friend from childhood, a simple man in complicated times, telling me that he had about finished his project of rereading a list of one hundred Great Books ("If it's on the best-seller list I don't bother"); that he dreaded going to work some days to face the racist talk; that he was proud that Rosemary and her daughter were teaching in all-black inner-city schools, especially when their husband and father was "pretty much a reactionary" banker; that his vote would go to Jerry Brown or Paul Tsongas, if either made it through the primaries.

"The problem is, people don't read anymore," he said. "They've made up their minds and they don't want to hear any arguments." We were fumbling for our keys, the last of the lights having been shut down.

"I'm afraid it's worse than that, pal. Worse than we could have imagined."

"Yeah?"

"Rickwood's gone," I said, "and nobody plays pepper anymore."

CHAPTER TWENTY-THREE

The Liberals

In the early weeks back home I spent a lot of time in the archives of the public library, a grim old stone building facing onto Linn Park, in a room as cold and still as a morgue, scrolling through microfilms and reading from musty typed dissertations dryly recounting the horrors of Birmingham's past. There seemed to be no end to the ugliness. The Klan, Bull Connor, bombings . . . U.S. Steel's stranglehold on the economy, the silence of the church, the absence of moderate voices, strident editorials in the daily newspapers . . . child labor, epidemics, strikes. Often, emotionally spent after hours of reading bad news, I would bolt from the dank basement, gasping for fresh air, yearning now more than ever for daffodils, for robins, for baseball, for some sign of hope.

"My God, didn't *anybody* care?" I said on one of those mornings to Dr. Marvin Whiting, the library's archivist. He smiled, spun away, and soon returned with a thin booklet bearing the title *Voice in the Storm: The Button Gwinnett Columns Written During the Civil Rights Struggles and Other Writings,* by one Charles F. Zukoski, Jr., a.k.a. Button Gwinnett. Whiting said that Zukoski was a crusty old fellow, maybe dead by now, who had come by a few years earlier to drop off a typed autobiography for filing away in the archives; that he had been the first mayor of Mountain Brook, had taken to writing columns for a free weekly newspaper over the mountain, and ultimately had been fired from his job at a downtown bank for his liberal opinions. The booklet had recently been published by the library's own press. I paid Whiting my five dollars, stuck *Voice in the Storm* in my pocket, and poked around town for the rest of the day. Only that night did I open it and begin to read.

Zukoski was born in St. Louis in 1898, got a law degree at Harvard, returned home to practice law for five years, but in 1926 accepted an offer to begin a trust department at the First National Bank in Birmingham, a city barely fifty years old, still something of a pioneer outpost, with the largest Klan membership in the United States. He and his bride, a St. Louis girl named Bernadine Edom, herself a graduate of Washington University and politically liberated in her own right, soon settled in among the elite over the mountain.

A *Voice in the Storm* indeed. "In the late summer of 1948, it became apparent to me that victory in the late war had not solved, and in fact in some ways had magnified, the troubles of our society," I read. The Cold War was on, and racial inequality appeared to be the next major domestic issue. "I felt restive over the situation and desirous to have some say as to some of the things that were wrong and what could be done about them." So Charlie Zukoski banged out some essays and ran them by a neighbor who published the Shades Valley *Sun*, a neighborhood weekly normally bloated with social goings-on. Zukoski proposed a regular column under the pseudonym Button Gwinnett, the obscure Georgian signer of the Declaration of Independence, and to his surprise he got the go-ahead.

On the day before Charles Zukoski's fiftieth birthday, in September of 1948, with Harry Truman threatening to dismantle Jim Crow and with the Dixiecrats seceding from the Democratic party, the inaugural Button Gwinnett column appeared in the *Sun,* accompanied by the first of many disclaimers from the editor ("Another of our editorial policies has been to steer clear of the ugly, unpleasant side of the news. However . . ."). In it, "Button Gwinnett" spoke broadly, as in an overture, of the

"spirit of unrest and dissatisfaction which grips men everywhere," of the "imbalance of wealth," of "past injustice," and
of the need to "be faithful to the fundamental principles of truth
and right." It was in the spirit of Thomas Jefferson and other
"revered fathers," he wrote, "that I will have my little say."
Soon he was off and running, a voice in the storm, taking the
only public liberal stance in town. He jumped the Klan, Connor,
and McCarthyism; even pointed out the unnecessary pressures
on young people inherent in having sororities and fraternities at
Shades Valley High School. He championed Truman, school desegregation, family planning, the United Nations, the Warren
Court, the hiring of black policemen, and the annexation of
neighborhoods like Mountain Brook.

"In all that time I only occasionally missed a weekly column," Zukoski recounts in his booklet:

> The authorship of the articles was a carefully guarded secret
> between George Watson [the publisher/neighbor] and me, for
> some of the views I expressed on economic, and especially on
> racial, questions were bound to be viewed by the essentially
> conservative readers of the paper and by my superiors and the
> Board at the Bank, as radical if not downright heresy. At times
> I was accused of writing the column, but always I had to deny
> it. At times customers of the Bank wrote to my superiors con-
> demning me, but always I had to say I was not the author. If
> I had admitted it, I would have had to discontinue the writing.

The writing was pontifical, a far cry from Ralph McGill's
wonderfully crafted vignettes in the Atlanta *Constitution,* and it
was impossible to guess how many people in the *Sun*'s audience
of some thirty-five thousand unsolicited "subscribers" actually
read it; but at least it was there. Now and then one of the essays
would be picked up and reprinted in, say, the Montgomery
Advertiser—never by the Birmingham dailies—or be used to fire
the rabble at Klan meetings. Mail would drift in, addressed to

"Comrade Gwinnett," railing for his dismissal; but for the most part Zukoski's pleadings fell upon deaf ears. The power brokers over the mountain simply ignored him; and when he was forced to stop writing the column in 1958, few seemed to notice—it was like the tree falling, unheard, in a distant forest. He was dismissed from the First National Bank in 1962, a year earlier than planned, not necessarily because he had been revealed as Button Gwinnett but because he was spending his days on the job preaching what was regarded as blasphemy.

As it turned out, Zukoski was very much alive. When his beloved Bernadine died in 1990, he moved out of the big house in Mountain Brook into an exclusive retirement home, Kirkwood-by-the-River, stuck back in the woods beside the little green Cahaba River, where many of Birmingham's wealthy go to die. Now he was nearing ninety-four, surrounded by books and Chippendale, and from this new bunker he continued to lob mortars. I had heard that he was more cantankerous than ever these days, partially because he had to shout to hear himself at meetings. Indeed, I thought he might never find room for me on his appointments calendar; first he had made a trip to New York, alone, for an annual meeting of the Council on Foreign Relations (he and his wife had founded a branch of the CFR in the forties); there had been surgery to relieve the pain in his spinal column, requiring a month for recovery; then he needed a few days to compose a letter to the editor of the *News* in which he addressed the problem of the federal deficit and the "failure of American society as a whole, not just Birmingham, to deal with the problem of race and minorities" in the wake of the Rodney King affair. More often than not, his phone would go unanswered.

Finally, on a balmy morning in June, I found myself sitting across from Birmingham's oldest surviving savant. Wearing thick glasses, his ears stuffed with the same high-powered hearing devices worn by Reuben Robinson, his hair gone wild and white, Zukoski sat like a deposed king in a high wing chair in front of a wide window revealing dappled leaves rustling in the summer breeze. He wore a striped long-sleeved shirt, gray gabardine slacks, white running shoes, and a bolo tie secured by the sort of pewter clasp you find at the Phoenix airport gift shop. Parked next to the door was his collapsible wheelchair, ready to go at a moment's notice, like a fireman's waders. Let's make this quick, he said.

He had never fooled himself into thinking his views would be welcomed in Birmingham. "The city might have looked and felt somewhat midwestern, because of its heavy industries," he told me, "but it was southern just the same. They had a segregated society, and they liked it that way. I talked to friends who said, 'I know you're right, but I've just been raised in a different culture and I can't accept it.' It was a plantation culture without the plantations."

What rankled him the most was the failure of others who had come down from the North to join him in the fight for change. "Those industries were started by people from the North, U.S. Steel and the others. They had been educated in the North and should have known that some change must be made here, but they had gotten so acclimated to the society down here that they just didn't do it. I'm talking about people like Oscar Wells, who was president of our bank. I'm talking about people like Crawford Johnson, who was head of the Coca-Cola industry in this state. I'm talking about the people who were sent down here by U.S. Steel. They were from the North, transplants, and they should have known better."

It must have been lonely, I said. "There were very, very few liberals here at the time. I had gone to Harvard at an early age, had become a Unitarian there, had become a liberal there, and I saw the problems of the country and certainly of the Birmingham community. Maybe a dozen of my friends were liberal, at best. Abe Russakoff, my personal physician. Paul Johnson, the lawyer [who eventually would be kicked out of the family law firm]. Jim Head. If there were more in the community, I didn't know about them. It was different in Atlanta, and I'm not sure why. The leaders in Atlanta realized they faced a very serious problem, and they dealt with it more realistically. [Mayors Ivan] Allen and [William] Hartsfield were enlightened men, but our leaders here were unwilling to see that the times had changed, that we had to change, that we had to treat the blacks and other minority groups fairly and equally. They just refused to see that here.''

Zukoski's involvement didn't end on the pages of the Shades Valley *Sun.* In addition to starting the Birmingham branch of the CFR, he was one of the founders of the Birmingham Symphony, the Birmingham Music Club, the local mental health association and industrial health council. He and his wife were always meeting with book clubs and school advisory groups and planning commissions and, more quietly, clandestine biracial gatherings. In 1951, presumably before they caught on to him, he was named ''Best Citizen'' of Birmingham. After the 1954 Supreme Court decision on school desegregation, he helped organize a fully desegregated two-day institute at Birmingham-Southern on ''Negro Progress in Alabama and Its Effect upon Race Relations'' that drew nearly one thousand people, half black and half white, and went off without a hitch in spite of Bull Connor's blustering about ''Commies.'' After his departure from the bank in '62 he and his wife, who together had started the first family-planning program in Birmingham, signed on as volunteers with a Boston foundation and traveled the world for the next twelve years, developing family-planning programs. And always, at home or on the run, he found time to write lengthy letters to the editor of the *News.* In the case of one, an impassioned two-thousand-word response to the Sixteenth Street Baptist dynamiting, he eagerly sought a co-signer from the ranks of "leaders"; but only his friend Jim Head, owner of a downtown office-supply firm, would step forward.

We kibitzed for a while, but Zukoski had begun deflecting talk of the past. He was frosted that George Bush "wouldn't even sign the endangered species law" at the recent conference on world pollution in Brazil. It looked as though the door was open at the White House for a Democrat this time. How did he feel about Richard Arrington, after a dozen years in office? "I know him pretty well. On the whole, he's been a good mayor. He's made some mistakes, been subject to some just criticism, but on the whole he's been a good mayor and he's tried to bring the two races together. He's been fair to the whites. It's the council I'm worried about. They run everything in the interest of the black people now, but I'm afraid they're not looking out for *all* black people."

Abruptly, he said, "I'm sorry, but I've got to go."

"Oh. Lunchtime already?"

"No." He checked his watch. "I have another appointment in about ten minutes."

"An appointment?"

"I'm very busy, you see."

He walked across the room, wincing from the pain in his back, and when he reached the wheelchair he popped it open. He allowed me to open the heavy door, and when he was sure I had locked it properly he began pushing the wheelchair down the carpeted hallway as though he were an orderly rather than a resident. A pair of women with blue hair greeted him as he made his way to the elevator, but he did not speak to them. "These are not congenial people," he whispered, once we were alone. "They haven't been enlightened."

.   .   .

In ways reminiscent of the Communist witch hunts of the fifties, the careers of Birmingham's few outspoken liberals in those days were either destroyed or seriously derailed. They were boycotted, defamed, fired, run out of town, or ostracized. Most of them were dead or long gone by 1992: Chuck Morgan was preparing to retire to Destin, Florida, on the Gulf beaches, after years in Washington with the ACLU; Sid Smyer, the realtor whose epiphany came when he saw the Freedom Riders story splashed across Japanese newspapers, died before some sort of racial balance came to his town; Henry King Stanford, president of Birmingham-Southern College when it was one of the few safe havens for liberals, was chased out of town. Given the time and the place, it had taken more courage for them to act on their convictions in Birmingham than had been required of Ralph Mc-Gill in Atlanta.

One of the last of the old liberals still active was Zukoski's friend Jim Head, eighty-eight, a shambling bear of a man who was still going in to work early every morning at Head Office Supply after seventy years on First Avenue. Head, the son of a Kentucky insurance salesman, had spent his life immersed in progressive civic works: founder of the local chapter of the National Conference of Christians and Jews, finance chairman of John Kennedy's campaign in Alabama, a force behind the Metropolitan Audit in '58, a liberal voice in the Young Men's Business Club, a member of the Civil Rights Commission, now active in planning the Civil Rights Institute. His business had been boycotted during the early sixties ("Aw, hell, I didn't miss any meals"), and he had learned a valuable lesson when he resigned from the Downtown Club over its refusal to add a Jewish member: "You don't do a damned bit of good, resigning."

For a couple of hours one morning in the spring, in a cubicle at Head Office Supply adorned with a pen-and-ink drawing of JFK, he reminisced. When a health officer in the thirties said the cause of a typhoid epidemic was unsanitary conditions in the local dairy barns, the response was not to clean up the barns but to take the man to the woods to be tarred and feathered. The Metropolitan Audit had been regarded as a "Communist plot." Early Birmingham wasn't a city but a "mill town." He blamed the lawyers and the preachers for the city's reluctance to change: "The attorneys knew the legal and the pastors knew the moral, but they were both afraid their 'clients' would disown them." The newspapers were guilty on the same grounds: "I asked [*News* managing editor] Vincent Townsend one time why he didn't point out Birmingham's problems, and he said, 'We tried that one time and in sixty days lost forty thousand subscribers, and we aren't about to make another goddamn foolish mistake like that again.'" And he told of bringing McGill over once to speak to the Rotary Club: "He didn't say the word 'segregation' one time, just painted a picture that we've got half our population going to waste and we're stupid if we don't make out of them everything they can be. Everybody talked later about what a fine little talk he had given, but they didn't pay a damned bit of attention to what he said."

Head has lived in Mountain Brook for most of his life, and been a member of the Birmingham Country Club for sixty years. "I enjoy it," he said. "It's near to heaven over the mountain, with the dogwood and the azaleas and everything, but I've been such a damned cockleburr it's a wonder they haven't kicked me out. I have friends that I play golf with and they don't want to have anything to do with the city except criticize it. 'That damned place has gone to hell,' they say, except they sort of like the airport, the zoo, the Alabama Theater, the facilities. Understand, my friends are wonderful people, sensitive about a lot of things, but they aren't having any truck with this bunch of blacks. 'They're loud,' they say, 'they're different,' as are Jews and Catholics. It's a damned shame we migrated and left the city." The only reason he's not leaving, he said, to "give up, go down and live on the Gulf or go to Sausalito," is that he has "some unfinished business." He paused, raked a hand through his graying hair, and smiled. "What the hell," he said. "You keep on plowing."

The most visible of the scant number of white liberals in Birmingham's history, perhaps, is David Vann, a lawyer who will probably go down as the city's last white mayor. Vann, the son of a small-town Alabama lawyer and a descendant of the Cherokee chief James Vann, had barely turned thirty and was practicing law in Birmingham when the Freedom Riders came in 1961. "I think that's when the change really began," he told me. He and Sid Smyer and Chuck Morgan became the leaders of the movement to change the form of government, their immediate purpose being to dislodge Bull Connor and his boys from City Hall; and they succeeded, of course, around the time of the dogs and hoses in '63. Vann was everywhere in the spring of that year, advising Martin Luther King and then negotiating the desegregation plan that resulted from the Children's Crusade; and when Chuck Morgan departed and Sid Smyer died, he was left as the city's most prominent liberal. In 1971 he entered politics for the first time, winning a seat on the city council, and when the moderate Republican George Seibels stepped down in '75 after two terms, Vann succeeded him as mayor. He lasted only one term—losing, ironically, to his friend and fellow councilman the black college professor Richard Arrington, because of a racial incident.

"Well, that was a twist, wasn't it?" he was saying late one afternoon in August. Vann, in his late fifties, was right out of Central Casting: about five-nine and 260 pounds, hair swept back into a theatrical white mane, cotton cord suit and red suspenders, wheezing through a cloud of cigar smoke as he rocked back and forth in a high-backed tan leather swivel chair at a desk he bought from Chuck Morgan when Morgan left town.

"About four months before the election, a police officer killed a black girl. There'd been a shooting and a holdup at a 7-Eleven, and when the police got there the guy they arrested said, 'Be careful, there's a guy with a shotgun in that car.' It turned out that the guy had talked a young girl into getting his car for him and she had an Afro haircut. Boys and girls were wearing Afros at that time, so you couldn't tell 'em apart. Anyway, when the policeman saw a car move and somebody in an Afro raised up, he shot and killed her. I couldn't in all honesty fire the policeman for doing what he was trained to do, but the black community didn't see it that way. I didn't even make the runoff against Arrington."

Early in my stay, I had spent half an hour with Arrington in his office at City Hall, a cool and tasteful inner sanctum featuring a framed photograph of the young Malcolm X and a small bust of Martin Luther King, and I was impressed by his demeanor and apparent sincerity. Not surprisingly, as was the case with most other black public officials across the country, he stayed in office by getting all of the black vote and just enough of the white. He appeared to be anything but the leader of some nefarious black political machine, as many working-class whites felt, but rather the same pensive and shy man who had been a professor of invertebrate zoology at little Miles College. It surely had not been easy, being the first black mayor of Birmingham, but he had done a smooth job of rallying the pragmatic downtown white business establishment while at the same time fending off rumors of various improprieties almost from the start. The latest Justice Department "investigation" of his administration had to do, ironically, with the alleged mishandling of Civil Rights Institute funds—Arrington, in an ill-advised and demeaning move, allowed himself to be wrapped symbolically in chains before spending a night in jail rather than turn over his diaries— and that, like all of the other vague inquiries over the years, would be quietly dismissed for "lack of evidence." "I have no doubt it's a personal vendetta on the part of certain judges," he told me. "When I saw the files [through the Freedom of Information Act], I was amazed. They were trying to find things on my ninety-year-old mother."

Vann was a loyal Democrat to the core and, of course, felt Arrington was the target of a Republican vendetta during the Reagan and Bush years. "I've known Arrington for a long time and I don't believe he's a dishonest man. I shared some of my campaign money with him when we were running for city council, endorsed him in the runoff for mayor when he beat me, and I think he's been a successful mayor. It's tough being black. He's a very bright guy who's been able to have a key core of white businesspeople supporting him. He's created an economic development program; he's kept the city moving. It's sad now to see this federal investigation splitting the city. You investigate a guy for seven or eight years and you can't get enough to indict him? They've left him swinging in the wind. They named him as an 'unindicted co-conspirator' in one case and never put on one bit of evidence against him. And, of course, he couldn't defend himself, because a nonindicted co-conspirator can't even have a lawyer in court."

He pointed out that there had been several black mayors around the country, that even Andy Young had been investigated while mayor of Atlanta, but there had been no similar investigations of white Republican mayors. "It's a completely politically controlled process. The Justice Department had been here before I left City Hall, when Jimmy Carter was in the White House, and when they charged us with discriminatory hiring practices we complied with everything they said and they left. Then Reagan won and they came back again, about as soon as Arrington went in, and this time it was white firemen saying *they* had been discriminated against. So the Justice Department switched sides and joined the white firefighters, and that tells me that something political happened. They decided there were more white folks in America than black folks, and they wanted to make sure that every white voter knew they were on the white folks' side. It's the power of the presidency. If the President says, 'Let's don't have an investigation of Iraq,' there will be no investigation of Iraq because the attorney general is in his Cabinet.''

My request for a half-hour chat had stretched past two hours, and Vann's secretary had already left for the day. ''There's some integration going on at Vestavia High, but they all happen to be fullbacks and ends,'' he said as he went around the office, shutting off the lights. Would there ever be another white mayor in Birmingham? ''It wouldn't be an easy thing— might take some restructuring. We've got thirty-four governments. We'd be bigger than Atlanta if we didn't spend so much time fighting each other.'' Had whites calmed down on the race issue? ''I had a cousin lose his job last year because he tried to hire a black person. His company said they already had enough blacks, and they got angry with him about it. So that's still with us.''

As he locked up and we headed for the elevator, he said he would soon be moving to city offices so he could fully qualify for his pension. He was divorced now, but the Vietnamese orphan he had whisked away on the last flight out of Saigon was a freshman at Birmingham-Southern (Lee Van Kim, renamed Michael Lee Vann), and the boy was important to him: ''My ex-wife has custody, but he comes around to stay with me until he can't stand the cigars anymore.''

The minute we hit the sidewalk, virtually deserted at dusk, a homeless man appeared out of the bushes along Birmingham Green and approached us. ''Excuse me, Cap'n, but you look like a big man,'' he said to Vann, waving an empty vial of Antabuse, explaining his difficulties: he'd get drunk if he didn't have it, but nobody would give him a refill because they said his Medicaid had stopped, and they wouldn't even let him spend the night at the Jimmy Hale Mission. Vann listened patiently, taking in the beard and tattooed arms and distended belly and wild eyes, then excused himself to go back into the lobby of the Frank Nelson Building. I told the man who Vann was. When Vann came back to the sidewalk, he handed the man a scrap of paper with the name and office number of a lawyer and said, "Be there at eight in the morning. That's exactly what this lawyer does." The man said, "Bless you, Your Honor, bless you—mighty fine city you got here," and went trundling off around the corner.

The best of the dissertations I was reading in the archives had been written by a man named Bob Corley, now head of the National Conference of Christians and Jews in Birmingham, and when I went by to meet him we discovered that we had much in common. Corley was twelve years younger, but he had grown up in Crestwood, been a member of Woodlawn Methodist, and attended Minnie Holman and Woodlawn High. He had even bought his house from George Quiggle, now an Episcopal priest, who was a mere tyke living next door to us in East Lake before we moved to Woodlawn; his best friend was Don Shockley, whom I had known as a YMCA football player, now a Methodist executive in Nashville; and a younger brother of his once had been road manager for a friend of mine, the country singer Ronnie Milsap. The one major difference between us, though, was our upbringing. The word "nigger" had not been allowed around his house, and his parents were volunteer workers in the early sixties for the moderate mayoral candidate Tom King (defeated by the Connor machine) and for the campaign to change the form of city government.

Now, at forty-four, Corley was the most prominent of a small cadre of native-born liberals who had been politicized during the troubles of the sixties. Amiable, soft-spoken, well-read, he not only served as a healer as head of the NCCJ but also was president of the Birmingham Board of Education, served on the board of the Civil Rights Institute, and found time to lecture on urban history at UAB. He had, in fact, just been elected to the Woodlawn High School Hall of Fame, along with the legendary Alabama all-American tailback Harry Gilmer. That's what I get for becoming a writer and leaving town, I thought—I had never received so much as a single piece of mail from the school in the nearly forty years since my graduation—and I listened to his story with some envy and a certainty that I would have come around much faster if the air had been calmer around my house when I grew up. I had felt the same as I watched my friend Howell Raines ascend in the hierarchy at the New York *Times;* Howell was from white working-class folks, too, near Dynamite Hill, but his parents had been much more genteel and supportive than mine. Both Corley and Raines, not to overlook Wallace Graddick, had gone to Birmingham-Southern during the hard times when it was a virtual boot camp for liberals.

Although Corley's parents "vote Republican now and repeat all of the stuff about Mayor Arrington," their tolerance when he was young had made the difference. "They certainly taught me not to hate anybody," he was saying. "I can't say for sure when I got politicized, but it could have been the day in '65, when I was a junior, and the first attempts were made to integrate Woodlawn High. A caravan of white students from West End, which had already been integrated, came charging across the lawn with a Confederate flag, trying to get us to join them, leave school in a boycott. The administration had gotten the Warblers, the football team, and all of the male faculty to block the doors so nobody could get in or out. Anyway, I went home that night, turned on the television, and saw my school on 'Huntley-Brinkley,' and realized that I was a part of something bigger and more important than I'd thought of at that point."

Brother John Rutland had been run off by then, but now there was a different attitude at Woodlawn Methodist, where Corley was president of the MYF and thinking of becoming a preacher. "George Quiggle was one of a number of young ministers working with the youth program there by then. I learned 'red and yellow, black and white' there, like you did, but I had my whole thinking shifted by some reading material the national Methodists were providing us, about race and brotherhood. Some of the adults got very upset, of course. I remember leading a discussion where the issue was 'If the people in Russia were starving, should we send them food?' We were saying yes, of course, they're fellow human beings; but a lot of the adults said, 'If Communism can't feed its own people, we should stand back and let 'em starve.' The older folks were still hanging on. But this was my group, my generation, and we were the ones who were going to have to deal with these issues."

He certainly understood the opposition faced by liberals in the state of Alabama during those days. As a part of a program called Boys' State, he spent a day inside the statehouse in Montgomery in the summer of '65. The Detroit civil rights worker Viola Liuzzo had been killed that spring during the Selma-to-Montgomery march; and when the Boys' Staters tried to introduce a simple resolution acknowledging her murder and condemning the Klan, they were gaveled down. "Finally, a friend of mine just went up and grabbed the microphone out of frustration and started screaming 'You bunch of brush apes!' at the top of his lungs. It was quite an education, to see what happened when you tried to bring up those issues in this state." For that reason he decided against going into the ministry ("I saw how far away I was from the thinking of most folks in the state"), switched to history and political science, toyed with the idea of becoming a lawyer, and finally got a Ph.D. in history at the University of Virginia. "By writing my dissertation there, I figured I could answer some of the questions I couldn't answer in high school while it was happening. That's when I came to grips with who I was."

Although he was part of a sadly small band of white people

in the city who were liberal and would openly stand up for their beliefs—not four hundred people showed up at Linn Park for an impromptu appearance and brief talk by Democratic candidate Bill Clinton on the day before, whereas late in the summer President George Bush would draw twenty thousand wildly cheering supporters at a mall—Bob Corley gave me a glimmer of hope for Birmingham. It was a good sign, he said, that ''a lot of people really got upset'' over the flap at Shoal Creek Country Club in 1990, just as they had over Arrington's grandstanding in wrapping himself in chains for his symbolic trek to jail. ''You see people standing up now like they wouldn't in the sixties,'' he said. ''The local television news last night was about Rodney King, but they led off with film from the riots here in '63. We'll never live that down, it seems, but that's all right. I'm not sure Birmingham is any worse than other places in the country about race these days—in fact it might be better. At least now, when things happen, we talk about it.''

CHAPTER TWENTY-FOUR

Last Notes
from Home

Who can blame the city for being paranoid, after what happened in the sixties? "You get a brick thrown or a policeman injured, and it'll be on CNN for three days," the *Post-Herald* has quoted a director of the Southern Poverty Law Center's "Klanwatch." Back in April of '92, a thirty-six-year-old homeless black man was stabbed to death by a gang of skinheads beneath one of the bridges over the railroad tracks downtown. The Associated Press says there are about a hundred members of the local Aryan National Front, mostly kids from screwed-up families on the city's rough edges who are into skinhead haircuts, storm trooper boots, swastikas, heavy-metal bands like Final Solution, and Third Reich rhetoric. "I needed a place to stay and they gave me one," says one teenaged boy, jobless and flopping in a commune. "They're teaching me things about life, things my parents don't have time for." Their stories are similar to those of the old Klansmen, and their leader is a thirty-four-year-old who is in and out of prison on gun and drug charges.

Now, on a Saturday in June, there'll be two rallies downtown—skinheads at noon, the hastily formed Coalition Against Hate Crimes later—and nobody is taking any chances. The papers have asked people to stay away from downtown (as if anybody goes there anymore on Saturday); many of the city's twelve hundred homeless have been bused away for the day; even the library has been closed; an area of ten square blocks, taking in Sixteenth Street Baptist and Linn Park, is cordoned off with yellow police-line tape; and it will cost the city fifty thousand dollars in overtime pay for police protection. "I'm praying for rain," an officer says.

The cops can't keep everybody out. While they're busy waving the skinheads—easily identifiable by their dress, the Nazi flags, the old cars and pickups decorated with racist decals—through a checkpoint on the edge of Linn Park, a crowd of media and FBI agents and counterprotesters begins to swell. The totals: forty-four skinheads, four hundred others, three hundred cops in riot gear bristling between them. Angry shouts from the crowd, most of them young blacks: "Hey, you skinhead motherfucker!" "Come over here, you white trash!" "Hey, hey, ho, ho / Racist crackers got to go!" I'm startled when I hear my name called; it's my son David, in a Malcolm X cap and his familiar hiking outfit of boots and black denim, a Teflar helmet and a water bottle dangling at his side. He's there passing out Socialist Workers Party literature, has been frisked by the cops, will help carry a banner reading "Stop Racism and Fascist Violence—Justice for Rodney King." "Cops asked about the helmet," he says. "Told 'em I'm a prudent man."

Photo opportunity. By one o'clock everything centers on the obelisk at Linn Park, a Confederate memorial, where the skinheads are trying to hold their rally. A police helicopter directly overhead accomplishes two things: ripples two dozen black-and-red Nazi flags and the white satin robes of a dozen Klansmen, also drowns out the "*Sieg heil*"'s and everything else the skinheads are trying to say. On the other side of portable chain-link fences, Muslims are taunting even the cops: "Why ain't you workin' in Homewood today, you Oreo?" Cops scan the rooftops for snipers. Police radios crackle. An old black woman snaps at the Muslims, "Y'all just go home now—go home," as they break away, form their own march, and begin raging through the streets with the media in pursuit. By two o'clock it's over, no harm done; cops sit on the grass at Linn Park, eating sandwiches, waiting for the counterrally to begin.

David and I spend the rest of the day together. We're sitting on the worn steps of Sixteenth Street Baptist as the counterprotesters queue up. There are black preachers, David Vann, Bob Corley in a Boston Red Sox cap, Episcopal priests in collars and Nikes, and what I call the NPR (National Public Radio) Crowd: new jogging outfits, L. L. Bean gear, blue blazers and khaki trousers, sentimental "Peace" and "Equal Rights Amendment" buttons. The crowd reaches three hundred, evenly divided by races. There are speeches, an orderly walk of five blocks, with everybody singing "We Shall Overcome," and more rhetoric at Linn Park about Birmingham's past and hopes for the future. David and I run by the Socialist Workers headquarters in a narrow brick building across the tracks, where he turns in the banner he has been holding all day, then proceed to a Tex-Mex joint at Five Points South. The SWP turns out to be as dogmatic as the Republicans and Democrats, he says, and he doesn't know how much longer he'll fool with them. Better this than golf, we agree.

I've said all along that if David reaches the age of thirty he's going to be fine, and I think he'll make it. It's been a rough road for him, my only son, since my leave-taking when he was only ten: lonely childhood exacerbated by divorce; first my drinking and then his drugging; his suicide attempt at nineteen; washing out of Sewanee and the Marines because of drugs. We've always talked, though, unlike my father and me, and our walk of the Appalachian Trail in '84 bonded us forever. Now he's twenty-seven and getting his act together: gangly and good-looking, no more booze and drugs, two straight years on the same job as a waiter at the only classy restaurant in town, an eclectic reader with friends of all stripes, hanging around Birmingham so he can finish up at UAB. Like his father and his grandfather, he'll never hold down a "job" as we define it, never be status quo. His flirtation with the Socialist Workers Party is more of an inquiry, I think. When the dust settles, he'll probably line up with the far left of the Democratic Party. Birmingham could have used him in the sixties.

My three daughters couldn't be more different from each other. Lisa, at thirty, is married to a co-worker in the Family Ministry of the Crusade for Christ, sort of a feel-good yuppies-for-Jesus organization; once her husband finishes seminary in Dallas, they'll settle in Little Rock and start a family where it's safe. Molly is turning twenty-one and about to graduate from Rhodes College in Memphis, in sociology and anthropology, and she won't be long for Birmingham; she's the liberated woman, tall and beautiful and bright—made a beeline to Dachau when she arrived in Germany to study, will walk the Appalachian Trail with David in the summer of '93. And then there is Martha, the most fortunate of them all due to her parents' marriage: four-teen, slim and quick, being educated at one of the best schools in Atlanta (private, but twenty-five percent minority), absolutely color-blind when it comes to race. The one thing I learned, as the son of parents who gave up on me when I chose a less-traveled road, is to give them a long tether and watch them dance. It's been a hell of a show.

A story from one of my landladies in Birmingham, who once owned a beauty salon catering to wealthy women from over the mountain: "When they went off on their vacations to Hilton Head they insisted that their 'girls' go with them. My girls were black, so about dark I'd put a bunch of 'em in my car, and off we'd go. It was a sight. Here I was, a white woman driving across Alabama and Georgia all night with four or five black girls in the backseat of my car. We'd be going through small towns and I'd make 'em scrunch down and hide under blankets. That was in the fifties and sixties. I tell you, it got scary.''

It dawns on me, after reading the *News* and *Post-Herald* regularly through the spring and summer, that women are relegated to the inside pages just as black people were in the days of "What Negroes Are Doing." Now and then a woman is pictured on the front page, usually a teacher or a "homemaker" or a serial killer in Nevada, but for the most part they are found inside in the sections devoted to food, religion, and social doings. One Sunday an entire page is filled with the names of every young woman being "rushed" by sororities at Auburn and Alabama. The major exception is the secretary in the athletic department at the University of Alabama who came to work one day with a black eye, said basketball coach Wimp Sanderson did it, and got him fired. Some letters to the editor have said what a shame it is that such a fine coach should have his career end over something so trivial. This comes at a time when Auburn is being investigated for buying football players, and I just bought a bumper sticker at the Auburn exit on I-85: "We May Pay Our Players, But We Don't Beat Our Women."

There's no way we're going to miss this. Susan and Martha come over from Atlanta to watch my fifty-two-year-old sister tap-dance with her group from Time Step Studio on the stage of the Alabama Theater. More than a thousand tickets have been sold, proceeds going to the fund for the preservation of the ornate old Alabama, the only remaining movie palace in downtown Birmingham. "Joyce," I say, "this is like my being invited to pinch-hit at Rickwood." We've all settled into the front rows when a spotlight is thrown on the apron of the stage, and suddenly the mighty Moeller organ rises and the strains of "Stars Fell on Alabama" thunder through the house. I feel like an icicle is being dragged up my spine. And then the curtains fly open and there is my sister—front and center, hoofing away in a skimpy white sequined outfit and an electric-blue boa and a tiara denoting her as the dean of the ensemble—and I jump to my feet, raise my arms, and lose it: "Yo, Sis! Hit it, Joyce!" For nearly two hours they pound the boards, from "Lullaby of Broadway" to an intricate hand-jive number featured in *The Will Rogers Follies,* and afterwards we repair to a pizza parlor in Mountain Brook. It isn't Sardi's, but it'll do.

On a Sunday night in May of 1992, Ivan Allen III, oldest son of Atlanta's celebrated mayor during the sixties, put a pistol to his head at the family farm in western Georgia. His suicide came just at a time when I was discovering exactly how much the lack of civic leadership had so hobbled Birmingham throughout its history. I had met Ivan III only to shake hands while I worked on the book with his father twenty years earlier, and as I read the Atlanta papers on the morning following his death I was astonished at the depth of his involvement behind the scenes. He was a major mover and shaker and fund-raiser for a boggling number of civic projects, from the 1996 Olympic Games to the Boy Scouts, and yet few outside of that great body of altruistic business leaders in Atlanta seemed to know him except as "Mayor Allen's son." For months I tried to find out why he killed himself. Did he have a fatal disease? Did he feel unappreciated, living in his father's shadow? Was there a personal problem? I finally determined that the answer was as simple as it was incomprehensible: he loved his city too much.

Piper Davis hasn't read *Only the Ball Was White,* the book about baseball's Negro Leagues, but he doesn't have to. He lived it. Born Lorenzo Davis seventy-five years ago, in a coal-mining town west of Birmingham called Piper, he began playing with barnstorming black teams when he was still a teenager. His peak year was in 1948, when he was player-manager for the Birmingham Black Barons: he led the Negro American League in batting with a .353 average, saw his team lose what amounted to a Negro World Series to the fabled Homestead Grays, and was the first professional manager for a local sixteen-year-old named Willie Mays. In 1950 Piper became the first black player signed by the Boston Red Sox organization, but he was abruptly released six weeks later even though he was leading the Class A Eastern League in hitting, and never got a shot at the major leagues. Well past his prime, he averaged .300 in the Triple A Pacific Coast League during the fifties before coming back home. He retired in 1986 after nearly thirty years of scouting for big-league clubs, running a bowling alley, managing the black team at Stockham, even touring as an "administrative assistant" with the Harlem Globetrotters.

On a humid June afternoon we are sitting in the cool living room of his house in the hills above Legion Field—when he bought it in 1970 he integrated the neighborhood—going through the scrapbooks his wife kept during all of those years. Here is Piper playing for the Globetrotters in his younger days; Piper in the Caribbean winter leagues; Piper with the Black Barons and young Willie Mays; Piper being named Senior Citizen of the Year by the United Negro College Fund. He takes a slender dark cigarillo out of his mouth long enough to show me that he can still bend over and not just touch his toes but lay his palms out flat on the floor. "Used to do this one, too"—he kicks out his leg like a Rockette—"but my dog got excited, jumped all over me, made me quit."

It's been a full life, he says, no complaints. He is a joyous man, tall and wiry, married to the same woman for fifty-five years. The week before, there was a call from a newspaper reporter in Baltimore, trying to bait him into saying bitter things about how the Red Sox never gave him his chance, but he wouldn't bite. "I just told her what the Red Sox told me: 'economic reasons.' I think they were a little embarrassed that they hadn't signed any black players when there was already some of 'em in the big leagues at other places, folks like Jackie Robinson and Satchel and Hank Thompson. Shoot, there was something to that 'economic reasons.' I was making a thousand dollars a month playing winter ball down in Venezuela, and they didn't want me doing that." In fact, he says, he had already turned down the St. Louis Browns before Boston came along, for the same reason.

When I tell him I regret that I, as a white boy from Wood-lawn, was never allowed to go out on Sundays to watch the Black Barons play, he shrugs. "You missed a lot of baseball, I can tell you that for sure," he says, laughing. Not many white fans came out, and the seating really *was* reversed at Rickwood on those days: whites in the uncovered concrete bleachers in right field, maybe five thousand blacks under the roof when there was a big doubleheader against a popular team like the Indianapolis Clowns. "We'd be responsible for the visiting team's schedule. Kansas City Monarchs, for instance. We'd book 'em all around our neck of the woods for that week. Play a doubleheader at Rickwood Sunday afternoon, run over to Tuscaloosa for another game that night, then start working our way down the road all week. Montgomery Monday, Mobile Tuesday, New Orleans Wednesday, then swing on around to Little Rock, working our way to Memphis." How many games did he play in his lifetime? "Nobody but the Lord knows that. A bunch."

"Tell me about Willie," I say.

"Which one?"

"Well, the kid."

He takes me back to 1948, to a seedy hotel in Chattanooga where the Black Barons are staying after a game. "It was rough for Negroes back then. Seems like there was always teams wandering around, just looking for a place to spend the night, and here comes a bunch that somebody'd rounded up to go out on the road and play some games. One of 'em was Willie, just a kid, still playing ball for the same high school [Fairfield Industrial] where I'd played. I said, 'Boy, don't you know you can't play no more high school sports if you're out here playing for money?' and he says, 'I don't care,' and I just left it at that. Next weekend we're in Atlanta and here they come again, looking for rooms, and I say, 'Well, I see you're still out here,' and he says, 'I ain't gonna be for long if they don't pay me more money.' He wanted to play for the Black Barons, see. To make the story short, I told him if he could play and if his daddy would let him play and if he'd quit playing high school ball, then I'd see him at Rickwood Sunday morning at eleven o'clock." Piper takes a drag on his cigar. "The boy could play, all right."

"What about the 'other' Willie, the star?"

He frowns. "He's still got a place, you know, up on Red Mountain. One time a few years ago I got a call from him, said he was having some folks over, come on up. So I go up there and we greet each other and I don't see a single soul I know, can't even find Willie anymore, so after a while I just walk out. Willie doesn't exactly stay in touch. He just left and got in with a different bunch of folks, I guess."

The Yellow Pages of Atlanta and Birmingham show these numbers under "Churches." Atlanta, with roughly triple the population, lists 1,532 churches plus 24 synagogues. Birmingham lists 1,126 churches plus 4 synagogues. There's a billboard you can hardly miss on I-20, nearing Birmingham: "Jesus Is Lord Over Pell City."

On one of my trips back home to Atlanta for the weekend, I stop off in Carrollton, Georgia, for a visit with my old friend Joe Cumming. He was the southeastern bureau chief for *Newsweek* in Atlanta during the days of the civil rights movement, and as such spent a lot of time in Birmingham. "There was always this envy of Atlanta,'' he tells me, ''and sometimes it got unreal. I remember interviewing one of those young go-getters with the Young Men's Business Club, one of those groups, and he was all pumped up about Birmingham's future after the trouble died down. 'No, you see,' he said, 'we want to be the Atlanta of the South.' ''

It was bound to happen sooner or later. My brother-in-law and I have managed to miss each other throughout most of my stay in Birmingham, but on a blustery night in July it becomes unavoidable. My Martha is with me on this trip. Yesterday Joyce took her to the Birmingham Country Club to loll about the pool all day, and now she is having us over for a dinner of roast beef, green beans, mashed potatoes, the works.

Jim comes in from work while Joyce and her daughter, Debbie, are cooking and setting the table. We have always tried to be civilized out of deference to Joyce—my sister, his wife—usually talking sports and the weather. He tells me that the highlight of their golfing trip to Aspen last week was playing in a foursome right behind Gerald Ford, the former President, and I don't touch Ford and golf and Aspen.

Then he says, ''What's this book going to be about, Paul?''

''Leaving Birmingham,'' I say.

''I mean, what's it *about*?''

''Me and Joyce, Mama and Daddy, old friends, steel, all of that. And 1963.''

The veins in his neck glow and he sucks on his teeth, as on the night of the Democratic Convention in '68. ''Looks like Birmingham will *never* live that down, doesn't it?''

''Well, I tell you, Jim, I've been spending some time in the archives, and it's even worse than I imagined.''

''That's history.''

''Can't write about Birmingham without it.''

''Why don't y'all write about positive things?''

"Ain't much positive about Bull Connor."

He's been trying to read the sports pages of the *News*, but he lets the paper go limp. I hear Joyce and Debbie clucking in the kitchen. I see Martha, seated in a chair across from me, grinning and rolling her eyes.

"It's more of this negative press," he says. "I guess it sells more books if it's negative. I'm a positive man. I believe in a positive outlook on life, positive thoughts, positive actions."

"A white boy can do that."

He lets it slide. "You want some dirt, how about Arrington? I can't believe what he's getting away with."

"I've checked him out. He's okay."

"Yeah, but where there's smoke, there's fire."

"Not when somebody else made the smoke."

We will get nowhere with this. He growls once more about negative reporting—even he, an Auburn man, can't understand the fuss about firing Wimp Sanderson because "they *say*" he hit his secretary—and everybody is relieved to hear Joyce announce that dinner is served. Debbie blesses the food, Jim says the meat's too dry, and I find that my appetite is gone. I wonder if I will ever eat at my sister's table again.

CHAPTER TWENTY-FIVE

Other Voices: An Uneasy Peace

Mimi Tynes

The first Martin Luther King Day breakfast I went to was about five years ago. It was held on the day observed as the holiday, at the Harbert Center in downtown Birmingham. Sam Pettigrew, pastor of Sardis Baptist Church, was the speaker and gave a rousing presentation. There was an overflow crowd, a pretty good mixture of whites and blacks, and I remember going away thinking this was a marvelous event where whites and blacks were coming together to celebrate something significant. There was such a big crowd that after that first year they had to move it to the Civic Center to accommodate more people.

Over the last several years, though, it seemed like the programming and the speakers became more black-oriented, illustrating some of the cultural differences between the white community and the black community. The speeches went on and on, making the program so long that it was quite difficult to sit through it all. The subject matter was more divisive, going back again to all the wrongs of the sixties and earlier. I began wishing that the whole event could live up to its name—Unity Breakfast—and focus on some of the many positive efforts going on in this community today and how we can work together even more effectively to move forward.

In terms of positive efforts going on today, I'm particularly partial to Leadership Birmingham and YLF. Several other excellent programs are under the banner of the NCCJ. One is the Coalition Against Hate Crimes, which offers a variety of prejudice-reduction workshops for community or employee groups. Another is Anytown, Alabama, a thirty-plus-year-old concept within NCCJ but just four to five years old here. It is an intensive week-long summer camp program for teenagers focused entirely on prejudice reduction and celebrating diversity. Here, it also has an Anybuddy component that is a year-long support group for Anytown alumni and their friends. They are involved in a number of school-related prejudice-reduction efforts in the Birmingham area. I am particularly proud of two Anytown graduates from Mountain Brook High School who are attending Smith College. They are actively involved in bringing some of the same NCCJ prejudice-reduction workshops to the Smith campus.

Another wonderful effort is Mayor Arrington's Birmingham Plan. Arrington enlisted the cooperation of key business and community leaders in developing ways to increase and ensure the participation of minority contractors and businesses in contracts let by the city, to improve the retention and recruitment of women and minorities in corporations and businesses in the area, and to improve the opportunities of women and minorities to get loans and other banking assistance in starting and maintaining businesses.

It seemed to me that fewer whites were attending the Unity Breakfast over the years. Last year, I didn't go at all because I didn't feel like sitting through the same kind of program again. I also have not made the effort to express my feelings to anyone involved in planning the event, so I shouldn't complain behind their backs. That's wrong of me, because we need to find more reasons to come together, do things together. I wish we could have more frank interracial conversations about how we really feel now about race relations. I should be asking my black friends what they feel really needs to be done to further the development of a truly open community. I am also interested in their feelings about whether or not there are areas and times when it is okay to prefer to be with people who share similarities of race, gender, religion, occupation, or whatever.

One of the issues that has come up, along that line, is membership in country clubs. I can see the point of view of members of a country club who say it is a private club and therefore members should be able to invite people they want as members. My problem is that, regardless of what is being said, we are still living in a community where very few minorities, particularly blacks, would be considered, and it's solely because of the color of their skin. I hope we are getting closer to the point where people are associating with each other more in business and other settings where you get to know your friends and associates and soon you want that person to be a part of whatever group you're in because you simply enjoy that person's company and individuals can be considered on their merits regardless of the color of their skin. Of course, that goes back to what the issue is all about, anyway. Even if we have made progress, all of us have prejudices of one kind or another. Not enough people are willing to take the steps necessary to bring about those kinds of social changes—some, simply because they feel other areas involving race relations are much more of a priority.

Listen to me, still talking about the "black community" and the "white community"; but, realistically, that's where we are. The polarization is worse, in some ways, and maybe that's another stage we have to go through before reaching one of more harmony. Another thing that bothers me is that there is a reluctance to constructively criticize someone who is black because you are afraid it will be interpreted as racist or prejudiced. We need to get to the point where we can all be considered on the same level playing field.

Many folks in Mountain Brook don't feel comfortable at all about what's going on in City Hall. In terms of the city council, now that members are elected by district instead of in a general election, there seems to be much more of a tendency by each councilor to take care of the people in his or her own district and focus less on what's good for the community as a whole.

In terms of the mayor, many feel very strongly that a lot going on in Arrington's administration is wrong. I haven't heard any specifics, but there is very definitely that perception. Speaking for myself, I have been extremely impressed with Arrington the times that I've been part of small groups he has spoken to. I feel Birmingham has been quite fortunate to have someone with his integrity and intelligence as mayor. It is hard for me to think that he is not an honest and aboveboard person. I wish he would say publicly that he will not tolerate corruption on the part of anyone in his administration. I do know several members of his administration, and I have great respect for those I know.

Arrington has taken a leadership position on a number of issues, in addition to the Birmingham Plan, that have been beneficial to Birmingham and shown that he thinks of the good of the entire area and not just the part within the city limits. Taking the airport out from under just the city and having an airport authority really made sense, as does his suggestion to do the same with the zoo. There are a number of facilities where Birmingham is paying its unfair share. The Art Museum is another example: does it belong to the city of Birmingham, or the community of Birmingham?

Am I liberal? That's a hard question to answer. In some ways I'm liberal, I guess, and in others I'm pretty conservative. I'm more conservative economically. I tend to agree that it's better for individuals to be involved as much as possible in solving problems rather than having government solving them, that individual effort to create jobs and wealth and goods is more effective. At the same time, I know there are issues that individuals and local communities cannot or will not tackle without pressure or authority from a higher level. Leadership Birmingham and Youth Leadership Forum reminded me that it took government intervention to ensure civil rights. They and all the organizations

I've been associated with have also shown me that things really get done when individuals with a common interest come together and really care about making change happen, that today it often takes public and private partnerships to make a dent in the serious and complex problems facing us, and that there are thousands of people in this and every community working very hard to make a difference.

At this point in my life, I am taking a break from that level of community involvement; but I do intend to pick up the pace again. I think and I hope I will always feel a commitment to make a contribution to my community. And I guess it's important to say it again: when I say "community" I mean all of Birmingham, not just Mountain Brook.

John Porter

It's wishful thinking that we are now beyond racism, that we are now reconciled. There was a time when some young blacks and even some of the older folks voted for George Wallace on the basis of that symbolism, that hope, wanting to believe that the hating days were over. The young ones today say, "Oh, no, no, no, I've been to high school with whites, and I'm an equal now, and blah-blah-blah." And things do appear to be okay for a while. You get your degree and you get a job and you're working alongside the white fellow you came up with through the training program. But then, suddenly, he moves on up the ladder and you're left sitting there. It's the "glass ceiling." These black kids come to me, as their pastor, and they break down and start crying. They've followed all of the rules, done everything right, but now they find they're stuck because they're black. It's racism of a different kind.

There's a saying in the black community: when we're invited into a room, the party's over. Take banking, for instance. I guess there was a time when banking was fun, and certainly profitable, but the S&Ls came along and stole all the money and made things difficult for the rest. For the few who are left behind, the regulations have become so stringent that the fun has been taken out of banking. So I expect to see a few black bank presidents come along now, because the party's over in the banking industry.

It's the same way with the cities, with Birmingham. Once it becomes difficult to run a city, when the city is already dead or dying, that's when we become mayor. The city will have deteriorated, the whites will have left and taken the money with them, so what you end up getting to be head of is a shell. You have to make out of this shell what you can, and there's not very much you can make out of anything without some money. In some cities, like Toronto, it's been different. In Toronto they just went in and tore out the inner city and built this huge mall in its place, did everything downtown and caused a refurbishing of the city. But in Birmingham, the whites just ran off. Toronto is broader, international, more sophisticated, while Birmingham still has all of that old money and the old ways die hard. Someone once said the reason we didn't get the Atlanta airport is that we wouldn't agree to have one bathroom. We lost the whole airline thing over segregated bathrooms. The old-money folks didn't want any changes—they liked it the way it was.

With what they've had to work with, considering white flight and the eroding tax base, I think Arrington and the other blacks at City Hall have done a herculean job. Dick has been as good a mayor as we have had or will ever have, although today he would get only a few white votes. Even if nothing has been going on, these investigations sure make it appear to be, to the white folks. The blacks were happy at first, figured with a black man at City Hall they'd be taken care of; but Dick realized very early that he couldn't be mayor without the power structure. So he sort of backed up and came back again, this time courting the power structure, and I think he's been effective. He's a very firm man—he'll take a stand and die if necessary—but in that way he's not a very good politician. A politician must be flexible, but Dick is intensely loyal and will hold to a position even to the detriment of his own career. He's made some choices of staff that weren't good. With a good politician, if your best buddy messes up you've got to put a little distance for the sake of the cause. There were some people around the mayor who shouldn't have been there, but he chose them anyway, like he was saying, "I'm going to lift you up on your feet and then you'll walk." Well, if a guy's a crook lying down it's a good chance he's going to be a crook standing up; but Dick would take the chance because he's a very loyal person.

It's amazing that the system still works for some people. The system is still in place, even with a black-majority city council. On the council the whites are strong and very verbal, and you can be assured they get what they want for their communities. The better parks and schools are still in the white areas.

In many ways there has been tremendous progress and improvement, but in many ways things are worse. It's gone from being blacks and whites to being haves and have-nots. The poverty is just tragic. People are poorer now than they were when we were growing up. They're like migrants. As a pastor, sometimes I'll hear well-meaning people say, "I want to help a really, really poor family. Can you tell me where to find them?" I say, "No, I can't, because they moved last night." There's a poverty of spirit that exists in the black community, among the low-income, and the best reason I can find for Birmingham not blowing up after the Rodney King decision is that we're not as big as Atlanta or L.A. and our low-income housing is spread around so that people there can't be anonymous. It's not that poor blacks have gone to sleep, are docile and happy now; it's that nobody wants to get caught and go to jail.

Then there are the winners, the black elite. I have a lot of them in my congregation—doctors and lawyers, people who have made it and moved all the way out to Hoover and Pelham and

Inverness. Even now there's a joke that you've got to have a credit card to join Sixth Avenue Baptist. We used to be known as the "sophisticated shoutin' church," full of domestics like my parents who all worked for rich white people like the Martins; but we don't shout like we used to do. We're near the expressway, making it easy for them to come from over the mountain, and instead of shouting "Amen!" during the presentation they'll wait for you to finish preaching or singing and then stand up and clap for five minutes. They're professionals with "servant spirits," bank vice-presidents and doctors who are out there in tennis shoes and jeans directing traffic and parking cars on Sunday morning, working with the Scouts, tutoring, and so forth. I've seen the whole transition.

If there's anybody who has an opening to the white community, I guess I'm it. I'm going to the funeral today for Gilbert Guffin, one of the early teachers at Samford University, as an honorary pallbearer. I'm on the board there, and on many other interracial boards. In these situations I would be lying if I were to say I'm completely comfortable. A part of this is me and the experiences of half a lifetime. There's a desire among some to have an open, diversified community, but I don't think they work as hard for that as they once did to keep the code. There's still the white flight, still the school system, still the old white money, still the racism. But you're going to hit racism almost anywhere. I would invite any black to come and live in Birmingham, in spite of these things, because the housing is open and the school systems are good and the city has great potential. You can pretty much live where you can afford to live in Birmingham these days.

New People on the Block

When my father died in the spring of '88, and my mother was led back to the "retirement home" to live out the rest of her days, the doors to their last house were locked and the utilities were turned off, and dust began to cover Daddy's piano and Mama's sewing machine and the framed family pictures virtually covering the walls and the incredible collection of junk in the basement that he had never even considered throwing out. I drove over there a few times, to sort through the things they had left behind, never feeling any particular emotions about the place. It might have been different had it been the house in Woodlawn, where all of my childhood memories were, but this house had been theirs, not mine. I had been but a guest from time to time, assigned to sleep in my old bed in a room that Mama had preserved like a museum, "Paul, Jr.'s room"; but the bed sagged now, and the planes kept me up most of the night.

It had befallen Joyce to clean out the place and put it on the market. Money was tight and interest rates were out of sight, no thanks to Daddy's hero Ronald Reagan, but still we felt the house would move fairly quickly. It sat on about an acre of land, on a quiet street (except for being in the main flight pattern of the airport), a carpeted three-bedroom brick split-level with two baths and a full basement. Good schools, a public golf course, East Lake Park, and public transportation were close by. We figured it would fetch around sixty thousand dollars. Joyce got it spruced up, and we waited for somebody to come along.

Months passed, then one year, and then two, before Joyce finally called me one day in June of 1990 with the news that a middle-aged couple with two or three children—she didn't remember exactly how many—had bought it and were tickled to death. He worked in transportation for the city, she as a clerk with the federal government, and two of their kids were still in school, a lot like it had been with our family. Their names were Lawrence and Rosa Baylor. Joyce had met them at the closing and they seemed to be—what else?—"nice." Then she told me, almost in a whisper, "They're colored."

Well, now. How many times had I sloshed my whiskey around in a jelly glass, bit my lip, slumped deeper into the faux Naugahyde recliner in the paneled den while my old man interrupted his pounding of the piano and looked at the framed photographs of George Wallace and Lester Maddox, to talk about how "the niggers are taking over"? This was a sweet irony indeed, that the integration of the neighborhood had begun at Daddy's house. More than once during my sojourn in Birmingham I had cruised past on my daily meanderings, noting the shiny new chain-link fence surrounding the backyard, seeing that the grounds in general were neater than I had ever seen them before, and I was more than a little eager to know who these people were.

One time my wife and I ran into a woman who had previously owned our house in Atlanta and the first thing she said was "Don't you just love that big master bedroom?" It was like a violation of privacy, none of her damned business anymore; and I had that in mind as I pondered how to go about this. I had already checked the phone company and found that the Baylors had an unlisted number, making me wonder if their arrival in the neighborhood had caused trouble; so one day I spent a couple of hours composing what I hoped would be a letter they couldn't refuse. "This will seem a strange request," I began, then laying it out about me and my old man's racism and the irony of their buying the house, adding some ingratiating liberal ideology ("We're not black and white, just people trying to live productive lives and do the best for our families"), closing with a request that maybe they could call or write me in the next week or so. I mailed the letter and waited to see what would happen, if anything.

Three weeks later, when there had been no response, I rolled the dice, bit the bullet. I had managed to finagle their phone number, and at dusk one Wednesday in the middle of August I dialed it. The phone was answered by Lawrence Baylor himself, and in a rush I introduced myself and babbled like a fool with effusive apologies: sorry about getting your phone number but it beats showing up at the door unannounced, hope I'm not disturbing dinner, wouldn't blame you for hanging up, you probably don't want any trouble, curiosity got the best of me, this is for history, could we please meet? Lawrence Baylor waited patiently for me to finish.

There was a long pause. I heard kids' voices and the clattering of dishes in the background. Finally, he said, "We got your letter. Matter of fact, I was going to call you today, but I got to running all over town looking for some parts."

"I know this is an imposition," I told him.

"Well, we been thinking about it."

"And?"

There had been a *lot* of thinking about it. Things were going smoothly, he said, but there were many considerations: their children, their jobs, their new neighbors, their privacy, their time. Unable to decide, he and his wife had finally taken my letter to his mother, who still lived in Ensley, in that area on Seventeenth Street near the gutted Ensley Mill, and asked her to be the arbiter.

"Mama said it seemed okay to her," he said.

"Great. When?"

"We work late during the week, both of us," he said. "How 'bout some Saturday?"

My father would have been interested to know that the Baylors had fled their rapidly decaying neighborhood across town in West End because, although they certainly didn't put it that way, the "niggers" were taking over. They had integrated that neighborhood, too, in fact, in the mid-seventies, but it had steadily declined and now had become a place of drugs and crime and poor schools. "We had our share of West End" is the way he put it. Lawrence, whose grandparents had been sharecroppers near Mobile and whose father had come to Birmingham to work in TCI's rail yard in Wylam, was a truck mechanic at the city garage. Rosa, whose family had come to Birmingham from the textile town of Forsyth, Georgia, "looking for a better way," was a clerk for a government welfare agency, much the same sort of job my mother had held, in the 2121 Building downtown. They were in their mid-forties, with sons twenty and fourteen and a daughter who was ten. They had specified to a real estate agent that they wanted a house on the east side of town, a substantial house near good schools, and Rosa fell in love with this place the second she saw it.

It was a balmy Saturday in late August when I visited, with high cumulus clouds and isolated rainstorms across town—the day when George Bush would bring his presidential campaign to the Galleria mall over the mountain in the afternoon. When I rolled up in front of the house and parked half on the grass and half on the narrow, twisting asphalt street, just as I always had on my fitful visits over the years, the Baylors' oldest son, who had been preparing to drive away with a friend, cut the engine of his '72 Pontiac and went inside to fetch his parents. A commercial jet, its landing gears and flaps down, roared over the rooftop like a runaway semi. In the driveway were a gray '87

Buick sedan and an '85 Chevrolet pickup, so well preserved that they looked like new.

Lawrence Baylor opened the glass outer front door and stepped onto the bricked porch, with his wife right behind him. My initial reaction to seeing them for the first time was that they weren't so much African-American as simply people of color— every bit as upwardly mobile and middle-class as my parents had been during the fifties. Some mingling of blood through the generations had left them and their children with chocolate skin, and their living and working beside white people since the fall of segregation had flattened out their speech to a basic soft south- ern drawl. Even in their dress they were pure American subur- banites hanging around the house on Saturday: she in a shiny light blue jogging outfit, he in a polo shirt and beige cotton slacks, both in running shoes. A bit formally, as though they had prepared for this visit, they summoned their children for intro- ductions to "Mr. Hemphill." The kids were mannerly, full of "nosir"'s and "yessir"'s, taught to shake hands and look an adult in the eye. When they disappeared, Rosa Baylor suggested that we sit in the living room.

There was much small talk of the house and the yard, for starters. Rosa, like my mother, kept the two chairs and the sofa in the living room covered with clear vinyl. Lawrence was still finding tools in the basement, making him think that my father had perhaps been a carpenter, and every spring bulbs that he didn't know about would burst into bloom. He had put up the fence, he said, so his beloved dog, a fearsome shepherd-collie named Bud, wouldn't bother the neighbors. The same rust- colored carpet covered the living room and dining room (I didn't want to know about the blood spot where Daddy fell and died); the same stained louvers covered the windows in the den. Rosa had hoped to no avail that my sister would leave the piano be- hind, or make an offer; and she agreed with me that my mother's brocaded and tasseled pull-down lamp in the living room was tacky, but she had kept it because visitors seemed to love it. Lawrence said the bedroom in the front at the end of the hall, *my* bedroom, had been assigned to his daughter because, well, little girls need to be close to their fathers.

I said, finally, "When I saw that your number was unlisted, I didn't know what to make of it."

"Oh, that's nothing," he said. "My oldest boy had started getting too many undesirable phone calls, late at night."

" 'Undesirable phone calls.' I've got a teenager, so I know what you're talking about."

"Got that problem whipped. Now, if I could just do something about cigars."

"You too? My daddy was born with a cigar in his mouth."

"Seems like we've got lots of things in common, your daddy and me."

"There was whiskey, too," I said.

"Aw, I gave that up when we moved here. Seemed like it was getting in my way."

"Fresh start in a new neighborhood, right?"

"That's right. That's exactly right."

Rosa Baylor seemed impatient with the chatter. She smoothed the top of her jogging outfit and said, "You wanted to know how it was, integrating the neighborhood."

"Yes, I do."

"The neighbors came over to welcome us the very first day. In fact, there's a mother across the street with a daughter the age of ours, and she and I take turns driving the girls to school. It's been no problem at all."

"Well," I said, "I never knew them very well. Just my parents, and the way they felt."

"If there's any of that, I don't know. I go through the basement to the car, drive to work, and get home at dark."

.   .   .

We left the house and walked into the yard to say our good-byes. As it was with my parents, the husband left the church-going to his wife, who was still a member of her church of many years several miles across town in Powderly. They would not be going to the George Bush rally that began in an hour at the mall over the mountain—didn't even know about it, in fact—because of a church picnic at the state fairgrounds. Rosa had already yelled out to the kids that it was time to start thinking about leaving, and Lawrence was roughhousing with his dog through the new fence in the backyard, when I waved a farewell and eased away from the last house my parents had called home.

If there was a single moment of my entire stay in Birmingham when I felt that the struggle had been worth it, this was it. My head reeled when I ticked off the mindless antagonisms in the city's past: Louvenia and her swollen feet; Bull Connor and his dogs and hoses; the Klan with its ropes and dynamite; Brother John Rutland's wasted career; the systematic exclusion of half the population. Most of all, I thought of how this one simple issue—of treating others like fellow human beings—had poisoned the relationship between me and the one person I wanted to love and honor and respect most of all: my father.

But now, as my parents' last house faded away in the rear-view mirror, I felt an elation—a feeling that all of the blood and the tears shed over all of the years had been worth it, that finally justice had prevailed. It appeared to me that the new owners of the house at 403 North Eighty-ninth Street had found peace there, had taken their rightful place in the world, and that they weren't likely to be leaving Birmingham any time soon.